$MART MONEY MANAGEMENT

ENTREPRENEURIAL PERSPECTIVE OF FINANCIAL INDEPENDENCE

NASSER SALEM ABOUZAKHAR

Cover image by: Yesna99 – 99designs.com
Book design by: SWATT Books Ltd – swatt-books.co.uk

Printed in the United Kingdom
First Printing, 2024

ISBN: 978-1-9989984-2-5 (Paperback)
ISBN: 978-1-9989984-3-2 (eBook)

Nasser Abouzakhar
Manchester

Dedication

To all those who are seeking financial freedom.

To Yema and Baba who passed away in 2020 and 2017.

To my wife Fathia and my adult sons Adrar, Axcel, and Efaow and daughter Natir the youngest; without their support, this book would not have been written.

Acknowledgements

Many people helped me make this book possible, and I offer my thanks to all of them. I would like to thank my family for my pleasurable life and their tireless support and love throughout my life. Fathia, my wife, thanks for her patience, encouragement, and understanding while I worked on this book. She was able to make challenging times enjoyable. Fathia and my adult sons have played a significant role in making this adventure happen and completing this project. Their constructive comments and feedback on the selected topics and elaborated ideas are highly appreciated. They are very supportive business partners.

Thanks to Sam Pearce, my publisher, for her support and significant advice and to Yvonne Doney, the book editor, who has been an outstanding resource. Thanks to Rosie Stewart for providing the necessary checking and support related to copyright material and getting all required permissions for many images used in this book from different publishers and online sources, ensuring everything is in the right place.

I would like to thank the service staff at Black Sheep Cafe on Deansgate in Manchester for the hospitality, relaxing music and nice Soya Cappuccino they prepared for me while I was writing this book. Thanks to the Go Falafel on Deansgate for the quality falafel, which I enjoyed eating for years at Parsonage Gardens, not far from their takeaway shop, or elsewhere before I headed to Black Sheep Coffee.

Most quotes from notable people given throughout the book have been taken from the following sources:
https://www.goodreads.com/quotes/
https://quotefancy.com/
https://www.brainyquote.com/quotes/
http://www.quotss.com/quote/

Definitions of technical terms have been taken from the following Cambridge Dictionary website:
https://dictionary.cambridge.org/dictionary/english/

All reviewers, thank you for your important comments and constructive criticism of the book and your invaluable reviews.

Praise for Smart Money Management

Smart Money Management: Entrepreneurial Perspective of Financial Independence"
by Dr. Nasser Abouzakhar is a meticulously crafted guide offering readers a profound
exploration of personal finance, wealth management, and strategic investment practices. With
clarity and precision, the book draws upon Dr. Abouzakhar's successful entrepreneurial
experiences. Its twelve chapters cover a wide spectrum of financial topics, beginning with
the fundamental role of money in our lives and progressing into essential aspects of financial
independence. The author provides practical insights into improving income, managing
debt, saving, and budgeting while delving into the intricacies of investment principles,
asset diversification, and real estate. The concluding chapter offers a real-world example
through the lens of Anzar Property Group, Dr Abouzakhar's family business, providing a
tangible application of the book's teachings. This guide is an invaluable resource for readers
seeking both knowledge and practical strategies for mastering their financial journey.

Farshid Amirabdollahian, Professor of Human-Robot Interaction, University of Hertfordshire

Smart Money Management offers perfect knowledge and skills, including practical and
sustainable strategies to make money and manage financial resources. Across twelve chapters,
the book discusses the characteristics of money, its importance and role in progressing financial
situations and fulfilling needs, monetary systems, financial independence, and skills required
to pursue the same diverse strategies for improving income, including financial planning
and making living expenses affordable. Furthermore, the book sheds light on savings and
budgeting and their impact on daily lives, future strategies and finances, unmanaged debt and
its problems, overspending, creative financing, and investment and asset diversification, thus
incorporating discussions on risks and their management. Last but not least, the book zeros in
on principles of real estate investment as one of the popular investment vehicles, property market
assessment and know-how required for successful investment, factors influencing the property
market and investment business, and investment financing concluding with the operations of
Anzar Property Group as a case study. Smart Money Management will be useful reading for
students, particularly those from economics, finance, real estate and business administration and
management disciples, researchers, academics, business owners and investors, and policymakers.

Kwasi Gyau Baffour Awuah, Associate Professor in Real Estate &
Land Development Processes, University of Salford

In Smart Money Management, readers are presented with an extensive resource that equips them with essential knowledge and skills for effective financial management and wealth creation. Through twelve insightful chapters, the book explores the fundamental characteristics and significance of money, emphasising its role in advancing financial situations and meeting diverse needs. It navigates through crucial topics such as monetary systems, financial independence, and the acquisition of skills necessary for implementing income-enhancing strategies, including financial planning and optimising living expenses. The book also dives into practical aspects like the importance of savings and budgeting, shedding light on their impact on daily life and addressing challenges related to unmanaged debt and overspending. Creative financing, investment strategies, and the value of asset diversification are thoroughly discussed, incorporating insights into risk assessment and management.

A significant focus within the book is dedicated to the principles of real estate investment. Readers gain valuable insights into property market assessment, the essential know-how for successful investment, and the myriad factors influencing the property market and investment landscape. Concluding the journey is an in-depth examination of investment financing featuring a case study on the operations of Anzar Property Group. Smart Money Management stands as a versatile resource, catering to a diverse audience that includes students specialising in economics, finance, real estate, and business administration. It is equally beneficial for researchers, academics, business owners, investors, and policymakers seeking a comprehensive guide to financial mastery, skillfully combining theoretical concepts with practical applications.

Laythan Barrett, Senior Mortgage Advisor, Prestige Private Finance

Nasser Abouzakhar's 'Smart Money Management' provides a concise, actionable guide to achieving financial independence with an entrepreneurial twist. It utilises straightforward language to promote a strategic approach to wealth. The book highlights practical examples, case studies, and straightforward strategies for devising finance plans, smart investments, and developing diverse income sources. It uniquely combines financial expertise with entrepreneurial tactics to encourage dynamic money management, making it a vital resource for aspiring individuals targeting financial freedom and wealth expansion.

Steve Porter, Founder of PPS Property Management Ltd

Contents

Abbreviations

AFFO Adjusted Funds from Operations

BMV Below Market Value

BREEAM Building Research Establishment Environmental Assessment Method

CBD Central Business District

CGT Capital Gains Tax

CPI Consumer Price Index

CRA Credit Reference Agency

DIP Decision in Principle

EPC Energy Performance Certificate

FCA Financial Conduct Authority

GDP Gross Domestic Product

GHG Greenhouse Gas

HMO House in Multiple Occupancy/Occupation

HMRC HM Revenue & Customs

LTV Loan-to-Value

MITR Mortgage Interest Tax Relief

NAV Net Asset Value

NBFI Non-bank Financial Institutions

NRLA National Residential Landlord Association

ONS Office of National Statistics

OPM Other People's Money

PED Price Elasticity of Demand

PES Price Elasticity of Supply

PIN Property Investor Network

PRA Prudential Regulation Authority

REIT Real Estate Investment Trust

RHI Renewable Heat Incentive

ROI Return on Investment

SA Serviced Accommodation

SDLT Stamp Duty Land Tax

SVR Standard Variable Rate

SWOT Strengths, Weakness, Opportunities & Threats

UKHPI UK House Price Index

INTRODUCTION

Money moves from those who do not manage it to those who do.
Dave Ramsey

Understanding how to manage your money is an essential aspect of your life. You may rely on the state welfare system or family members or friends for financial support in unpleasant circumstances, but you must be prepared for such situations. Therefore, taking care of your own finances should be a priority in your life. Managing your income and dealing with expenses and debt requires a good understanding of money management and financial knowledge. Luckily, many available tools can help you understand how to manage your money, such as budgeting, income statements, and balance sheet to manage your assets and liabilities, etc. We cannot escape the reality of the economic situation and its factors, such as inflation and interest rates, which affect our lives and can influence our behaviour socially, mentally, and towards money.

Money is not unmanageable; understanding how to manage your money would help you tackle your financial challenges, make better financial decisions, and improve your future financial well-being. Lack of financial knowledge could lead to various problems, not only economic but also social, which can have a knock-on effect on people's mental health and well-being. When we buy goods or services, we regularly make financial decisions about whether or not those goods or services are essential for our families or us and whether or not we can afford them. Regardless of whether people are better off or less well-off, understanding their financial situations and how to manage and control their money is vital for making such decisions.

You must gain control over your money or the
lack of it will forever control you.
Dave Ramsey

In our world, there are some bad rich people, and it is they who make money look bad. There are many benefits of accumulating wealth if done correctly. Nothing is wrong with that, especially when wealthy people play a positive role in their communities, serve their society, and make a difference. Happiness and money can coexist harmoniously, make life more enjoyable, and discover the undiscovered. It is possible to live a balanced life between pursuing growth and selflessness, and, at the same time, embrace and leverage the existing systems, whether these are financial or democratic

Managing your income and dealing with expenses and debt requires a good understanding of money management and financial knowledge. Luckily, many available tools can help you understand how to manage your money, such as budgeting, income statements, and balance sheet to manage your assets and liabilities, etc.

Lack of financial knowledge could lead to various problems, not only economic but also social, which can have a knock-on effect on people's mental health and well-being.

Happiness and money can coexist harmoniously, make life more enjoyable, and discover the undiscovered. It is possible to live a balanced life between pursuing growth and selflessness, and, at the same time, embrace and leverage the existing systems, whether these are financial or democratic political systems.

political systems. However, this requires a change in mindset or even rising above your school of thought and belief that you can change circumstances the way you wish and for the better. This book is not about becoming rich super-quick in a week or a month, so if you want to get rich quickly, it is the wrong book and it doesn't cover gambling. It is designed to provide you with the necessary knowledge and skills to manage the commodity that is money. So, this is the right book for those who want a practical and sustainable strategy for managing and making money. It is helpful to university or college students who are studying business or finance-related courses.

Our politicians, employers, household, or family members or partners can make decisions that could influence our personal financial decisions and behaviour towards money. Therefore, we must have a financial plan and strategy to deal with unpleasant or unforeseen situations, cope financially, and become economically independent, as follows:

- developing proper financial plans;
- identifying opportunities for improving our financial situation;
- managing our debt and expenses;
- making informed financial decisions;
- getting on top of our finances and having options;
- dealing with financial challenges.

Being financially knowledgeable is important, especially during tough times and certain economic events, such as recession, increased interest rates, or inflation. Such events could have an impact on your money, financial plan, and the economy in general. This book covers those issues and provides real-life scenarios and practical numerical examples to help you understand the concepts of those events and learn how to deal with them when they occur. You will appreciate the challenges associated with inflation and how it affects prices and the cost of living. You will know why keeping money in your bank account during high inflation or low interest rates offered by banks is not a wise financial decision. You will also figure out how to deal with high-risk investments, make informed financial decisions, and understand the advantages of diversifying your investments. For example, you will understand that when you put your money into what you believe is a profitable investment, it is likely that you will lose most or all of your money due to high risk.

If you are born poor, it's not your mistake.
But if you die poor, it's your mistake.
attributed to Bill Gates

Any kind of financial decisions we make, whether related to savings, budgeting, mortgages, personal loans, investments, or anything else, are affected by many factors. These factors could be political, economic, social, or technology related (Shipman and Stone, 2019). You need to be aware of those factors and any imminent changes in the world before making any financial decision. For example, as a property investor in Manchester, I have to consider the development projects planned and published by the city council.

I need to be aware of the demographic changes, such as longevity or fertility rate in the city, before I invest in new buy-to-let properties and decide what kind of properties would suit different communities and households.

Governments change their economic and social policies, which could have a knock-on effect on your financial decisions. Any changes in policies by your government related to social housing, welfare matters, or tax or changes in interest rate by the central bank could affect your decisions about various financial issues such as buying a new residential house or selling your home, your savings or investments, etc. Due to limited resources, squeezed budgets, and social changes, even welfare countries that were generous in their social benefits have started recently shifting to become more restrictive and less helpful regarding their support to those most in need. Such changes could contribute to people who are looking for better alternatives and opportunities having to make complex financial decisions.

The financial services sector and many financial firms offer the public different financial products, banking services, private pensions, investment funds, credit loans, etc. Due to the deregulation of non-high street lenders, many private financial firms offer the public a broader range of financial facilities. Financial businesses provide those products to their customers to ensure they receive appropriate services and help them achieve their financial goals. Governments try to ensure that less well-off households can access essential financial products such as basic bank accounts (BBAs) or savings accounts and can apply for other types of services. All these services allow people to carry out basic transactions, such as depositing and withdrawing money, transferring money, applying for loans, making payments, etc.

The way we manage our finances and make financial decisions can affect and be influenced by others. Financial decisions about how much we spend, save, or invest and what economic choice to make could positively or negatively impact others, such as households or other family members and their finances. The effects of financial stress can be exceptionally high financially and emotionally for families, especially when decisions are not made collectively. We must know the complexity of money management and our financial decisions. It is becoming essential to learn how to develop financial plans and strategies and how they can be affected by other forces, whether political, economic, social, or technology related.

> *A person who won't read has no advantage over one who can't read.*
> Mark Twain

The technology significantly changes how financial service providers and banks operate and how business is carried out. Almost all banks have moved many of their financial services to online delivery. They invested a lot of capital to improve the quality of their online services, develop new online platforms for banking, and have a presence on the internet. However, they have to deal with many cybersecurity challenges to ensure the safety of their customers and the security of their accounts and online transactions. They aim to minimise the risks of cyber attacks, prevent cyber threats and criminals from accessing their systems, and protect them and their customers against online attacks.

Any changes in policies by your government related to social housing, welfare matters, or tax or changes in interest rate by the central bank could affect your decisions about various financial issues such as buying a new residential house or selling your home, your savings or investments, etc.

Using new technologies such as fintech (financial technology), blockchain, and mobile apps has helped banks improve the quality of their services, access new markets, and provide better service to their clients. These technologies have changed the way banks operate and also helped entrepreneurs, investors, and traders to grow their businesses at a faster rate. Online financial services such as payments, crowdfunding, and peer-to-peer lending allow entrepreneurs to borrow money to develop their products, services, and companies and investors to grow their asset portfolios. The recent advances in internet technologies and web applications have provided many opportunities for entrepreneurs to have an online presence and use social media for marketing themselves and their products and services. Examples of those opportunities and online business ideas include, but are not limited to:

> Online financial services such as payments, crowdfunding, and peer-to-peer lending allow entrepreneurs to borrow money to develop their products, services, and companies and investors to grow their asset portfolios. The recent advances in internet technologies and web applications have provided many opportunities for entrepreneurs to have an online presence and use social media for marketing themselves and their products and services.

- delivering online training courses;
- publishing their books;
- setting up their own media channels on YouTube;
- setting up online businesses on social media networks such as Facebook;
- offering digital marketing services;
- selling products on Amazon or eBay and services on social networks and using online subscriptions;
- setting up an e-commerce website to sell products or services;
- developing mobile apps.

Chapter One discusses the importance of money in our life and how it is vital in progressing our financial situations and fulfilling our needs and commitments. It covers the history of the monetary system, how money is used to carry out financial transactions and the main characteristics of money. We use money to value products and services, carry out daily transactions, and pay for our living expenses. The flow of global wealth relies on the transactions used to pay for required commodities and consumed products and services. This chapter introduces the money flow cycle, the main inflation challenges, and its impact on people's money. Managing cash flow, borrowing, investing, and risk and return-related matters are also covered.

> We use money to value products and services, carry out daily transactions, and pay for our living expenses. The flow of global wealth relies on the transactions used to pay for required commodities and consumed products and services.

Chapter Two introduces the subject of financial independence, which requires various skills that can be learnt and mastered. Financial independence or freedom requires paying a personal price and doing what the majority of people are uncomfortable doing. This chapter discusses how investing in financial education is crucial to improving your financial skills and achieving your goals. It covers the principles of financial independence, the importance of investing, and the skills needed to help you develop innovative ideas and explore possibilities for developing solutions to existing problems or seeking investment options. A dedicated section about financial stress management is introduced, including the measures that can be followed to avoid stressful situations and minimise financial risk.

> Financial independence or freedom requires paying a personal price and doing what the majority of people are uncomfortable doing.

Chapter Three discusses improving income, dealing with financial commitments, and making living expenses affordable. Such issues are becoming increasingly crucial to meeting our personal and family financial needs and achieving our financial goals. Different approaches to improving our financial knowledge and skills are covered through learning and accessing financial and money management resources available to everyone. Keeping part of our income aside is vital for saving and dealing

> Keeping part of our income aside is vital for saving and dealing with unexpected events and future consumption.

with unexpected events and future consumption. This chapter introduces the main principles of income and wealth, the impact of inflation on your income, and financial planning concepts. Different financial strategies for improving your income and a financial planning process called GROW A+ are discussed.

Chapter Four covers saving and budgeting, their importance in our daily life, and their impact on our future finances and plans. We have to be careful not to overspend and make sure that we use budgeting to spend our money wisely, monitor our cash flow, and control our finances. The influences and motivations for saving and its role in improving our financial situation and planning for the future is covered. Out-of-control spending could lead to stressful financial situations and unhealthy habits. Therefore, you must monitor your budget, expenditures, and debts and develop a proper financial plan to deal with all those matters. This allows better management of your income and expenses and helps you achieve your financial goals. Some real-life scenarios about saving and budgeting, supported with numerical examples, are also presented.

Chapter Five highlights the problems associated with unmanaged debt and issues with overspending by households on expensive products and services. Spending on unnecessary items is inappropriate for those with limited financial resources and could lead to unpleasant financial situations. Therefore, managing our money appropriately and developing a financial plan could help us avoid unhealthy habits and personal economic problems. Learning how to manage expenses, especially during uncertain times, and monitoring credit reports could help you access credit, apply for a mortgage, or invest in the future. This chapter covers debt management and how to deal with financial obligations such as loan payments, mortgage commitments, etc. This should help you avoid damage to your credit reports and the risk of financial losses, maintain vital financial status, and build a growing asset portfolio.

Chapter Six introduces creative finance, which uses financial opportunities and techniques to raise capital and manage good debt. Creative finance should help you to manage your finance by producing financial statements, including profit and loss (or income) statements and balance sheets. This chapter discusses my wealth generation engine, which provides a financial strategy to develop a financial plan and help build a multi-stream income strategy. The main phases of designing and building a successful investment portfolio using creative financial planning are introduced. This chapter presents examples of income-producing property investment and buy-to-let property deal evaluations to help you understand the principles of creative finance.

Chapter Seven focuses on the principles and concepts of investment in modern life, which are essential for improving your financial knowledge about investing in general and building your asset portfolio in particular. Inflation is dangerous and could lead to unpleasant situations; therefore, this chapter will introduce real-life scenarios and numerical examples of the impact of inflation on savings and income. Knowing how to measure the performance of an investment, using the necessary financial tools, and managing risk is crucial. Moreover, getting the essential knowledge from available resources can help you make informed decisions, minimise inflation's impact, and not rely on speculation. The 5-step investing process, which covers the main investment rules and guidelines, is discussed.

Chapter Eight is about investment and asset diversification, which aims to help you understand how to manage risk by investing in different asset classes. Investors must be prepared, before investing, to analyse investment options and select the business strategy that works for them. They must understand how to deal with varying market conditions and challenges, develop multi-asset portfolios and aim for multiple income streams. This chapter discusses the importance of seeking opportunities to build a robust business plan using various investment strategies, helping investors to improve their revenues and establish a resilient, healthy, and diverse portfolio. Interested individuals must gain the necessary skills and knowledge to conduct their investment activities. Examples of asset classes such as real estate, REIT, commodities, stocks, and diversification benefits are introduced.

Chapter Nine covers the principles of real estate investing, the property market assessment and the knowledge and know-how investors need to gain to build successful investment businesses. For example, the buy-to-let market entails investing capital into an income-generating property that can achieve a good return on investment (ROI) and yield. A modified version of Porter's Five Forces model is introduced to help investors assess the property market and business strategy. This chapter presents a business philosophy for real estate investment that we use for our family business before we select and decide on a deal and allocate the necessary resources. For instance, before deciding whether to invest in buy-to-let properties, we have to consider issues such as proximity to a CBD, property location, local amenities to the property, level of demand, etc.

Chapter Ten discusses the economic factors influencing the property market and investment business. Economic factors such as interest rates, government rules and regulations, building material costs, local authorities policies, etc., are introduced. Property markets change cyclically between four phases: expansion, hyper-supply, recession, and recovery. This chapter will cover the property life cycle, the issue of supply and demand in the property markets, the factors affecting the economic conditions in terms of prices, and investors' and developers' behaviour. The relationship between supply and demand and their effects on real estate prices and the property business are covered. This chapter also discusses the main challenges in the property market, such as the housing shortage and its implications, inflation, etc., and the tools governments and central banks use to deal with these challenges. The challenge of raising funds by real estate investors from available sources and lending options, such as banks, non-high street banks, funding circles, Angel investors, etc., are discussed.

Chapter Eleven focuses on real estate investment and finance, including the opportunities available for property investors and the challenges associated with lending that investors face. It demonstrates how investors use creative finance to fund their development projects, conduct investment activities, and leverage to grow their business without using much of their capital. However, property investors have to deal with many financial challenges, such as raising funds, allocating necessary financial resources to projects, getting business loans, inflation, etc., which require attention and skill, proper plans, and informed decision-making. This chapter covers those challenges and their impact on real estate investment and economies during different market conditions. This requires a good understanding of the financial markets, the costs associated with lending and debt management, property accounting, and risk management.

Interested individuals must gain the necessary skills and knowledge to conduct their investment activities. Examples of asset classes such as real estate, REIT, commodities, stocks, and diversification benefits are introduced.

A modified version of Porter's Five Forces model is introduced to help investors assess the property market and business strategy.

Economic factors such as interest rates, government rules and regulations, building material costs, local authorities policies, etc., are introduced. Property markets change cyclically between four phases: expansion, hyper-supply, recession, and recovery.

Property investors have to deal with many financial challenges, such as raising funds, allocating necessary financial resources to projects, getting business loans, inflation, etc., which require attention and skill, proper plans, and informed decision-making.

In this chapter, real-life examples will show how investors can leverage and arrange funds from available banking and lending institutions, using various financial products to help them expand their businesses.

Chapter Twelve, the final chapter, introduces our family property business, Anzar Property Group, which focuses on buy-to-let business and property development. Anzar Property Group focuses on four main activities: operations, finance and accounting, investment, and IT management. These activities help the business to grow and the management team to implement its business strategy and deal with daily operations and challenges. This chapter covers the whole story of this family business, the company's structure, and the skills gained by the business members who manage multiple property companies. Real-life scenarios supported with examples of successful investment deals are presented, including some media and social responsibility activities and contributions to society.

A business that makes nothing but money is a poor business.
Henry Ford

Chapter Twelve, the final chapter, introduces our family property business, Anzar Property Group, which focuses on buy-to-let business and property development. Anzar Property Group focuses on four main activities, operations, finance and accounting, investment, and IT management. These activities help the business to grow and the management team to implement its business strategy and deal with daily operations and challenges.

MONEY

1

We use money to fulfil our daily financial commitments and to allow us to carry out our transactions offline and online. Money plays a significant role in keeping our economies growing and our finances moving forward, allowing the flow of wealth worldwide. Businesses use money as a standard measure to value their products and services, and people need money to pay for them. The more money we have, the higher the affordability of those offered products and services. This chapter teaches you about money, its main characteristics, how and where people use money, the monetary system, and how modern financial transactions are carried out. Because we live in an interconnected world, our financial decisions can have a significant impact on many entities, including corporations and governments; therefore, the money flow cycle and main types of marketplaces are covered.

The main challenges associated with inflation, its effects on people's savings and investments, and the significant role of supply and demand in inflation are discussed. The principles of managing cash flow, borrowing and investing are also covered. This chapter highlights the main concepts of risk and return and how using multiple streams of income and asset classes helps offer different types of revenues to minimise risk.

> Money plays a significant role in keeping our economies growing and our finances moving forward, allowing the flow of wealth worldwide.

> The more money we have, the higher the affordability of those offered products and services.

1. WHY MONEY?

People who become rich through their own efforts have tended to devote a great deal of time to learning about money, what it involves and how to deal with it. This helps them gain understanding of the way to manage money and the tools available to support them in achieving that. Understanding money and its laws, how it grows and flows, and discovering its philosophy is essential to anyone who wants to improve their financial situation and the lives of their families. Money can be a source of good for you and your family, have a positive impact on your community and society and create a lasting legacy. Self-made wealthy people may be the minority but they have a completely different view of money from the rest of the population simply because they have selected a different and challenging path. They had to make sacrifices, experience worry, and often live outside their comfort zones to face and deal with the pressures. They had to deal with many challenges during their early business life, but once established, they can enjoy every stage of its development and growth. It is a choice, but is it worth it? Of course, I can tell you from experience that it is worth it!

You have to make sacrifices at the beginning to save, learn, and get ahead of your competitors, whether or not it is about money; this is what most successful people do when they start their business lives. It seems better to take some carefully calculated risks and invest some time in research than to keep sacrificing the rest of your life, struggling for money to make ends meet

> Understanding money and its laws, how it grows and flows, and discovering its philosophy is essential to anyone who wants to improve their financial situation and the lives of their families.

> You have to make sacrifices at the beginning to save, learn, and get ahead of your competitors, whether or not it is about money; this is what most successful people do when they start their business lives.

while making others wealthy. The difference is that those who managed to become wealthy decided to step outside their comfort zone while the majority felt that uncertainty and discomfort were too high a price to pay. During 2022–23, due to the UK's cost of living crisis, many employees from different sectors, such as healthcare, education, transport, etc., went on strike, taking to the streets to ask their employers and the government to increase their wages. People are struggling because of the lack of money and limited options, despite many being highly qualified and spending years at universities studying difficult subjects. The major problem is that universities don't teach their students how to make money or use the knowledge they learnt at university to set up their own businesses and become financially independent. Millions of students graduate every year worldwide, and only the minority make it and manage to build successful businesses a few years after graduation. It is not the graduates' fault or their lack of abilities; it is the education systems designed and built to offer them as a labour force to the competitive markets, convincing them that wealth is beyond their reach and they exist only to serve others.

Individuals use their money in different ways, depending on their financial abilities and circumstances. Some work hard to earn their living, some work smart, and others work hard and smart. If 'Money doesn't buy happiness', then why do people feel happy when receiving their wages at the month's or week's end? The majority of people take the same paths in life: they follow the mainstream education system to obtain a college diploma or a university degree in order to get a job, work for a private company or in the public sector, and receive a monthly salary. Sometimes, they have to borrow to pay for essentials and can run up bad debt. Those who work smart know the difference between good and bad debt and borrow to pay for investments and accumulate assets that produce income, grow more significantly, and expand. You are not born and do not exist only to work day and night, stuck in the hamster wheel, worrying about money all the time, paying off debt, and trying to make ends meet. We all have a purpose in life; we have to

- play a positive role in solving big problems;
- develop cost-effective solutions;
- take care of ourselves and the people around us;
- improve the quality of people's lives;
- support those in need; and
- serve the growth of our communities and contribute to society and humanity as a whole.

To achieve that, we need to make use of the available resources, develop the required skills, understand how to monetise that situation and operate creatively. Money is the fuel that keeps our economy moving and financial life progressing. It is a central aspect of our daily business activities, an essential part of life, and is used to exchange for food, clothes, transport, energy, healthcare, etc. Money incorporates all aspects of finances that matter to you, including, but not limited to, your lifestyle, family living expenses, daily transactions in exchange for products and services, and legacy. People have used money for thousands of years and played a role in the flow of wealth between individuals, generations, and nations. Wealth is the value of assets you, a group, business, or nation own. Money is widely recognised as a measure of value against any commodity and serves its owner(s) to pay for

---

Sidebar notes:

People are struggling because of the lack of money and limited options, despite many being highly qualified and spending years at universities studying difficult subjects.

If 'Money doesn't buy happiness', then why do people feel happy when receiving their wages at the month's or week's end?

Those who work smart know the difference between good and bad debt and borrow to pay for investments and accumulate assets that produce income, grow more significantly, and expand. You are not born and do not exist only to work day and night, stuck in the hamster wheel, worrying about money all the time, paying off debt, and trying to make ends meet.

Money incorporates all aspects of finances that matter to you, including, but not limited to, your lifestyle, family living expenses, daily transactions in exchange for products and services, and legacy.

goods and services based on their level of supply and demand. Part of any government's job is to liaise with its central bank to print and supply money, whether a physical coin, note, or digital currency and manage its monetary policy. The money a government applies represents the amount of money circulating in a particular economy. The main characteristics of money are as follows:

Money is widely recognised as a measure of value against any commodity and serves its owner(s) to pay for goods and services based on their level of supply and demand.

- being acceptable and usable: coins are made of precious metals or base material;
- having equal value: money retains a fairly stable value with which to build wealth;
- the ability to withstand damage: can be used frequently;
- easily carried and transferable: money can be stored and transported from one place/bank account to another;
- easily divided: for example, £10 can be exchanged for 2 x £5;
- limited supply, to control inflation.

Money is used as a universally agreed method of exchange and carrying out trade. It is a trusted, standardised measure of value, which can be stored and retained for the future. Inflation can harm the value of money by reducing its purchasing power; in other words, increasing the prices of products and services. Lower interest rates encouraging lending and supply of money plays a role in raising inflation and, consequently, the devaluation of money. During periods of inflation, we strategically enhance our property portfolio by implementing value-boosting renovations. This not only contributes to the appreciation of property values but also positions us to command higher rental rates. By leveraging long-term appreciation, we establish a competitive edge over other rental properties in the market. With our continuous desire to grow our business, we add value to newly purchased properties, fit quality kitchens and bathrooms, improve the quality of life of our tenants, and attract more potential customers, increasing the rents and the value of those properties.

Inflation can harm the value of money by reducing its purchasing power; in other words, increasing the prices of products and services. Lower interest rates encouraging lending and supply of money plays a role in raising inflation and, consequently, the devaluation of money.

Inflation of money is ultimately a reflection of life's purpose of progress and evolution. The desire for growth makes human beings want to continually increase prices and quality of services.
Rob Moore, in his book *Money*, 2018

Society should benefit from wealthy people who know how to make money and accumulate wealth professionally. Because they understand the system and have access to resources not available to everybody, they can serve their communities and make a difference in their society while enjoying life and building a legacy; some can make money only to give large amounts of it away. Warren Buffett donated over $50 billion to charities and foundations for various good causes during his business life. The wealthy should understand their social responsibilities and the positive impact they can have on their communities without major sacrifices. Giving back and helping communities achieve their goals and scale their passion, whether in sports, culture, music, education, or developing businesses, is nice. A balanced

Society should benefit from wealthy people who know how to make money and accumulate wealth professionally. Because they understand the system and have access to resources not available to everybody, they can serve their communities and make a difference in their society while enjoying life and building a legacy; some can make money only to give large amounts of it away.

life between seeking wealth and contributing will help society to develop, flourish, and move forward. The education system can play an important role by supporting curricula with successful stories and good examples. Life is not just about becoming wealthy or super rich as, unfortunately, some people think; it is much more than that.

2. THE MONETARY SYSTEM

The monetary system started thousands of years ago and has gone through multiple milestones in its evolution and development, as shown in Figure 1.1. Around 6000 BC, the barter system was the dominant cashless system available for people to exchange goods and services. Around 3500 years later, commodity money was used as a trusted currency to trade and exchange. Metal money was introduced in about 1000 BC as an easy and practical solution, but it was impractical for dealing with large amounts. However, about 1600 years later, paper notes were introduced to overcome the problems associated with metal money. During the 1970s, electronic transactions became popular, and people started to use credit cards to access short-term credit to pay for goods and services. In the 1990s, digital money was introduced, and online payment systems made it easy to carry out electronic transactions as part of the services available on the World Wide Web. If the pound sterling's value changes, the value of the digital money holdings will change concomitantly. Digital money can have its own currency and acquire a real value, similar to scarce metals like gold or precious minerals such as diamonds.

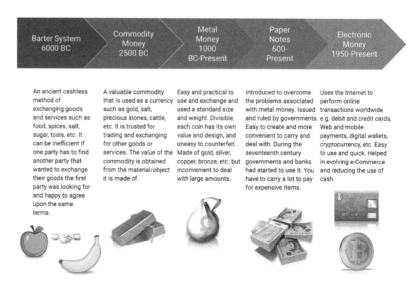

Figure 1.1 The evolution of the monetary system

Individuals and governments started setting up banks to manage people's and organisations' money, and process their daily transactions. Banks provide financial services to their customers, such as saving and borrowing money, withdrawing money, paying for goods and services, and investment options to those pursuing profit. However, the value of money in exchange for goods and services could be affected by various economic factors and events, such as inflation. Inflation can seriously affect the value of money and change the prices of goods and services in a market economy over time.

It took banks a while to convince customers to use plastic cards for electronic payments. Credit cards represent the dominant transaction payment method used on the internet today. With only a very small delay, you can use your credit card(s) to transfer money securely anywhere in the world. Money loves fast decisions and the internet facilitates that. The buyer sends the credit card details to the merchant/seller, who contacts a financial system involving intermediaries such as banks to receive the payment. The internet was a game changer in the money world. According to ukfinance.org.uk, contactless payments increased by 12% in 2020 in the UK; that is, to 9.6 billion payments.

Only relatively recently, during the 17th century, governments stepped in to centralise the supply of cash. The main advantages of using cash are that it provides some anonymity, the bank doesn't come into the picture, and no third party is involved in the transaction. All currencies require supply control and security enforcement to prevent cheating. Organisations like banks control the money supply and add anti-counterfeiting features to physical currency. On the other hand, online payment systems use various application protocols designed to accept online transactions and handle secured electronic payments. However, such payment systems provide less anonymity because the banks can track all transactions.

Nowadays, online credit card transactions are the dominant payment method, but not all e-Cash technologies manage to survive. PayPal survived because it quickly offered its services to mobile phone users. In using PayPal, you do not provide your credit card details to the seller or service provider. PayPal receives the buyer's credit card details as an intermediary, approves the transaction, and notifies the merchant. The online seller or service provider does not receive the buyer's details. If the payment server goes down, the payment cannot be arranged. The most serious problems are identifying theft, payment fraud, and lack of anonymity because the bank can track all your transactions/spending.

Cryptography was introduced to overcome the limitations associated with the current electronic payment systems. It uses P2P (peer-to-peer) networks, so it does not require a central server and avoids real-life identities altogether, but it is not anonymous to the same level as cash. Cryptocurrency is a decentralised digital money using blockchain technology and cryptography to encode the rules for creating the currency and carry out secure online financial transactions. Using blockchain and cryptography helps prevent double-spending, i.e., using the same coin for two payments. Cryptocurrency was introduced in 2008 as secured digital money and operates independently of any government, central bank, or central authority.

Satoshi Nakamoto developed the first working cryptocurrency, known as Bitcoin. He had to learn from multiple electronic payment technologies to create Bitcoin. In Bitcoin, all transactions and events are recorded by trusted nodes, managed by 'miners' instead of central servers. In Bitcoin, the protocol allows user-to-user transactions and doesn't differentiate between merchant and user, i.e., the senders and receivers have the same level of anonymity. Bitcoin uses the blockchain as a ledger to record all

Money loves fast decisions and the internet facilitates that. The buyer sends the credit card details to the merchant/seller, who contacts a financial system involving intermediaries such as banks to receive the payment.

The main advantages of using cash are that it provides some anonymity, the bank doesn't come into the picture, and no third party is involved in the transaction.

Cryptography was introduced to overcome the limitations associated with the current electronic payment systems. It uses P2P (peer-to-peer) networks, so it does not require a central server and avoids real-life identities altogether, but it is not anonymous to the same level as cash.

Bitcoin transactions securely. Nakamoto designed Bitcoin to be completely decentralised and to operate without a central authority.

Bitcoin is an implementation of Wei Dai's b-money proposal on Cypherpunks in 1998 and Nic Szabo's Bitgold proposal

Satoshi Nakamoto

3. MONEY FLOW CYCLE

As individuals, our financial decisions can significantly affect our local communities, the wider society, and the economy. We are economically connected to our governments, including central and local governments and their organisations and companies, as well as private corporations. This includes state-owned companies, state agencies, and privately owned financial and non-financial institutions. To develop a proper financial plan, manage your money, and build wealth, you must understand these three sectors' connectivity (individuals, financial and non-financial firms, and government) and economic interdependence and how goods, services, and money flow between them (Shipman and Stone, 2019). Figure 1.2 represents an economic model that shows the links between all three sectors and the circular flows of money in opposite directions.

> To develop a proper financial plan, manage your money, and build wealth, you must understand these three sectors' connectivity (individuals, financial and non-financial firms, and government) and economic interdependence and how goods, services, and money flow between them (Shipman and Stone, 2019).

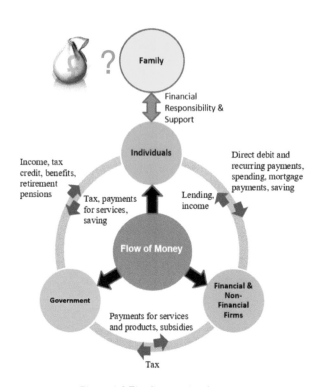

Figure 1.2 The flow cycle of money

Expenditure in one sector becomes an income for other sectors, and after a full circle the money returns to the starting sector to be spent again. When individuals spend more money on goods and services, this increases the profits of corporations. This will have a positive impact on the amount of money in the form of tax that the government receives. Figure 1.2 shows that when you spend your money or savings to buy goods or services, it flows into privately owned or state-owned firms and the payments are transferred to financial institutions. You receive employment or self-employment income, investment returns, loans, etc., from those firms. This cycle of money and its flow speed creates energy, significantly affects cash and its value, and has an impact on the economy as a whole.

In successful economies, money is in circulation, flowing fast and continuously, allowing the economy to progress and trading activities to increase. During recessions, central banks tend to intervene by printing more money to inject cash into the economy to minimise the impact of the recession. Adding cash to the economy must be well controlled and managed effectively to avoid any economic issues and problems associated with significant currency devaluation. Although saving is an important step in financial planning and money management, there are more useful approaches than keeping money standing still and extreme saving and disallowing money to exchange and move freely. This differs from what money is for and is not meant to be! The more it flows, the more rewarding it becomes, and the more energy it produces, the better for all entities involved in those transactions.

To be on the safe side financially and able to build your wealth, you must ensure that you receive a level of income that allows you to save and invest regularly. The higher the income, the better the opportunity for saving and investing in multiple passive income streams, and ensuring that your bank account is healthy and regularly charged. Investing in assets is the best strategy and fastest way for money to move constantly, accelerate its flow, and build wealth. Like many wealthy individuals, you only need a little cash to start a business and develop your multi-asset portfolio. Of course, this requires changing your mindset and lifestyle to explore the world outside your comfort zone. You must select the right marketplace for your investment to achieve that. The marketplace is where individuals and businesses offer their products and services and meet with potential customers interested in those products and services. The two main marketplaces are as follows:

- The online marketplace: based on e-commerce and web content to offer your products and services. Potential customers have access to your online business and have the option to select from your offered products and services.
- The offline marketplace: physical places are used by sellers and customers to meet and do business. The offline marketplace allows customers to meet the sellers and see their products or discuss their offered services before purchasing.

Money in the form of taxes on your income or payments for certain services flows from your bank account to the government. This includes savings kept in public banks, payments for council tax, and rental payments if you live in council properties or social housing. There is money flowing in the opposite direction to your account from the government. This includes income if you work for the government, benefits, tax credits, retirement pensions, etc. The money flows into the government from corporations in the form of corporation tax but also goes in the opposite direction in the form of payments for services and products or subsidies paid by the government to private corporations.

4. IMPACT OF INFLATION

Inflation is a rise in price levels of goods and services over time and a fall in buying power associated with economic growth and money supply. Understanding how inflation affects savings, real estate prices, and the value of money over time is crucial. Hyperinflation in the early 1920s led to an uncontrollable economic situation in Germany and was one factor that enabled the consequent rise of fascism. It is remembered as one of the most challenging periods in modern German history, with economic instability that contributed to the Nazi party winning the elections in 1933. During this challenging period, the currency lost most of its value and wages were paid to workers in large baskets by their employers. The hyperinflation made it difficult for ordinary Germans, the working class in particular, and their day-to-day survival was hard and required much effort to obtain even basic needs. The higher the inflation rate, the higher the prices and the lower the purchasing power of your money. This could devastate people who rely on their monthly or weekly wages to pay for their living expenses, feed their families, and make ends meet.

In a BBC interview, Mr Simon Clarke, the treasury minister in 2022 during Boris Johnson's government, expressed his view about pay rises and inflation. He was against employee pay rises amid the soaring inflation rate in 2022. According to him, any high pay rises could push prices up. However, the Trades Union Congress (TUC) argues that energy prices push inflation, not pay rises. In June 2022, the Bank of England predicted that inflation could reach more than 11% and was proved correct; by the end of 2022, inflation had reached 11%. Central banks can control inflation by raising and lowering short-term interest rates, which are always used for this purpose.

Inflation reflects the change in the price of a basket of goods and services consumed by the public during a specific time and is represented using a measure known as the CPI (Consumer Price Index). The CPI measures track inflation by monitoring and reporting a country's monthly cost of goods and services.

Supply and demand of certain commodities play a significant role in changing inflation rates. For instance, factors such as rising property prices, oil or gold prices, and labour costs can impact inflation. Monitoring inflation changes over time helps investors plan for the future and prepare for any opportunities or guard against unpleasant times. For instance, inflation analysis helps real estate investors to predict the amount they need at a particular time during inflation to keep the same buying and investment power.

Understanding how inflation affects savings, real estate prices, and the value of money over time is crucial. Hyperinflation in the early 1920s led to an uncontrollable economic situation in Germany and was one factor that enabled the consequent rise of fascism.

The higher the inflation rate, the higher the prices and the lower the purchasing power of your money. This could devastate people who rely on their monthly or weekly wages to pay for their living expenses, feed their families, and make ends meet.

Inflation reflects the change in the price of a basket of goods and services consumed by the public during a specific time and is represented using a measure known as the CPI (Consumer Price Index). The CPI measures track inflation by monitoring and reporting a country's monthly cost of goods and services.

Monitoring inflation changes over time helps investors plan for the future and prepare for any opportunities or guard against unpleasant times.

5. MONEY AND CREDIT

Money is a lubricant that plays a significant role in keeping investors moving forward and allowing the flow of wealth around the globe. The world community has recognised it as a standard measure of value for goods and services and daily financial transactions. Economists use money to measure the GDP (gross domestic product) for countries and the purchasing power of people and to control price stability. Investors do not work for money; their money works for them. They rely on their bank accounts to carry out financial transactions. Today, money is issued by central banks in a physical or digital form and deposited by people in their bank accounts. Gold is considered good money, whereas currency is called bad money.

Currency is not a reliable indicator of value because it can lose its value due to inflation, economic downturn, or both. Active investors know what makes real money and where to invest and store it. This protects their asset wealth and ensures that the value of these assets increases. During the 20th century, new money transaction methods, such as electronic transfers, digital money, online transactions, and credit cards have emerged.

Banks issue credit cards that can be used as an interest-free loan tool or a flexible borrowing service for a limited period. Individuals can use credit cards to borrow money from banks, which they can use within a specific limit to pay for products or services. They can be used for payment without actual money being paid upfront, allowing cardholders to raise capital for free (although some credit cards do have an upfront fee). However, any late payments of such debt would lead to high interest charges and could have a knock-on effect on the following payments and damage to the individual's credit report. Moreover, lenders are reluctant to approve loan applications to individuals with significant outstanding debt. Therefore, to minimise risk, lenders will look at a borrower's credit report and history. Although money and credit offer purchasing power to people, they are different. Table 1.1 highlights the significant differences between money and credit.

> Investors do not work for money; their money works for them. They rely on their bank accounts to carry out financial transactions.

> Currency is not a reliable indicator of value because it can lose its value due to inflation, economic downturn, or both. Active investors know what makes real money and where to invest and store it.

> Lenders are reluctant to approve loan applications to individuals with significant outstanding debt. Therefore, to minimise risk, lenders will look at a borrower's credit report and history.

Table 1.1 The distinction between money and credit

Money	Credit
Physical money in the form of coins and notes that are used as a medium of exchange	Virtual money in the form of credit cards or loans that can be converted into cash
Maintained by people and banks as a physical cash	Offered by banks to people in the form of loans with interest, i.e. not free
Accessible cash to buy goods and services	Accessible money through credit cards or loans
Used by a limited number of customers who withdrawn cash; consumed on a daily basis	The majority of credit transfers use electronic transactions
A lot of cash is required to buy expensive goods and/or services	You do not need to have a lot of cash to buy expensive goods and/or services
No extra costs or interest charges are involved in using cash from your debit/savings accounts	There is a cost associated with using credit until it is paid back
There is no limit to using your money	There is a limit to using credit

Experienced property investors know how to use multiple credit cards to pay for property deposits when access to cash is limited. Depending on their credit limit, two or three credit cards can be used to pay for the deposit of a particular property deal that requires quick action. A few more credit cards can be used to pay off the debt of those existing credit cards in the following months to avoid interest charges. It is one of the skills mastered by very few investors to get funds from third-party institutions to finance their investment projects and build their portfolios. This can be a tricky payment process as it requires attention, careful planning, and money management skills to avoid late payments and any issues in one's credit report and scores.

One of the valuable features of using a credit card is that cardholders can claim their money back if the product/service has not been delivered by the supplier, service provider, or merchant. UK credit cardholders are protected and can recover their money between the value of £100 and £30,000 under Section 75 of the Consumer Credit Act when things go wrong. Some credit card providers offer extra purchase protection above the standard cover. However, you are not protected in all cases, so there are situations where you may not be able to claim a refund.

Cardholders should ensure they use credit cards responsibly, in stages, i.e., one project after the other, and for building cash flow and capital. Although no interest charges will be incurred if the balance is fully paid off within the stipulated time and the agreed credit limit is not exceeded, interest would build up on any unpaid amount. If the borrower chooses to repay only the credit card's minimum monthly payment to avoid a charge, interest will build up upon the remaining outstanding balance. Figure 1.3 shows the credit card transaction process and the main steps associated with this process. Many credit card suppliers have different offers; users should always check their monthly credit card statements, as this will reveal whether a fraudster has used their card to make purchases in their name or carry out fraudulent transactions.

> Although no interest charges will be incurred if the balance is fully paid off within the stipulated time and the agreed credit limit is not exceeded, interest would build up on any unpaid amount.

> Many credit card suppliers have different offers; users should always check their monthly credit card statements

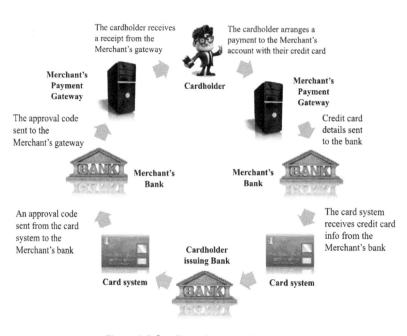

The cardholder receives a receipt from the Merchant's gateway

The cardholder arranges a payment to the Merchant's account with their credit card

Merchant's Payment Gateway

Cardholder

Merchant's Payment Gateway

The approval code sent to the Merchant's gateway

Credit card details sent to the bank

Merchant's Bank

Merchant's Bank

An approval code sent from the card system to the Merchant's bank

The card system receives credit card info from the Merchant's bank

Card system

Cardholder issuing Bank

Card system

Figure 1.3 Credit card transaction process

A 0% balance transfer offer from a credit card issuer allows a cardholder to move an existing debt from one credit card supplier to another. It is a helpful way to manage existing debt, but individuals must monitor their credit card activities to avoid unauthorised access to their accounts and money. If cardholders use their credit cards regularly, this encourages the suppliers to send them offers for finance and/or to increase their credit card's balance limit to a more significant amount. Credit card suppliers tend to compete to provide customers with the best deals in terms of credit limits, annual fees, and interest rates. Therefore, cardholders must manage their credit card properly and stick to the rules to avoid financial difficulty and unnecessary trouble. Also, cardholders and investors, in particular, must make sure they play the game carefully, otherwise the outcome is painful. Credit cards are helpful for

- short-term financing;
- building a credit history;
- buying products and services and, most importantly, buying assets.

Individuals must monitor their credit card activities to avoid unauthorised access to their accounts and money.

Cardholders must manage their credit card properly and stick to the rules to avoid financial difficulty and unnecessary trouble.

6. MANAGING YOUR CASH FLOW

Income is an essential aspect of personal finance and represents the money you receive from your employment or self-employment in return for work. You use your income to pay for your living expenses, such as food, transportation, utility bills, etc. You must manage your costs by controlling your outgoings and increasing your income to as high a figure as possible. This would allow you to save part of your earnings to use or invest in the future. However, there are many tools that you can use to manage your money; for example, budgeting can help you monitor and regulate expenses and allocate available cash and savings toward unexpected events, emergencies, or investing in tomorrow. One of the main tools you can use to plan your finances is the cash flow statement (or income statement), which shows the flow of your incoming and outgoing money during a specific time, such as a year or month, as shown in Table 1.2. Knowing the details of your income and financial commitments in terms of deductions, such as the tax you pay, social insurance, or pension contributions, will allow you to determine your net income and develop your financial plans.

You must manage your costs by controlling your outgoings and increasing your income to as high a figure as possible. This would allow you to save part of your earnings to use or invest in the future.

Knowing the details of your income and financial commitments in terms of deductions, such as the tax you pay, social insurance, or pension contributions, will allow you to determine your net income and develop your financial plans.

Table 1.2 Cash flow statement

Cashflow statement	
Income and Expenses	**Cashflow**
Income	
Your salary	
Income from investments	
Part-time job	
Deductions	
Net income	x
Expenses	
Rent	
Council tax	
Food	
Utility bills	
Car finance	
Clothes	
Internet and Phone	
Leisure	
Other	
Total spending	y
Surplus (+) / Deficit (-)	= x - y

The difference between the disposable or net income and the total spending amount determines whether or not a surplus is left at the bottom of the cash flow statement period. The cash flow statement can be checked to know whether or not you are living within your means and how to plan for the future.

You must consider investing in assets that generate profits and passive income, such as properties, and manage your liabilities. Liabilities include goods or services often resulting from unwise spending, leading to unnecessary debts and fees.

Keeping your expenses below received income is vital to long-term financial stability and security and avoiding unnecessary debt. This is a key step towards saving a part (20–30%) of your after-tax income, investing in assets, building your income-producing assets portfolio and generating wealth. To achieve that, you must use the available tools that can help you monitor and manage your finances consistently. You can use the cash flow statement to monitor the inflow and outflow of your money to help you manage your finances and budgeting. To use the cash flow statement correctly, you have to record all the sources of income, such as your salary from employment, self-employment, benefits, or returns from investments, including any deductions such as the tax on investments or contributions to private pensions.

To get an accurate figure of your disposable income, you have to consider the tax as part of the deductions, which may not be due on parts of the income until the end of the tax year. All parts of the income are added together, minus any deductions, to represent your net income. The second part of the cash flow statement lists all outgoings or expenses such as rent, food, utility bills, etc. The difference between the disposable or net income and the total spending amount determines whether or not a surplus is left at the bottom of the cash flow statement period. The cash flow statement can be checked to know whether or not you are living within your means and how to plan for the future. Having a surplus will determine how much you should be able to save every month or year and, consequently, how much you can invest.

Aiming for multiple sources of income can help you improve your lifestyle, effectively manage your debt and expenses, and ensure regular savings. Managing debt, keeping expenses lower than income, monitoring the budget, and careful investing are all crucial for building your assets portfolio. You must consider investing in assets that generate profits and passive income, such as properties, and manage your liabilities. Liabilities include goods or services often resulting from unwise spending, leading to unnecessary debts and fees. Lack of financial knowledge such as income statements, budgeting, and money management burdens individuals.

7. BORROWING MONEY

You may need to borrow money for many reasons: for instance, if your income is insufficient to cover your expenses, to finance a range of purchases, to fund an investment project, etc. If you're borrowing money from a bank, you should expect to pay interest on the borrowed money. Although inflation has, at the time of writing, made it difficult for households to make ends meet in terms of the rise in the cost of living, reducing the value of their money, experienced investors are using this opportunity to find good deals, borrow lots of money to fund their investment projects, and grow their portfolios and revenues. Although inflation is not good for most people, it is suitable for borrowers, especially those using borrowed money for investment purposes. As investors, we borrowed millions from different lenders to fund our real estate investment projects; some of the money was borrowed during inflation times in 2022 and 2023, which we used to grow our property portfolio.

Incurring managed debt allows people to receive funds that are inaccessible to anyone else and to raise funds or buy products or services whenever needed. However, they have to repay their debt out of the money they get from their future earnings. For instance, if the borrowed money was used to finance a buy-to-let property, then part of the generated rental income can be used to pay monthly interest or to repay the capital plus interest if it was a repayment loan. Consider buying a large residential house to rent part of it and increase your disposable income. You will reduce the cost of living in this large property if the monthly mortgage payments are less than the rental income you receive at the end of each month.

Of course, debt is bad and could lead to problems unless adequately invested to generate income. Bad debt is the kind of debt that is used to buy unnecessary stuff, often known as consumer debt. Examples of consumer debt are buying a large-screen TV, designer clothes, or expensive furniture just to show off. The major problem occurs when such goods are bought by people who cannot borrow, do not qualify for a credit card, and cannot afford to repay their debt. Unfortunately, due to lack of money management skills people tend to misuse the money they have access to whether it is council benefits, loan schemes offered by credit unions, universal credit, overdrafts, or even child benefits. This makes people unable to make their loan payments on time, which would lead to more problems. Banks can add extra fees to those individuals on top of their regular interest payments to minimise risk. Therefore, it is necessary to keep the debt and its costs controlled and well managed using different aspects of debt management to minimise personal risk.

> Although inflation is not good for most people, it is suitable for borrowers, especially those using borrowed money for investment purposes.

> Banks can add extra fees to those individuals on top of their regular interest payments to minimise risk. Therefore, it is necessary to keep the debt and its costs controlled and well managed using different aspects of debt management to minimise personal risk.

8. INVESTING MONEY

Investing is an important aspect of building wealth for the future and achieving financial independence. Increasing income, managing savings, and budgeting are vital for achieving your financial goals. If you have managed to build up good savings, it is time to move forward on your investment and financial independence journey. There are various investment vehicles available to select from, such as stocks, real estate, REITs (real estate investment trusts), commodities, cryptocurrencies, etc., and there are always suitable investment options. Investing long term and building a diversified portfolio is always good to ensure good returns and minimise risk. Moreover, having the proper financial knowledge, doing your due diligence and researching higher-return investments will positively impact your investment outcomes and financial independence journey.

Investing your money could be a challenging task initially, but using the right resources and getting the necessary knowledge and information will help you in your investment journey and make it easy. Building a successful business requires discipline and perseverance. Successful investors generally use a variety of opportunities depending on whether the economy is doing well or badly and feel confident operating in both situations. For instance, property prices tend to increase when the economy does well; active investors use this market situation to refinance or remortgage their properties to raise funds and reinvest them to grow their portfolios. During an economic downturn, property prices fall, making it an opportunity for investors to get good deals. We bought many of our properties during recession times. Most people think there are no opportunities for investment when the markets are depressed and prefer to avoid taking risks. However, regardless of how the economy is doing, there are always investment opportunities, even during unpleasant periods such as recessions.

Making money is common sense. It's not rocket science. But unfortunately, when it comes to money, common sense is uncommon.

Robert Kiyosaki

Building your multi-asset portfolio requires multiple skills and good knowledge of money management. Knowing how to reinvest raised funds from capital gains and profits to grow your asset portfolio and build wealth is essential. Individuals who start early in investing are often more knowledgeable about money and business management and willing to take risks. Investing requires a disciplined individual to acquire investment knowledge and business skills; the primary skills are listed below.

- Willingness to learn: many educational resources about investing and finance are available online for anyone interested in improving their knowledge.
- Developing a long-term strategy: investing requires a long-term business plan and discipline to achieve optimum results.

Sidebar notes:

Investing long term and building a diversified portfolio is always good to ensure good returns and minimise risk.

Most people think there are no opportunities for investment when the markets are depressed and prefer to avoid taking risks. However, regardless of how the economy is doing, there are always investment opportunities, even during unpleasant periods such as recessions.

Building your multi-asset portfolio requires multiple skills and good knowledge of money management.

- Managing credit and debt: to ensure good credit history and high credit rating scores, investors must monitor spending and keep debt under control.
- Financial management: developing financial and investment goals and budget plans, managing income and reassessing net worth and financial situation, and re-evaluating asset portfolio to ensure growth.
- Risk management: awareness of PESTEL (political, economic, sociological, technological, environmental, and legal) risk analysis, investment diversification, and investment exit strategy and options.

Investors often receive income from their assets, such as cash, property, stocks, commodities, and investment funds. Successful investors establish effective strategies to build their assets portfolio to generate profits through passive income. They keep their liabilities, such as credit card debts, unnecessary goods, etc., minimal. This ensures their investments are under control and meet their financial objectives. An individual's net worth is the value of their assets minus their debt liability. A healthy net worth is essential, especially when applying for a mortgage or personal or business loan. Therefore, you must ensure that your debt liabilities are not more than 40–45% of your assets. Banks check the net worth before deciding on your mortgage or personal or business loan application.

During a recession, most immature investors turn to a defensive mode and focus on defensive equities of companies such as healthcare, food, or telecoms, whose shares exhibit low volatility and whose earnings are unlikely to be affected by the downturn. However, intelligent investors who tend to do well when the economy grows can also do well during an economic downturn. As economic growth starts to slow, commodities and house prices fall and become affordable to investors who are well prepared for such periods. For investors who started their investments during the recession, their average annual return would be higher than those who started when the economy peaked.

> *Buy when everyone else is selling and hold until everyone else is buying. That's not just a catchy slogan. It's the very essence of successful investing.*
> J. Paul Getty

Ultimately, the main goal of your investment is to build a portfolio of high quality that produces passive income and dividend-paying stocks and to retire whenever you want to. Investment platforms, such as Dividend Aristocrats, Yahoo Finance, Investopedia, etc., provide useful information to all levels of investors, experienced and beginners. These resources present recent developments in the investment world and analyse and rank stock companies according to their dividend returns, growth rate, and growth history. Such resources are helpful for long-term investment, building quality portfolios, and learning about stock companies and their dividend payouts. Investing is different from speculation, but most people need help to understand the difference. Investing is a long-term business that requires researching and analysing the markets based on specific criteria to know

Successful investors establish effective strategies to build their assets portfolio to generate profits through passive income. They keep their liabilities, such as credit card debts, unnecessary goods, etc., minimal.

Investing is a long-term business that requires researching and analysing the markets based on specific criteria to know how they perform.

how they perform. This is to identify the investment opportunities using various factors, select the right strategy, and implement it at the right time.

9. RISK AND RETURN

Taking risks is an essential step for you if you are seeking success and financial rewards. This would allow you to gain a significant advantage over your competitors. Successful entrepreneurs tend to be disciplined, have a professional work attitude, and are prepared to go the extra mile to achieve their business goals. Different asset classes have different levels of risk, but there is no riskless investment, and the higher the expected return, the higher the risk attached. Therefore, risk management is vital for any investor to reduce any potential losses and maximise the likelihood of positive outcomes. You must acquire the necessary skills to manage and keep the risk of failure as minimal as possible. You have to be aware of the risk of losing out if your business fails to achieve its predicted profits due to unexpected changes in the market or economic circumstances.

Investment risk is the likelihood of financial loss rather than an expected return from a particular investment. Risk management is about identifying, forecasting, and evaluating a financial risk likely to happen to a business and its earnings and resources. In this way, you can minimise potential losses caused by negative factors and maximise the possibility of positive results and events. Investments that promise high income, such as a stock market, are often considered high risk. Medium-risk assets such as property usually provide a steady and medium income level.

Your ability to manage risk should allow you to enhance your financial skills and capabilities, improve your money management abilities and make the most of funds available for investment. Consider the following two strategies to keep your investment risks as minimal as possible and avoid the impact of market fluctuations.

- Lengthening your investment time: investing long term can help you in risk tolerance and mitigation. For instance, investing in equity (or stocks) would often lead to positive returns. Investing in real estate is less volatile than REITs equities, but both provide an attractive return potential over the long term.
- Diversifying your investment: investment diversification is about managing risk by accessing new markets or offering new services. Investing in different asset classes, such as properties and equities, helps spread your investment risk over multiple income streams from other types of assets and strategies. This is to build a diversified portfolio that contains various asset classes and keep risk as minimal as possible in case of economic downturn or market fluctuation.

Both strategies should help you manage your risk and develop a diversified portfolio of asset classes. Diversification can help you minimise the risk of your investments by spreading the risk in different asset classes, markets, commodities, or industries. This might require an asset allocation strategy to balance risk with returns by assessing the expected return percentage from each asset class. This would allow you to predict the overall returns

Different asset classes have different levels of risk, but there is no riskless investment, and the higher the expected return, the higher the risk attached.

Risk management is about identifying, forecasting, and evaluating a financial risk likely to happen to a business and its earnings and resources.

Investing in different asset classes, such as properties and equities, helps spread your investment risk over multiple income streams from other types of assets and strategies.

of the whole asset portfolio. The more financially able you are, the more likely you are to take on more risk and invest in multiple asset classes, such as equities, properties, gold, etc., without affecting your living expenses and lifestyle.

The more financially able you are, the more likely you are to take on more risk and invest in multiple asset classes, such as equities, properties, gold, etc., without affecting your living expenses and lifestyle.

> *Do not put all your eggs in one basket.*
>
> Unknown

You must prepare before investing your money, especially for the first time. Investing is about making money and producing a profit, which implies taking risks. This means you either profit or lose part or all of your invested money. The crucial step here is to manage your risk and assess your financial situation and resources before deciding which investment to select and making any financial decision. Investors use different investment strategies, also known as asset classes. Asset classes offer different types of revenues and are managed differently as well, as follows:

- Equities: investors buy shares of a company which they believe will grow and its shares will increase in price. Buying shares in a company makes them part owners of that business. Share prices tend to fluctuate rapidly and can be bought and sold through online stock market platforms such as https://uk.finance.yahoo.com/
- Managed funds: they are different investment markets that offer diverse options for investments. Busy investors and inexperienced individuals can invest in a managed fund that an experienced professional manages. The values of managed funds fluctuate depending on the value of the stock markets.
- Real estate: different options and strategies for investing in real estate exist. For instance, residential and commercial real estate can offer a good rental income. This type of investment requires a deposit of 20–25% of the property value to be paid, and the rest can be raised as a mortgage from a lending financial institution such as a bank or non-high street lender. Like any other investment, there is a risk because the property market and mortgage interest rates can change, including the costs associated with managing properties and tenants.

Residential and commercial real estate can offer a good rental income.

Figure 1.4 shows an example of a diversified investment and the expected returns from each type of investment. In this example, the investor allocated 70% of their portfolio to real estate, 20% to managed funds, and 10% to equities/shares. The real estate class generates an 8% return (or yield), managed funds generate a 10% return, and equities a 12% return, as shown in Table 1.3. This makes the average expected returns of all three asset classes 10%.

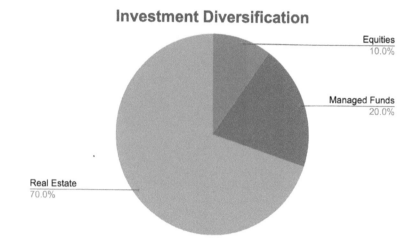

Figure 1.4 Investment diversification

Table 1.3 Portfolio investment returns

Asset Class	Investment Percentage %	Expected Returns %
Equities	10	12
Managed Funds	20	10
Real Estate	70	8
Average Expected Returns		10

Active investors accumulate wealth and often aim for financial independence through receiving income from their profit-producing assets. They monitor their finances and investments regularly, manage their debt, and ensure their net worth is high enough to enjoy and show good financial health. Financial independence is important for successful investors to maintain a good living standard for themselves and their families without the need to work. They often have a financial plan that helps them monitor and assess their financial situation and achieve their goals of maintaining a good standard of living and supporting their daily living expenses during their early retirement and more.

10. SUMMARY

Money is vital in progressing our economies and fulfilling our financial needs and commitments. We use money to carry out daily transactions and value our products and services. The flow of global wealth relies on the transactions used to pay for those required commodities and consumed products and services. This chapter has covered the main characteristics of money, its importance, its impact on our daily lives and many other entities, such as governments and businesses. Wealthy people and organisations often have options for business opportunities and access to helpful business information and services. The monetary system, economic principles, and the role of supply and demand in inflation have been discussed. Risk and return and investing in multiple asset classes have been introduced. Investing requires financial resources and planning; furthermore, we need to figure out how to afford those resources and increase our knowledge of financial planning. This can be achieved by improving our professional skills, financial expertise, and commitment. This chapter also covered the main challenges of inflation and its impact on people's lives, savings, and investments. Therefore, it is essential to be well informed about those challenges and think seriously about how to manage money and have options in life.

Developing innovative ideas and exploring possibilities of what options are available for investment is vital for beating inflation. The next chapter introduces financial independence concepts and available options. The journey toward financial independence requires multiple skills, but self-discipline and taking action are also necessary. To achieve financial freedom, you must be prepared to pay a personal price and do what the majority are uncomfortable doing. Financial stress management and the main measures that can be followed to avoid stressful situations and minimise financial risk are covered. You will learn how earning your living without being forced to work for anyone else is something to consider in order to achieve your financial goals.

> Investing requires financial resources and planning; furthermore, we need to figure out how to afford those resources and increase our knowledge of financial planning.

> The journey toward financial independence requires multiple skills, but self-discipline and taking action are also necessary. To achieve financial freedom, you must be prepared to pay a personal price and do what the majority are uncomfortable doing.

FINANCIAL INDEPENDENCE

2

Money is only a tool. It will take you wherever you wish, but it will not replace you as the driver.

Ayn Rand

Financial independence (FI) is an attractive idea for people from all different backgrounds and cultures. However, FI requires multiple skills, which can be achieved through learning, discipline, and commitment. A practical and attractive financial plan is also required. People must educate themselves about managing their money and fighting financial illiteracy. This chapter introduces the principles of FI and basic concepts of money management and investment. This is to help you explore available opportunities and options to find innovative ideas and explore possibilities of what options are available for investment. This chapter ends with a dedicated section about financial stress management using four main measures that can be followed to avoid stressful situations and minimise financial risk.

1. FI Journey

FI is about being financially free and able to earn a living without being forced to work for anyone else. The journey toward financial freedom and making wise financial decisions is not an easy one and requires much effort, focus, and self-discipline. It requires working hard and serious commitment, learning new financial skills, and paying a personal price. To achieve financial freedom, you must be prepared to do, as I have said before, what the majority are unwilling to do. However, there is nothing that can stop you from achieving your dream, and the only obstacle is yourself. In this chapter, an answer to the question 'Why FI?' is provided with an explanation of how investment can help people achieve their dreams of FI.

It is not because things are difficult that we do not dare, it is because we do not dare that they are difficult.

Lucius Annaeus Seneca

FI is about being financially free and able to earn a living without being forced to work for anyone else.

It requires working hard and serious commitment, learning new financial skills, and paying a personal price. To achieve financial freedom, you must be prepared to do, as I have said before, what the majority are unwilling to do.

Many people need to develop their household budget and control spending. They might spend money on unnecessary things and need more money management skills. The majority need help understanding inflation and investment. Some spend hours watching TV programmes and on social media, which can be a waste of valuable time.

> *Rich people stay rich by living like they are broke and*
> *broke people stay broke by living like they are rich*
>
> Dave Ramsey

FI can change your life dramatically, but this requires a proper financial plan and SMART (specific, measurable, achievable, relevant, and time-bound) objectives. To achieve your financial goals and commitment, you must fully control your spending, explore possibilities, and seek opportunities and options to find innovative ideas to develop plans for your investment projects. Setting specific objectives is vital to make them measurable, and once they are measurable, they can be achievable and manageable.

> *You cannot manage what you do not measure*
>
> Peter Drucker

1.1. Why FI?

Is it true that money doesn't bring happiness? I think it does. It is a claim by many people without proper evidence or supported by data. Unfortunately, it is like many myths that people believe about life but which hinder their progress and keep them from achieving FI. Have you ever heard a wealthy person saying they are unhappy because of their wealth? I don't think so. Money alone doesn't bring happiness, of course, but the opportunities it brings can make a lot of difference to our happiness. I have had experience of different types of life: being overstressed and overstretched in a toxic working environment, making money for the top management while personally struggling to make ends meet, and the other, brighter side, and I can see the difference. Money can help us buy a thing that many people are struggling to get even though it is free but precious: time. Research published by the University of Pennsylvania in 2021 found that happiness increases with income until $100,000 is reached for the least happy group. However, for the happiest group, the association with happiness actually rises with income above $100,000.

In a standard economy and open labour market, employers offer jobs to their employees and negotiate their work contracts, rights, and obligations, including payment (De Henau and Callaghan, 2019). Employers aim to maximise the revenues of their businesses, while employees aim to maximise the income they receive in exchange for their effort, time, expertise, and skills. Labour protection laws tend to differ from country to country, and unions remain the entity with institutional power to negotiate employees'

Sidebar notes:

The majority need help understanding inflation and investment. Some spend hours watching TV programmes and on social media, which can be a waste of valuable time.

Money alone doesn't bring happiness, of course, but the opportunities it brings can make a lot of difference to our happiness.

Money can help us buy a thing that many people are struggling to get even though it is free but precious: time.

Employers aim to maximise the revenues of their businesses, while employees aim to maximise the income they receive in exchange for their effort, time, expertise, and skills.

rights, wages, and working conditions and times. Owing to a lack of fair regulations and political will to improve the situation and the weakened position of labour representation, job insecurity, limited resources to fund pensions, and wage inequality are rising in many developed and developing countries. All these factors can have serious consequences, particularly a negative impact on people's lives, stress levels, and well-being. This makes the topic of FI and self-reliance increasingly important.

They deem me mad because I will not sell my days for gold, and I deem them mad because they think my days have a price.
Kahlil Gibran

The long working hours and low-paid labour in both the low-skilled and high-skilled ends of the labour market and below-inflation-rate pay rises create the perfect conditions for labour abuses and severe exploitation to arise. The lack of proper regulations for addressing employment challenges leaves people vulnerable to modern slavery with limited choices but to accept such unpleasant situations, keep silent, and avoid the risk of losing their jobs. I hope that this chapter provides a simple answer to this problem. FI is using your financial literacy skills to generate sufficient income to live comfortably and meet your needs without being employed or dependent on others. It is about the independence, rewards, and opportunity provided to you.

> FI is using your financial literacy skills to generate sufficient income to live comfortably and meet your needs without being employed or dependent on others.

Time is more valuable than money. You can get more money, but you cannot get more time.
Jim Rohn

FI allows people to change their lives completely, empowers them to do what they want, sack their bosses, and end their inhumane treatment. When you are financially independent, you do not have to wait for anyone to give approval for holidays or permission to take a rest from endless work. FI empowers you by giving you many opportunities, much more than an average person can imagine. Also, FI can help you ditch your unhealthy pastimes, become a healthy person, able to help others financially and get rid of money worries. Instead, you learn how to develop good financial plans and adopt recognised investment strategies.

> FI empowers you by giving you many opportunities, much more than an average person can imagine.

It is a kind of spiritual snobbery that makes people think they can be happy without money.
Albert Camus

Making financial freedom a priority objective in your life will help you to achieve it. You do not need to over-complicate things; you just have to take it seriously, move step-by-step, and follow your developed financial plan and objectives. You need to be honest with yourself and about your beliefs because your behaviour and attitude will determine whether or not you will succeed in your FI journey. FI requires a clear road map, long-term planning, and adequate investment to build up income-generating assets and passive income streams. It is available to all people regardless of their background, culture, or belief and regardless of what they do. However, the earlier you start learning about money management, the sooner you become financially independent; therefore, you need to acquire the following skills:

- assess your financial situation;
- find ways to improve your income;
- develop a plan for multiple streams of income;
- develop and implement a saving strategy;
- manage your spending and debts;
- minimise your expenses;
- set a budget;
- learn about investment;
- invest in knowledge.

> *If money is your hope for independence, you will never have it. The only real security that a man will have in this world is a reserve of knowledge, experience, and ability.*
> Henry Ford

> *If you think education is expensive, try ignorance.*
> Robert Orben

During my early working life, I had to save aggressively, avoid nonsense spending, budget my expenses carefully, and manage my monthly salary and part-time income. I set up my small computer business in Tripoli in 1995. I invested most of my money into buying PCs to deliver my training programmes and the necessary furniture and equipment for the company. I had to close the business in 1997 before travelling to the UK for postgraduate study. If you understand and follow the strategies introduced in this book, you will do better financially in the future and will fundamentally change your perception of money.

> *It is not the strongest of the species nor the most intelligent that survives. It is the one that is most adaptable to change.*
> Charles Darwin

FI requires a clear road map, long-term planning, and adequate investment to build up income-generating assets and passive income streams. It is available to all people regardless of their background, culture, or belief and regardless of what they do.

If you understand and follow the strategies introduced in this book, you will do better financially in the future and will fundamentally change your perception of money.

Most people struggle not because they cannot make money or it is not easy to make or they do not understand managing it; they were not given the opportunity to learn how to make it. There is more than enough money in the world. In 2021, according to Wikipedia, there were 56 million millionaires, many of whom were self-made, with various skills and professions. Some are super-wealthy, offering diverse products and services and operating in different sectors. Most people need a clear direction for their life and support in money management and their long-term financial plans. They need to have the right mindset and know their priorities and goals in life. To achieve FI, you must learn how to manage money by improving your income, committing to saving, developing your household budget, and expanding your investing skills.

Being financially independent can allow you to support people and your favourite charities and organisations. In the *Cambridge English Dictionary*, 'financial' and 'independence' are defined as follows:

- Financial: 'relating to money or how money is managed'.
- Independence: 'the ability to live without being helped or influenced by others'.

So, FI is about managing your own money to cover your living expenses and live your life without being helped by others. Depending on how passionate and enthusiastic you are about becoming financially independent, achieving your goals in ten years or even less than that is possible. It is a difficult journey that requires a lot of learning and an extraordinary amount of work, but it is worth the effort. However, working hard for such an ultimate goal will depend on various circumstances and require serious commitment. Not many people are willing to give up spending their money unnecessarily to satisfy their unreasonable demands and unhealthy habits. What worsens things is the time unwisely spent on shopping, online shopping, and social media. If you are an employee, regardless of your salary, you are dependent on your employer for your living, which implies dependence on their support. There is a clear difference between a high-salary income from employment and long-term and self-made wealth. The *Cambridge English Dictionary* defines employment as 'work that you are paid to do for a particular company or organization'.

Like Warren, I had a considerable passion to get rich, not because I wanted Ferraris – I wanted independence. I desperately wanted it.'
Charlie Munger

1.2. Rat race

Employment often leads to unhappy and deeply dissatisfied employees working long hours for limited wages to feed their families and please their bosses due to a lack of options. It is often called the rat race because employees keep working tirelessly for long hours and compete with each other for little reward, long-awaited promotion, or fake recognition by their employers.

Most people struggle not because they cannot make money or it is not easy to make or they do not understand managing it; they were not given the opportunity to learn how to make it.

Most people need a clear direction for their life and support in money management and their long-term financial plans. They need to have the right mindset and know their priorities and goals in life.

Depending on how passionate and enthusiastic you are about becoming financially independent, achieving your goals in ten years or even less than that is possible. It is a difficult journey that requires a lot of learning and an extraordinary amount of work, but it is worth the effort.

Employment often leads to unhappy and deeply dissatisfied employees working long hours for limited wages to feed their families and please their bosses due to a lack of options.

Opportunity does not knock; you have to find it.

*If you don't value your time, neither will others. Stop giving
away your time and talents- start charging for it.*

Kim Garst

<table>
<tr><td>

The rat race is
commonly associated
with a monotonous
routine and dissatis-
faction with life without
time for enjoyment.

</td><td>

The rat race is commonly associated with a monotonous routine and dissat-
isfaction with life without time for enjoyment. Working as an employee for
someone else is a pointless pursuit. It means allowing your employer to set
your aims and objectives for you and allowing them to take credit for your
stressful job and efforts. Therefore, many employees trapped in the rat race
feel dissatisfied with their jobs and generally live unhappy lives. What makes
their situation even worse is that they feel hopeless because they cannot
escape their unpleasant situation and take control of their life and destiny.
Figure 2.1 shows the employment rat race and its futile financial cycle.

</td></tr>
</table>

*If you ask the CEO of some major corporation what he does,
he will say, in all honesty, that he is slaving 20 hours a day to
provide his customers with the best goods or services he can and
creating the best possible working conditions for his employees.*

Noam Chomsky

During the second decade of the 21st century, I was unhappy with my
employment and left it after I set up my property investment company. I
entirely oppose society's perception of the 9:00 am–5:00 pm abusive daily
rat race and their perception of money. I still remember when I became

financially independent. I started to value every minute of my life to the point I began waking up early, enjoying my daily early morning coffee, and working for myself with my family whenever we wanted to.

I still remember when I became financially independent. I started to value every minute of my life to the point I began waking up early, enjoying my daily early morning coffee, and working for myself with my family whenever we wanted to.

Figure 2.1 Rat race

Earn with your mind, not your time.
Naval Ravikant

2. THE BEGINNING

The question often presented is how to begin your self-employment or get the money to pay for a property deposit. Well, you need to learn how to save money from your current income-generating job. Any saved money could then be invested to make extra money, which can then be reinvested to make even more money, and so on. This requires a change in your spending habits, in your mindset, in behaviour, in lifestyle, and in dealing with money. Also, it requires discipline, learning about investment, building credit, managing the budget, and then reinvesting. Your mindset plays a significant role in achieving success; the rest is gaining knowledge and applying techniques. Unfortunately, changing your mindset from buying liabilities to acquiring assets is an unavoidable step in starting your FI journey. This might require

Your mindset plays a significant role in achieving success; the rest is gaining knowledge and applying techniques. Unfortunately, changing your mindset from buying liabilities to acquiring assets is an unavoidable step in starting your FI journey.

a change in your perception of money and behaviour adjustment in terms of making financial decisions.

You must acquire the financial know-how and necessary money management skills to maximise your income, implement a saving strategy, control your spending, and develop budgeting skills. Regardless of your current net worth, you must understand how to list your assets and liabilities to establish your balance sheet. Assets are the resources you own that generate income and can provide you with other economic benefits. Liabilities are financial obligations or debts you owe to others. Your net worth comes down to your balance sheet, i.e., your portfolio of assets and liabilities, as shown in Table 2.1. You will have a positive net worth if your assets exceed your liabilities.

Assets are the resources you own that generate income and can provide you with other economic benefits. Liabilities are financial obligations or debts you owe to others.

Table 2.1 Balance sheet

Personal Balance Sheet	
Date	DD/MM/YYYY
Assets	
Asset 1	A1
Asset 2	A2
Asset 3	A3
Asset 4	A4
Asset 5	A5
Total Assets =	**A1+A2+A3+A4+A5**
Liabilities	
Liability 1	L1
Liability 2	L2
Liability 3	L3
Liability 4	L4
Total Liabilities =	**L1+L2+L3+L4**
Total Equity (Net worth) =	Total Assets + Total Liabilities

Your liabilities to assets ratio and leverage ratio (see Chapter 4) determine your financial situation. Different financial tools and techniques are covered in this book. Adopting the investor mindset should help you manage your finances.

3. FI AND INVESTMENT

We must regularly reflect on our financial situation and understand where we stand and why we are in our current situation.

Becoming financially independent is a complex, time-consuming, and labour-intensive process and challenging at times, but undeniably rewarding. We must regularly reflect on our financial situation and understand where we stand and why we are in our current situation. Using the following basic FI algorithm, the four factors determining whether you are financially independent are your monthly income, expenses, assets, and liabilities.

IF your monthly income < monthly expenses
OR your assets < liabilities
THEN you are not financially independent

IF your monthly income > monthly expenses
AND your assets > liabilities
THEN you are financially independent

Therefore, to be financially independent, you need to have a higher monthly income than your monthly expenses and assets worth more than your liabilities at any point in time. An old saying opines, 'You have to have money to make money'. It is true. If you have to work overtime, go for it if possible. If you are in debt, then you must learn how to manage it and to keep it as low as possible as soon as possible before it gets worse.

To achieve FI, you need to explore possibilities and seek opportunities and options to find innovative ideas, as shown in Figure 2.2. You may identify the options available for investment, such as property, stocks, trading, pensions, bank account deposits, etc. You must conduct rigorous research about all selected markets or industries. It is essential to understand the difference between all of them, their strengths and limitations, and then select the one(s) that are likely to work for you. To take advantage of any investment option is to make sure that you have enough capital ready for investment. FI requires a change in mentality and in our way of thinking. Getting into the business of property investment requires a behaviour change. Figure 2.3 summarises the preliminary steps of becoming financially independent. This book covers various types of investments and asset classes but focuses on only one kind of investment: property investment.

> FI requires a change in mentality and in our way of thinking. Getting into the business of property investment requires a behaviour change.

Relinquish your attachment to the known, step into the unknown, and you will step into the field of possibilities.
Deepak Chopra

It's good to have money and the things that money can buy, but it's good, too, to check up once in a while and make sure that you haven't lost the things that money can't buy.
George Lorimer

Figure 2.2 Exploration of possibilities

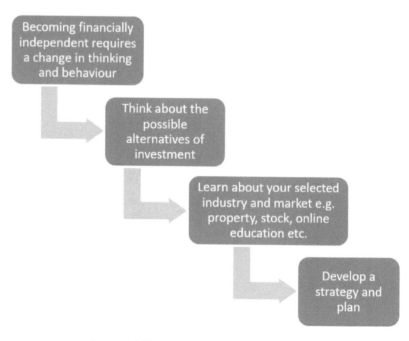

Figure 2.3 The preliminary steps of investment

FI requires a financial plan, strategy, and budget.

- **FI strategy:** An FI strategy aims to help you achieve your financial goals. You need to identify and select the appropriate strategy to move forward. Each strategy has its strengths and limitations.

- **FI plan:** To address all aspects of your financial situation and to know when money is coming in and going out. It is to help you save money and organise your finances. This is to manage your spending and your selected investment option.

- **FI budget:** To view your current income and expenses situation. A budget helps you identify what money is coming in and going out.

Developing a financial strategy, addressing a financial situation, and managing a budget require much work but not necessarily an expert level of financial knowledge. Money management is a creative process for leveraging and requires a long-term plan, strategy, and careful investment over time. However, long term doesn't necessarily mean enjoying FI only when you retire; that is wrong. You deserve to enjoy financial freedom while you are young if you plan it right. The more extensive your portfolio, the more likely you will become financially independent earlier. The returns generated on your portfolio can change your life forever, before and after retirement age. Unfortunately, education systems worldwide do not teach money management; this is another crucial problem that requires tackling, but is beyond the scope of this book.

> Money management is a creative process for leveraging and requires a long-term plan, strategy, and careful investment over time. However, long term doesn't necessarily mean enjoying FI only when you retire; that is wrong.

Capital as such is not evil; it is its wrong use that is evil.
Capital in some form or other will always be needed.
Gandhi

4. MANAGING FINANCIAL STRESS

Financial stress is a common problem in modern life. Thinking about money and your own financial commitments and expenses, such as rent, regular utility bills, and debt can be stressful. The situation could worsen, especially when working for a ruthless employer in a toxic environment or trying to survive during tough economic times. Unfortunately, only a few employers can understand the needs of their workers and are willing to support them. The likelihood of experiencing stress and anxiety due to financial matters or income insecurity is very high. For most people, the most stressful issue is not earning enough money or, even worse, becoming broke. Lack of money and financial stress could lead to various problems, as follows:

> The likelihood of experiencing stress and anxiety due to financial matters or income insecurity is very high.

- making people feel overwhelmed, feel sick mentally and physically (weight gain or loss), and hindering their ability to think logically and function rationally;

- people feeling irritated and worried and losing their confidence; the decline in mental health would make it difficult for people to control their finances;
- affecting people's relationships, family connections, and quality of life;
- increasing the risk of depression and anxiety and decreasing the levels of enthusiasm and energy;
- affecting their immune system, which could lead to a behavioural disorder and unpleasant symptoms.

Financial stress is part of our life; it is unavoidable, and we cannot and must not deny it. Denying the reality of an unpleasant situation will only make things more complicated and even worse. However, we must deal with it, alleviate stressful conditions, and minimise its impact on our daily lives and families. This does not mean those who live a life of financial freedom are stress-free and vice versa. Living a simple life could be an option to eliminate stress and avoid financial struggles and hardship, but it is necessary to select the appropriate environment for such a life.

Denying the reality of an unpleasant situation will only make things more complicated and even worse.

> *The greatest weapon against stress is our ability to choose one thought over another.*
> William James

No one wants to be financially stressed or worry about money. Everyone deserves a stress-free and peaceful life full of joy and happiness. No one else will take care of your finances as much as you will, so you need to prioritise taking care of your finances. It is simple; you will become stressed if you do not manage your finances. Therefore, self-care is essential when it comes to finances and stress management. This means having complete control of the situation and your finances. It is useful to develop a strategy to deal with stress immediately, before it threatens your life and the situation runs out of control. There is no perfect life, but you need to be in control, prepared to eliminate the causes of stress, and have choices in life. It is essential to address the underlying problems of our finances before they get out of control and become difficult to resolve. There is a range of possible solutions to the problem of financial stress. This might require a brainstorming session to reach the roots of the problem and then follow through on actions and possible solutions. Figure 2.4 shows a model containing four main measures that can be followed to self-manage financial commitments, avoid stressful situations, and minimise financial risk. All four criteria are described below and supported with quotes by well-known figures.

It is useful to develop a strategy to deal with stress immediately, before it threatens your life and the situation runs out of control.

There is a range of possible solutions to the problem of financial stress. This might require a brainstorming session to reach the roots of the problem and then follow through on actions and possible solutions.

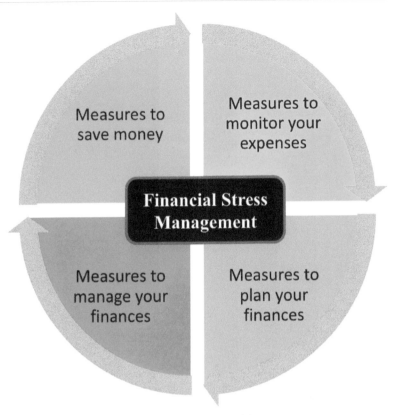

Figure 2.4 Managing financial stress

A wise person should have money in his head, but not in their heart.

Jonathan Swift

- **Monitor your expenses:** identify your main financial challenges, unnecessary commitments, and problems associated with income generation. Tracking your spending, credit rating, and history by keeping a detailed record of your outgoings is helpful. This could be achieved by regularly reviewing bank statements and examining transaction history. Avoid late payments, which can adversely impact your credit reports, by setting up automatic payments using direct debit or standing orders. Also, avoid overspending and too much shopping, prioritise your debts, and manage your budget regularly. This is to make sure that your incomings exceed outgoings.

> Tracking your spending, credit rating, and history by keeping a detailed record of your outgoings is helpful.

*A budget is telling your money where to go
instead of wondering where it went.*

John Maxwell

- **Develop a financial plan:** financial stress does not disappear over-night; it requires proper planning and thinking. Develop a plan to manage your income, expenditure, and debt and, most importantly, stick to it. It is helpful to devise a plan and review your financial situation regularly. As part of your plan, you can develop a clear list of financial goals and actions and ensure you work towards them. Focusing on priorities and what you want first and then the less crucial matters is essential. Financial preparation can help you recover quickly from financial hardships and economic downturns. You need to regularly review your plan and insert the necessary updates into it.

It is helpful to devise a plan and review your financial situation regularly. As part of your plan, you can develop a clear list of financial goals and actions and ensure you work towards them.

Planning is bringing the future into the present so that you can do something about it now.
Alan Lakein

- **Manage your finances:** Manage your financial commitments and reduce unnecessary stuff. Develop a realistic budget to maximise assets and minimise liabilities. Review your budget and look for ways to improve your finances.

It's not how much money you make, but how much money you keep, how hard it works for you, and how many generations you keep it for.
Robert Kiyosaki

- **Learn how to save money:** saving requires good financial skills, helps manage unexpected expenses, and helps you adhere to your financial plan. You must build an emergency fund for future urgent financial needs and challenging times. Do not punish yourself for unintentional financial mismanagement or deny yourself a treat; saving money can help you make some investments.

The competition level and business environment play a significant role in your success. For example, working in a rewarding market and serving quality clients in various parts of the globe will positively affect you and help you progress your career effectively.

Do not save what is left after spending, but spend what is left after saving.
Warren Buffett

Indeed, people with excellent credit scores and good jobs or stable employment and income will probably receive the best loan offers to fund their investment projects. However, your ability to earn a high income will depend on your acquired knowledge and skills as well as your contribution to the business market. This will allow you to save part of your income and get the best deals. The competition level and business environment play a significant role in your success. For example, working in a rewarding market and serving quality clients in various parts of the globe will positively affect you and help you progress your career effectively. This requires changing your attitude, increasing your skills, and making yourself visible to top employers in your industry. To get the best out of your upskilling activities and investment, there are various options available for you to choose from, depending on your needs. But you have to decide what to do next and what skill you need to improve to achieve your financial goals and maximise the return on investment (ROI) on your outlay. Convincing lenders of your financial abilities to fund your investment project is a good step toward FI.

> *Wealth is not about having a lot of money;*
> *it's about having a lot of options.*
> Chris Rock

5. SUMMARY

The journey toward FI requires multiple skills, which can be learnt, self-discipline, and serious commitment. To achieve FI, you must be prepared to pay a personal price and do what the majority are uncomfortable doing. Most people need more money management skills, spend their money on unnecessary things, and spend hours of their time on meaningless TV programmes and social media. They do not try to invest in financial education to improve their financial skills. Remember that the only obstacle to achieving your financial dream is yourself. Many resources are available for you to learn and practise to help you fight financial illiteracy and improve your financial skills and planning abilities. This chapter has introduced the basic concepts and principles of FI, money management, and investment. These skills help you develop innovative ideas and explore the possibilities of what options are available for investment.

> Many resources are available for you to learn and practise to help you fight financial illiteracy and improve your financial skills and planning abilities.

A section dedicated to financial stress management was introduced, including four main measures that can be followed to avoid stressful situations and minimise financial risk. You learnt that FI is about earning your living and obtaining money without being forced to work for anyone else and then using that money to fulfil your financial commitments. Therefore, managing income is vital in keeping your finances progressing to pay for products and services for yourself, your family, and the people you want to help. The next chapter covers various important aspects of income, the financial planning process, and investment philosophy. Issues about improving your financial situation and the impact of inflation on your finances are also discussed. The following chapter presents strategies for increasing your income and planning future milestones to achieve your financial goals.

INCOME AND INFLATION

3

We must think seriously about how to afford our living expenses, receive an income that can cover these expenses, and improve our financial situation. Learning about money and how to improve our income plays a significant role in managing our finances and improving our financial situation. Therefore, we must receive enough income to meet our daily needs and financial goals. This could be achieved by improving our professional skills, getting a higher paid job, understanding the tax system, and seeking other income streams, such as part-time jobs or exploring opportunities for investing in real estate or the stock market. This chapter highlights the difference between income and wealth, and passive and active income. Issues related to income and your lifetime, planning future milestones of your life to achieve your financial goals, and the impact of inflation are covered. The main issues to be aware of when you plan for your finances and various strategies for increasing your earned income are introduced. I also present my GROW A+ financial planning process, adapted from the known GROW model and my investment philosophy.

1. YOUR INCOME

Increasing income should be your core strategy for improving your financial situation. However, having multiple methods for managing income, such as managing debts, minimising liabilities and expenses, budgeting, raising savings income, and investing, is necessary to build your portfolio of assets and towards your ultimate goal of FI. These strategies are powerful and vital for your financial situation and lifestyle, the people or organisations needing your support, and those dependent on you. Before we proceed with our discussions about your income, let us agree upon the difference between income and wealth as follows:

- Income: a periodic flow of money such as a wage, rental income, or benefits from your government.
- Wealth: a stock of assets valued at a particular time that includes valuable possessions and money that have been accumulated over time.

Most people work as employees in jobs where they exchange their skills and time for money through wages. Paid employment from public or private-sector employers or self-employment is the primary income source for most people. Employees must wait a month to get paid by their employers and manage their income every month. This ensures that the earned income

If you are one of those who exchange time and labour for a monthly wage, regardless of the money you receive at the end of the month, then you are likely to be in the same position as most people.

will cover all their monthly expenses and that anything left is kept as savings. If you are one of those who exchange time and labour for a monthly wage, regardless of the money you receive at the end of the month, then you are likely to be in the same position as most people. This is a challenging position because, if you stop working and do not show up every morning, your employer can press the button to stop your income, and money stops coming into your bank account. This is the harsh reality that the majority are unable to think about seriously due to various reasons.

Investing in education and financial skills would help your plans for FI. You must learn how to improve your income and manage your expenses.

Investing in education and financial skills would help your plans for FI. You must learn how to improve your income and manage your expenses. You still work for an employer for a few years, especially after graduation. You might need such support to learn different skills through employment, whether technical, organisational, or management skills. Job markets are very competitive and require multiple skills and experience of the applicants. If you are one of those competent applicants with quality skills and manage to get a higher-paid job, that would help you plan your savings and manage expenses.

Many employers offer good training programmes for their staff to help them improve their knowledge about their work duties and enhance their work abilities. If you received an opportunity that is unavailable to others, such as a job offer from a reputable corporation or successful SME, you should take advantage of this. The higher your education and skills, the better your earnings and income, and the higher the opportunity to invest for a better lifestyle. For individuals, the two main types of income are as follows:

The higher your education and skills, the better your earnings and income, and the higher the opportunity to invest for a better lifestyle.

- Active income: earning from delivering a service for an employer or customer, i.e., receiving income for work in which an individual is actively involved, e.g., a job.
- Passive income: earning without participating or with little effort, where an individual is not actively involved, e.g., rental income or as a result of capital growth. Such an income requires some work and extra attention at the beginning to set it up.

Getting a good level of education and selecting a subject you are passionate about are essential for improving your employability and earnings. Acquiring entrepreneurial skills and investing in yourself can help you develop innovative and cost-effective solutions to your market problems and become knowledgeable in your business area. You can set up a business that delivers services or produces high-demand products and become financially independent. The higher the income you receive from your business, the more money you can save and invest.

Acquiring entrepreneurial skills and investing in yourself can help you develop innovative and cost-effective solutions to your market problems and become knowledgeable in your business area.

People are not the same; each person has their individual abilities and challenges, but there are specific steps each person has to consider during their financial freedom journey. Therefore, seeking better jobs with higher earnings is essential; however, having multiple sources of income does help to ensure a better living standard and the ability to save regularly. The following steps are significant to creating income, especially in your early working life, whether it is active or passive income or a combination of both:

- keeping expenses lower than income;
- having a spending plan;

- managing after-tax income savings regularly;
- monitoring the budget;
- working overtime, extra shifts, or second part-time job;
- investing carefully is a significant step toward creating income;
- developing a positive work attitude;
- developing a disciplined and professional life.

The more knowledgeable and experienced you are with transferable skills, such as problem-solving, sales, marketing, computing, and critical thinking, the more likely it is that you will get a well-paid job. What matters is the expertise and experience you developed over the years, which might give you an advantage over competitors. The kind of business activities you are involved in, the complexity of your tasks and the responsibilities you hold, and the demand for the business services or products you offer will determine the opportunities for you to obtain a higher salary. The level of market competition will determine the willingness of the business management to offer higher wages to attract talent and offer them additional benefits in order to retain quality employees and remain competitive.

What matters is the expertise and experience you developed over the years, which might give you an advantage over competitors.

The level of market competition will determine the willingness of the business management to offer higher wages to attract talent and offer them additional benefits in order to retain quality employees and remain competitive.

2. INCOME AND YOUR LIFETIME

It is helpful to know how your income from a job may change up and down during your lifetime and what can be done to improve the situation. Although income profiles vary significantly between individuals (for instance, highly educated professionals receive more earnings than those with lower skills), some patterns apply to most people. Your earnings are affected by different events and the skills and qualifications you gained, which may help you achieve higher wages over time. Therefore, you must take the necessary steps to plan early and build a robust financial plan. Figure 3.1 shows a generic curve that depicts how an individual's earnings change as they age, assuming they lived all their life working as an employee in a job for a company or for someone else.

Your earnings are affected by different events and the skills and qualifications you gained, which may help you achieve higher wages over time.

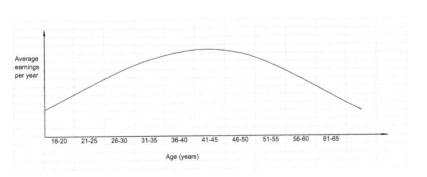

Figure 3.1 An individual's earnings working in a job

Figure 3.1 captures how individuals may begin working as low earners and then move to better income levels as they gain higher qualifications and experience. Finally, the curve turns down as they get older and retire.

Figure 3.2 shows a successful investor curve that depicts the change in their earnings over the years. It depicts multiple ups and downs and demonstrates that income is increasing all the time, even after their early retirement and probably after their death, if they had a proper legacy plan. Notice that the y-axis doesn't include any numbers for the average annual earnings. This was deliberate, to show you the difference between both cases, regarding how both perform financially, and avoid confusion.

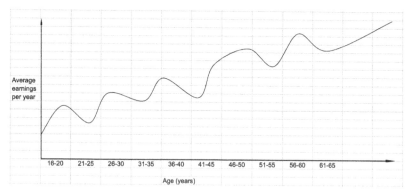

Figure 3.2 A successful investor's earnings

If you don't find a way to make money while
you sleep, you will work until you die.

Warren Buffet

3. FINANCIAL PLANNING

Financial planning is about preparing your personal finances for future milestones of your life and achieving your financial goals. You must set your financial goal(s), allocate the necessary resources, and make informed financial decisions to achieve that. Figure 3.3 shows what I consider to be the main issues to be aware of when you plan for your finances. The financial plan contains information about your current financial situation, short-term and long-term financial goal(s) and 'SMART' objectives, and strategies to achieve those objectives. The plan should include an assessment of your finances in terms of assets and liabilities and future expected milestones. You must review your financial plan every few months after significant events such as buying a house, marriage, raising funds for investment, investing in new assets, or any event that can have an impact on your finances.

The financial plan contains information about your current financial situation, short-term and long-term financial goal(s) and 'SMART' objectives, and strategies to achieve those objectives.

You must review your financial plan every few months after significant events such as buying a house, marriage, raising funds for investment, investing in new assets, or any event that can have an impact on your finances.

Figure 3.3 Financial planning pyramid

A decision-making model that can be used to support the development of your financial plan is known as the **GROW** (Goals, Resources, Options, What's Decided) tool (Shipman and Stone, 2019). This model's source is unknown but used in various contexts such as management, economics, and business. Figure 3.4 shows a modified version of the adapted financial planning and decision-making model, which has been adjusted to include a fifth stage: Assess and Adjust, or **GROW A+**. This additional stage of A+ is required to support the financial planning and decision-making process, indicating the importance of regularly assessing your financial plan and adjusting in case of unexpected events or changes to your situation. The function of each stage of the **GROW A+** model is as follows:

- Goals: to identify your financial goal(s) and objectives.
- Resources: your available resources in terms of assets that can be allocated to meet your financial goals.
- Options: prioritise your goals and develop strategies to pursue them and then compare and contrast those strategies.
- What's Decided: select the most appropriate option and develop actions to implement the selected option(s).
- Assess and Adjust (A+): you monitor the plan regularly and measure the performance of the implemented strategies using specific KPIs (Key Performance Indicators) to check:
  - if the selected strategies helped to achieve your goals;
  - if your goals and objectives have been achieved;
  - if you need to adapt to any changes and unexpected circumstances, and update your goals accordingly.

Figure 3.4 GROW A+ financial planning process. Adapted from the GROW model

4. ASSETS AND LIABILITIES

Assets are any accessible cash from active or passive income, savings, and personal assets such as properties, gold, or items that are convertible to cash. Starting to build up your assets portfolio year after year is an absolute priority and, without a shadow of a doubt, will pay off in future. Building your assets portfolio will set the foundation for your FI. Liabilities represent debts, regular financial commitments, and sometimes unnecessary expenses or fees. They are part of any investment business, such as mortgages or business loans, but often result from unwise financial decisions that burden non-business-oriented individuals. The two main types of assets are as follows:

Starting to build up your assets portfolio year after year is an absolute priority and, without a shadow of a doubt, will pay off in future. Building your assets portfolio will set the foundation for your FI.

- Financial assets: money in your bank account, savings, or funds that produce multiple income streams.
- Physical assets: such as real estate, gold, and stocks, which have to be sold to be converted into cash.

In the real estate business, billions of pounds of property transactions occur yearly. These investors have managed to build up a stock of profitable assets and create successful investment portfolios. Successful investors think about their investment philosophy when determining their approach to investing. As an investor of many years, my philosophy is to acquire assets of high demand, which produce high returns with manageable risks to meet my financial goals, as shown in Figure 3.5. In other words, to buy properties in good locations with an apparent demand, generate passive income and high yield, and achieve FI. Properties are physical assets that can produce a regular rental income without being sold. Assets such as money in a bank account are considered liquid assets because they can easily be converted

Properties are physical assets that can produce a regular rental income without being sold. Assets such as money in a bank account are considered liquid assets because they can easily be converted into cash.

into cash. Less liquid assets are such things as properties or gold because selling and converting them into predictable money takes time.

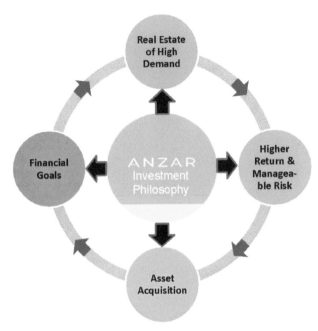

Figure 3.5 My investment philosophy

Of course, you are the most important asset, but if you are careless, and using simple maths and logic, you have fewer years to earn money as you age. Therefore, improving your value and increasing your income as early as possible, starting with early investing in knowledge and building a robust multi-asset portfolio is very important. Investing is a long-term game that implies long-term rewards that would improve your ultimate value. Why not join an investment networking group or subscribe to an investment YouTube channel, or why not develop a passive income-producing online course using your experience and valuable skills? Or why not have a part-time job during weekends to improve your income or cover your monthly mortgage? By now, you've probably thought of many other ideas unique to your circumstances and expertise.

> *When you make yourself so knowledgeable*
> *the market cannot disappoint you.*
> Nasser Abouzakhar

In other words, investing in knowledge will enable you to operate and succeed in all markets and economic situations. The more you invest in yourself today, the more valuable you become in future.

> Investing is a long-term game that implies long-term rewards that would improve your ultimate value.

> Investing in knowledge will enable you to operate and succeed in all markets and economic situations. The more you invest in yourself today, the more valuable you become in future.

5. INCOME TAX

Income for the majority of people comes from employment, but it may also be obtained from other sources such as benefits, pensions, savings, or investments. However, proactive investors often avoid working for others to earn their living unless their own companies employ them. Figure 3.6 shows personal income on the top, followed by other sources of income, such as government support to eligible people. The overall earnings result in the gross income, and then different taxes are deducted from the gross income. Finally, at the bottom is the net income, also called the disposable income.

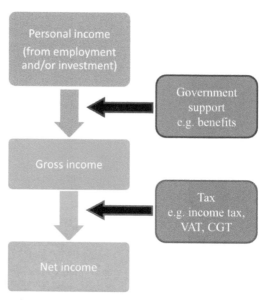

Figure 3.6 Steps of receiving income. Adapted from De Henau and Callaghan, 2019

It is helpful to know how much is received as gross income and what is actually transferred to your bank account as disposable income or net income for you to spend. Knowing how much tax you pay will help you understand your commitments as a citizen and explore alternatives to become more tax efficient, especially if you decide to start your own business, invest, or set up your own business company. You need to know how much tax to pay for any extra income from part-time jobs or profits you gain from future investments. Different countries have different tax laws for collecting tax revenues from personal income, social security contributions, small businesses, or large corporations.

Governments spend tax revenues on social protection and public services such as healthcare, education, social security benefits, defence, etc. Some countries don't tax certain earnings, such as pension contributions to encourage people to save for retirement, charity donations to support civil societies and communities, or investing in growing business companies. However, most countries use a tax schedule known as a progressive tax system.

> Knowing how much tax you pay will help you understand your commitments as a citizen and explore alternatives to become more tax efficient, especially if you decide to start your own business, invest, or set up your own business company.

A progressive income tax system is based on an individual's income, the income tax bracket they are in, and their ability to pay tax. This system imposes lower tax rates on lower-income earners than those on a high income, i.e., the higher the income received by an individual, the more tax they have to pay. The progressive income tax system is structured so that the taxable income is divided into brackets to cover a range of income bands. The UK's current tax system applies a specific rate of tax to each bracket as follows:

> The progressive income tax system is structured so that the taxable income is divided into brackets to cover a range of income bands.

- Personal allowance 0% rate (up to £12,570)
- Base rate 20% rate (£12,571–£50,270)
- Higher rate 40% rate (£50,271–£150,000)
- Additional rate 45% rate (over £150,000)

Let us assume that you have been offered a job with a salary of £30,000 per year, and you are under 66 years of age. In order for you to calculate the amount of tax you will have to pay by the end of the first year, you can use an online Income Tax Calculator available at www.moneysavingexpert.com/tax-calculator/. This online calculator would show you the breakdown results of tax payments, national insurance (NI) and net income, as follows:

- You earn £30,000 in 2023/24, and you will take home £2,064 a month from January 2024. Therefore, you will take £24,510 across the year. However, you would have taken home £2,035 a month for any period before January due to NI change.
- Over the 2023/24 year, you'll pay income tax of £3,486 and £2,004 in NI.
- This calculation takes into consideration the NI change in January 2024.

This calculator makes standard assumptions to estimate your tax breakdown due to many other possible variables. It assumes that you are employed, and because of the several changes to the 2023/24 rate of NI in the UK, the results from this calculator are approximate. Use your tax code and talk to the tax office for accurate results.

Based on the calculator results and calculations of the pay after income tax and NI contributions (NICs), the income tax system in England is less progressive than in Scotland. Had you lived in Scotland, you would have received a pay – after income tax and NIC – of £24,484 across the year with a total of £3,512 income tax and £2,004 NI.

Suppose your line manager has agreed; your monthly net pay will increase to £2,400 two years later (in 2025/26). Over these two years, inflation is predicted to average 10% per year. Using the following inflation calculation formula, the nominal value required at the time horizon is £2,559.36.

The nominal value required in 2 years = (Current monthly net pay + (Current monthly net pay x 12%)) + (Current monthly net pay x 12%)

= (2,064 + (2,064 x 12%)) + (2,064 x 12%) = £2,559.36

Using comparisons to other people's income to determine the quality of your income and to plan for the future financially is not enough. We need to know the purchasing power of the money we receive as income and what can be achieved.

This shows that in 2025/26, you will likely enjoy a lower standard of living (£2,400 is less than £2,559.36).

6. IMPACT OF INFLATION

Inflation affects the value of your income and the purchasing power of your money to spend on goods and services consumed by yourself or your family. Using comparisons to other people's income to determine the quality of your income and to plan for the future financially is not enough. We need to know the purchasing power of the money we receive as income and what can be achieved. This is in terms of products and services that we buy now and in the future, and the standard of living we aim for. To carry out such an assessment and determine the value of income we receive, we need to consider inflation, which reflects the continual rise of the prices of products and services over time.

Let's say a year ago the average price of residential property in Manchester was £260,000 and increased by 15% when measured again today. Due to the inflation rate of 15% after a year, the property price would be £299,000, as follows:

$$Property\ price\ this\ year = 260,000 \times (1 + inflation\ rate)$$
$$= 260,000 \times (1 + 15\%)$$
$$= 260,000 \times 1.15 = 299,000$$

This result shows that you would have to pay £299,000 for the same residential property that you could buy for £260,000 twelve months ago. If property prices in Manchester are predicted to increase by 10% in the following twelve months, in this case, the average property price will rise to £328,900 compared to its value of £260,000 one year ago, as follows:

$$Property\ price\ next\ year = 299,000 \times (1 + 10\%)$$
$$= 260,000 \times (1 + (15\% \times (1 + 10\%) + 10\%))$$
$$= 260,000 \times (1 + 26.5\%)$$
$$= 260,000 \times 1.265 = 328,900$$

This means the average property price will be 26.5% higher over the two years. The average property that cost you £260,000 twelve months ago will cost you £328,900 by the end of next year if the inflation is predicted to be correct.

If your monthly salary was £2,000 a year ago and is still the same next year, in this case the nominal value would be the same, i.e., £2,000. However, the real value represents a measure of how your standard of living has been affected over some time.

Inflation reduces the purchasing power of your money, so what is the difference between the real value and the nominal value of your money? The nominal value is the cash value of your money as it stands every time. If your monthly salary was £2,000 a year ago and is still the same next year, in this case the nominal value would be the same, i.e., £2,000. However, the real value represents a measure of how your standard of living has been affected over some time. Using the same inflation rate of 26.5% over the following two years, the real value, which represents the purchasing power of the achieved income, would be calculated as follows:

The real value of salary next year = Monthly salary
– (Monthly salary x inflation rate over two years)
= 2000 – (2000 x 26.5%) = 1,470

This means that the real value of your salary of £2,000 is 26.5% lower than your salary two years before, which is £1,470. The real value is calculated for a one-year-ago reference point. You must consider inflation, especially when your salary is kept the same over a long period or when just increased below or equal to the inflation rate; it is simply because it reduces the purchasing power of your money.

The following online calculator uses Consumer Price Index (CPI) inflation data from the Office for National Statistics from 1988 onward. The calculator uses the CPI as this is the measure used by the UK Government to set the Bank of England's target for inflation. Figure 3.7 shows an example of goods and services costing £1,000 in 1990, which would cost £1,996.98 in 2021. Inflation can seriously affect your cash savings and eat into the purchasing power of your money.

> You must consider inflation, especially when your salary is kept the same over a long period or when just increased below or equal to the inflation rate; it is simply because it reduces the purchasing power of your money.

What would goods and services costing

£ 1000   in 1990 ▾   cost in 2021 ▾ ?

Show amount

£1,996.98

Inflation averaged **2.3%** a year.

Figure 3.7 Inflation calculator 2023. Source:
https://www.bankofengland.co.uk/monetary-policy/inflation/inflation-calculator

7. UK GOVERNMENT SUPPORT DURING COVID-19 PANDEMIC

During the COVID-19 pandemic, the UK government provided full financial support to working households. Different support measures were made available to subsidise the income of eligible households, such as the Job Retention Scheme and the Self-Employment Income Support Scheme (SEISS). The Job Retention Scheme was a wage replacement for affected businesses that had their employees put on furlough. The SEISS also provided financial support for eligible self-employed workers affected by the pandemic (Cribb *et al.*, 2021).

When the schemes opened, eligible households could apply for and access the support because only certain groups of household workers were eligible (Department of Business, 2020). However, employees taxed and reported by PAYE on all categories of visas and any type of employment contract, such as full-time, part-time, zero-hour, etc., were also eligible for the furlough scheme (UK Government HM Revenue & Customs, 2020).

The furlough scheme protected the incomes of employees who could no longer operate. Initially, the eligible employees benefited from the payment of 80% of their wages paid by the government (Plummer and Palumbo, 2021). Many of those employees protected their jobs and maintained their living standards. They were able to spend for shopping on the high street in general and online in particular. This helped corporations maintain their profits, retain their employees, and pay their wages in response to the increased demand for their products (Shipman and Stone, 2019).

SEISS provided affected self-employed workers with payments worth 80% of pre-pandemic profits. The self-employed are individuals operating as contractors to perform a service or work for individual clients or corporations. Around 1.8 million self-employed workers were not eligible for support through the scheme (Cribb et al., 2021). This led to a heavy reduction in new entrants to self-employment, which shows an apparent injustice in how these workers were excluded. The government should have provided the desired support to all self-employed workers, instead of leaving more than 50% of them worse off due to the disaster (Blundell et al., 2021).

Employees eligible for the furlough scheme received most of their wages from employers/corporations and continued spending. Self-employed households were less affected by the pandemic than their employed counterparts, spending more and paying off debts. Corporations with furloughed employees could continue their businesses and keep their workforce. However, corporations with self-employed clients could not generate the same profits and continue business as usual.

During the COVID-19 pandemic, British households managed to repay record amounts of their debts on personal loans and credit cards as they stayed away from the high street during the lockdown (Partington, 2020). They received support from the government to cover different needs and protect them from COVID-19 challenges and social risks such as unemployment and poverty.

The COVID-19 job retention scheme provided by the UK government to replace lost income tends to favour high earners, while flat-rate benefits are less generous to low earners. Well-paid households could repay their debts through the money borrowed on their credit cards and loans during the coronavirus pandemic. Borrowing results in debt but enables households to smooth consumption during hard times, for example, in case it's difficult to access their savings. Interest rates on unsecured borrowing are usually higher than those for secured lending backed by an asset. Lenders assess loan applicants' creditworthiness and charge individuals different rates based on their credit scores.

> Interest rates on unsecured borrowing are usually higher than those for secured lending backed by an asset. Lenders assess loan applicants' creditworthiness and charge individuals different rates based on their credit scores.

8. DIFFERENCES IN HOUSEHOLD INCOME

Paid employment is the primary source of income for households in the UK, either in the form of paid salary by a public or private employer or earnings from self-employment business (De Henau and Callaghan, 2019). Households with skilled and experienced members who achieved quality qualifications can attain high income and stable employment. In the UK, households in highly qualified occupations are much better paid than those in less skilled professions. This enables them to aim for promotions at work, the best pension plans, sick pay, and paid holidays (De Henau and Callaghan, 2019). However, even if households receive a high income, they must manage their finances regarding spending, borrowing, budgeting, and investing for the future.

Lone-parent households are more likely unable to get mainstream credit and are often forced to use high-cost credit alternatives with higher interest rates (Shipman, 2019). When debts become difficult to repay, the household has to change their income or expenditure patterns, otherwise, the situation cannot be rescued (Shipman, 2018). Lone parents' families may be relying on the state for receiving long-term unemployment benefits and often have to make tough financial decisions. Long-term benefits paid by the state tend to be flat-rate, means-tested and are expensive and usually received by households who are less likely to be at work and, therefore, highly unlikely to repay their debts (De Henau and Callaghan, 2019).

Despite the importance of state support and benefits to replace lost income, lone parents are more likely to suffer financial stress and exclusion than other households, such as couples. Couple households can support each other financially and cope with unexpected events (Shipman and Stone, 2019). Being part of a couple can have implications for budgeting as living together is cheaper than living alone and can help the household budget due to the economies of scale in consumption and equivalence scales. A couple can use goods and services more efficiently than a single person or lone parent to attain the same standard of living (Lowe and Higginson, 2019). However, couples with dependent children are more likely to suffer a fall in income and an increase in spending due to extra financial commitments such as childcare.

Household expenditure is influenced by economic factors such as income and the costs of products and services (Lowe and Higginson, 2019). Due to increased inequalities in the UK, larger households need to earn more income to maintain a good living standard for their members (De Henau and Callaghan, 2019). This would have a knock-on effect on the household's standard of living, savings, pensions, and family's ability to meet their needs and commitments, such as repaying loans (Lowe and Higginson, 2019).

> Even if households receive a high income, they must manage their finances regarding spending, borrowing, budgeting, and investing for the future.

9. SUMMARY

Improving income and affording our living expenses and daily financial commitments is becoming increasingly important. This is to improve our well-being and financial situation, meet our personal and family needs, and achieve our financial goals. Therefore, improving our financial knowledge and skills through learning and seeking financial education is necessary. Fortunately, accessing financial knowledge and money management information is becoming possible with online resources and private training programmes. This chapter introduces the main concepts of income and wealth and financial planning principles. The issues of inflation and its impact on your money and financial situation and planning the future milestones of your personal financial life have been discussed. This chapter covered different financial strategies for improving your income and a financial planning process known as GROW A+.

> Improving our financial knowledge and skills through learning and seeking financial education is necessary. Fortunately, accessing financial knowledge and money management information is becoming possible with online resources and private training programmes.

We can accumulate part of our income for saving purposes to use for necessary consumption and unexpected circumstances in future. People tend to behave differently towards saving and spending their income. We must be careful not to overspend and avoid spending more money than we take in. To achieve this, we can use budgeting to ensure we spend our money wisely, monitor our cash flow, and control our finances. The next chapter covers the main concepts and principles of saving and budgeting, their importance, and their impact on our financial planning for the future. The influences and motivations of saving and its role in improving our finances and planning for the future are covered. The benefits of saving and budgeting are discussed in the following chapter to better manage your income and expenses and help you improve your financial knowledge. Some real-life scenarios about saving and budgeting supported with numerical examples are presented.

SAVINGS AND BUDGETING

4

If you would be wealthy, think of saving as well as getting.
Ben Franklin

Saving money is about accumulating part of an income over a certain period and keeping it safe. Bank saving accounts are often used to keep savings for future unexpected events and consumption before or after death. The percentage of individuals' savings from their income, why they save, and how to spend those savings can vary between cultures and societies. Sometimes we have to overspend due to unexpected circumstances, but we must be careful and avoid consistently spending more money than we receive. We can use budgeting to manage our spending, monitor cash flow, set financial goals, and keep our finances under control. This chapter introduces the main concepts of saving, its influences and motivations, and its role in improving our finances and planning for the future.

Saving and budgeting are challenging tasks that most people often feel uncomfortable doing because they require cutting back on what you think is necessary for living expenses and lifestyle. This chapter discusses budgeting principles and benefits to help you understand how to manage your finances, build your cash assets, and increase your net worth. It presents practical, real-life saving examples and budgeting scenarios. Using balance sheets and financial ratios should help you achieve your financial plan.

1. WHY SAVINGS

Saving plays a major role in managing your money and expenses, improving your balance sheet, and growing your net worth. To achieve that, you must commit to your saving strategy and manage your attitude towards money to change your behaviour and build the right discipline. Saving is the opposite process of borrowing to buy something now and pay for it later, which involves bringing forward consumption. Saving money is crucial not only for your future financial dependence, investment projects, and retirement but also to protect you from unforeseen expenses and emergencies.

Economic downturns and financial crises affect people's behaviour toward saving money. People tend to behave differently regarding what proportions of their income should be saved and how they spend the remaining income. However, during normal economic times and as a starting strategy, you

> Saving money is crucial not only for your future financial dependence, investment projects, and retirement but also to protect you from unforeseen expenses and emergencies.

You must have a proportion of your monthly income saved to build up your assets, deal with unexpected circumstances, and avoid unnecessary borrowing.

must specify a certain percentage of around 10–15% of your income to be saved monthly. You must have a proportion of your monthly income saved to build up your assets, deal with unexpected circumstances, and avoid unnecessary borrowing. If you are part of, or in charge of, a family, that may influence control over your expenditure and how much you can save. Having multiple regular savings by family members can help provide more financial security for the family.

Many people need more savings to cover emergency expenses and deal with crucial situations when necessary. The majority of middle-class and lower-income people tend to live beyond their means. I have visited many universities in Europe and the United States, and I noticed that most education systems do not teach their students how to manage their finances, including student loans, grants, income if they work part-time, and funds from family, if any. When I worked for my employer, helping the top management to become more prosperous, most of my colleagues had yet to learn about their pensions and how much they would receive when they retired. It is not in the employers' interest for their employees to become financially educated; otherwise, no one would continue working for them.

Most people tend to increase their expenses when they get a pay rise and often delay or forget their saving strategy. When they receive the good news about their pay raises, they start thinking about where to spend the incoming money. Any increase in expenditure will not help them save money despite the rise in their income and, hence, they lose the opportunity to build up assets. The ability to save will help people plan for their future and achieve their financial goals. People must behave wisely and responsibly with their spending, whether or not their financial situation has improved. Most people accept that they have to wait for 30 days to receive money, which is the only option available, and they never critically question why they have to.

People must behave wisely and responsibly with their spending, whether or not their financial situation has improved.

Do not save what is left after spending, but spend what is left after saving

Warren Buffett

Opportunities are available to everyone, but only those who care to look and are open to ideas can find them.

Having a clear vision and strategy for your financial future and building a successful investment business that provides a passive income will pay you for the rest of your life and help you achieve FI.

A small business owner who receives customers daily can generate income daily. Motivated business owners can decide when to double efforts and increase their daily income by, for example, investing in a newly developed marketing strategy such as social media to attract more clients. Such an effort and smart strategy will pay off for this business owner. Opportunities are available to everyone, but only those who care to look and are open to ideas can find them. The biggest mistake people make is feeling embarrassed or criticised because of their savings commitment or investment strategy. Having a clear vision and strategy for your financial future and building a successful investment business that provides a passive income will pay you for the rest of your life and help you achieve FI.

The habit of saving is itself an education; it fosters every
virtue, teaches self-denial, cultivates the sense of order,
trains to forethought, and so broadens the mind.

2. SAVING INFLUENCES AND MOTIVATIONS

Your decision about how much to save regularly and when to start saving will be influenced by different factors such as income, debt repayment, access to funds, job guarantee, and age. However, these factors might change at different times in your life. The higher your wage, the greater the opportunity that your income exceeds your expenditure and the better the situation to save more and grow your stock of assets. So, if that is the case, then the difference between the income and expenditure will be the net saving; otherwise, the net saving will be negative, and you be in deficit. Using net savings for investing will increase your income and eventually build up your financial assets. People have different reasons for savings and attitudes toward saving and use different saving patterns. This depends on their circumstances, financial plans, and age, but saving becomes more demanding as people age. This is to use their accumulated savings to cover their expenses in later life.

> Using net savings for investing will increase your income and eventually build up your financial assets.

Figure 4.1 shows what you can achieve if you implement a consistent saving plan of £1,000 each month or two or three months from your regular income to save a few hundred every month. The cash you managed to save will be transferred to your separate savings account. This is to build your stock of savings; however, you couldn't save in the seventh month but had to spend £2,000 to pay for a used car, meaning your stock of cash assets falls from £6,000 to £4,000. You needed the car to work part time with Uber as a weekend taxi driver and could pay for it using part of your savings. You continued your regular savings but needed to use an extra £1,000 from your accumulated savings to pay for a training course about investing in buy-to-let properties. Your savings stock falls again from £9,000 to £8,000. You started building your assets from the regular saved cash again until the last twentieth saving. The accumulated savings were £15,000, which is good cash you can use to pay as a deposit for a buy-to-let one-bedroom flat or residential property if you want to.

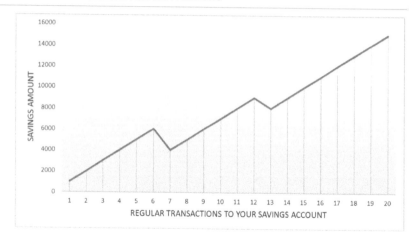

Figure 4.1 Regular saving

Many individuals cannot save from their income because they need more income to pay for their living expenses, and many others have expenditures exceeding their income. Most people, especially in developing countries, are struggling and tend to borrow to pay for essentials and to make ends meet. In general, saving money is about postponing consumption to a known or unknown future rather than consuming now. Stone (2019) suggests three main motives for households to save, as follows:

> Most people, especially in developing countries, are struggling and tend to borrow to pay for essentials and to make ends meet.

- Saving as a safeguard: this is to deal with unexpected circumstances and unpleasant events such as serious incidents. This is to meet unexpected financial obligations and protect themselves against those unwanted events.
- Saving for a certain purpose: this is to pay for a particular planned activity such as setting up a business, funding a training programme, paying for a residential property, etc. This is to meet specific long-term targets, often requiring lots of cash.
- Saving to build up wealth: this happens when there is no clear target and planned activity, such as paying a deposit for buy-to-let property to produce passive income and build up a future portfolio of assets.

> Regular savings help people postpone their consumption, have more significant cash assets, and achieve their financial goals.

In the UK, banks are regulated by the FCA (Financial Conduct Authority) to ensure that financial institutions adhere to the rules and regulations and to protect their customers. So, when you deposit your savings in a regulated bank, they are protected by deposit insurance schemes. This means that if for any reason you couldn't withdraw your savings, they are safe. People tend to increase their savings when they can, i.e., when their income rises. They select the banks which are offering higher interest rates for more returns. Regular savings help people postpone their consumption, have more significant cash assets, and achieve their financial goals.

> Starting early to save consistently despite a possibly low income and limited resources helps in learning to save, managing expenses, and then saving becomes a habit.

People think about saving or plan to save some of their income for different reasons, but it is essential to consider the right time and financial abilities. People need more financial resources to plan for saving and investing in the future. However, starting early to save consistently despite a possibly low income and limited resources helps in learning to save, managing expenses, and then saving becomes a habit. Those with good income or diverse portfolios of income-producing assets, such as real estate investors who use good debt for borrowing to build their wealth, often do not have problems with saving when they want to. This is because they have access to cash and financial resources, which can be used to save, reinvest, and grow their wealth.

3. SAVINGS SCENARIO

Saving is a challenging task that requires cutting back on unnecessary expenses to build your cash asset and increase your net worth. If you are serious about becoming financially independent, living below your means is often required. You must avoid unnecessary excuses for being unable to save because you cannot control your behaviour, restrict yourself, build the right attitude, etc. Unnecessary expenses such as long holidays, eating out, entertainment and media subscriptions, expensive cars, clothes, gifts, etc. can be controlled. Emphasising living below your means and implementing the right plan and saving strategy will positively impact your future financial situation.

> If you are serious about becoming financially independent, living below your means is often required.

You can change your entire life by saving smaller amounts consistently every month to start your savings journey using simple strategies. One way to achieve that is to use a standing order or direct debit to transfer a specific portion (for example, 10–15% of £2,000 is £200–300) of your income monthly to your savings account. This can be achieved by giving up one habit, such as smoking or eating out. You will not see the transferred amount and are obliged only to use the money left in your current account for the rest of the month. The earlier you learn this skill and start this process of saving and investing, the better, as this will enable you to accumulate a good amount in a few years and start an investment project.

> *Try to save something while your salary is small; it's impossible to save after you begin to earn more.*
> Jack Benny

In a few years, you will be surprised by how much you have saved and feel proud of yourself and the skills you learnt, but the earlier you start, the better. Starting as early as possible will have a positive impact on your savings account and on your FI journey. Regardless of your financial situation, regular savings using automated methods will help you achieve your financial goals, plan for early retirement, and quit the 9:00–5:00 rat race. Employees' contributions to their pension have fallen recently mainly due to low income, having too many expenses, or being unable to afford them. Figure 4.2 shows the average active pension pot sizes among female and male employees in the UK who are contributing to a private pension, adjusted for inflation from July 2006 to March 2020. Figure 4.3 shows the percentage of people (self-employed and employees) in the UK and the reasons for not contributing to a pension from April 2018 to March 2020.

> Starting as early as possible will have a positive impact on your savings account and on your FI journey. Regardless of your financial situation, regular savings using automated methods will help you achieve your financial goals, plan for early retirement, and quit the 9:00–5:00 rat race.

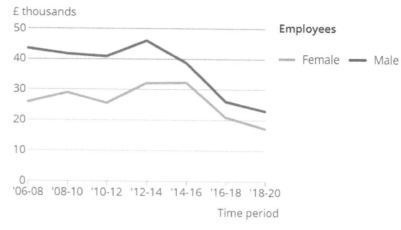

Figure 4.2 Average active pension pot sizes have fallen among employees contributing to private pensions. Source: Office for National Statistics – Wealth and Assets Survey

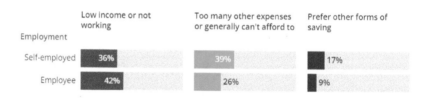

Figure 4.3 Reasons for not contributing to a pension. Source: Office for National Statistics – Wealth and Assets Survey

If you plan to retire early, you must save earlier than your peers. Your financial adviser should assist and guide you in selecting a suitable pension scheme to support your retirement and investment options.

Your pension funds will depend on your income, pension contributions, retirement age, and personal and family situations. Various factors play a significant role in determining your retirement and future financial plan. If you plan to retire early, you must save earlier than your peers. Your financial adviser should assist and guide you in selecting a suitable pension scheme to support your retirement and investment options. Your net worth and country of retirement would determine your minimum retirement age. In other words, the higher your net worth, the retirement lifestyle you aim for, and the cheaper your country of retirement, the earlier you can retire. The earlier you start saving for your retirement, the better, and if you haven't started yet the best time to begin your saving contributions was yesterday.

A simple fact that is hard to learn is that the time to save money is when you have some.
Joe Moore

In the UK, a workplace pension is a way of saving part of your income for your retirement that you arrange if you are self-employed or is provided by your employer if you are employed. It is about automatically saving a percentage of your income into a pension scheme. Often, your employer adds money to your pension scheme, and you might get government support through tax relief. Also, you receive extra government support for your pension if you work in specific sectors such as education, police, NHS (National Health Service), armed forces, or civil service.

4. BUDGETING

Spending money on expensive goods to show off ownership of luxurious products and maintain social status would force limited-income earners to borrow money they may be unable to pay back. Uncontrollable spending behaviours do not help people with limited financial resources to plan for their finances and future investments. To ensure you are saving your money properly, you need to know exactly where the money is spent. To achieve that, you can use a method for managing your expenditure and planning your finances based on your income: budgeting. It is a process of working on your expenses and spending behaviour and planning for the future.

Of course, sometimes we have to overspend due to unexpected circumstances, but we must avoid consistently spending more money than we make. To achieve that, you can transfer your monthly savings to a dedicated savings account using direct debit, regardless of how little they are. You may arrange the direct debit so that the monthly savings are transferred on a specific day of each month. This could be the beginning or end of each month, assuming you receive your monthly income at the end of each month. We must ensure consistent savings transactions, monitor our finances, and control our behaviour towards money in general and spending in particular. This allows us to manage our expenses and keep our finances under control. Successful investors and companies use budgeting to set financial goals, monitor cash flow, and track growth plans. This helps them

- develop a financial structure;
- achieve their business objectives and targeted revenues;
- manage their cash flow, expenses, and losses daily;
- deliver their services using cost-effective tools and systems;
- become successful in their competitive markets.

Many people lack financial knowledge and are unable to control their spending and debts from their credit cards, with the result that their finances end up in total disarray. With some financial skills and carefully budgeting their expenses, they should be able to repay their debt quickly. Seeking financial knowledge and understanding money management principles can help anyone regain control over their finances. There are many helpful budgeting templates or spreadsheets supported with graphical tools that we can use to help us manage our income and expenses in any given week, month, or year. Budgeting templates can help you monitor your expenses under specific categories such as rent, food, utilities, transportation, mobile, internet, etc., and how much you spend on average in each category each day or month.

Budgeting helps you learn more about your expenditure habits and understand how to regain control over your finances and any overspending.

> To ensure you are saving your money properly, you need to know exactly where the money is spent. To achieve that, you can use a method for managing your expenditure and planning your finances based on your income: budgeting.

> Seeking financial knowledge and understanding money management principles can help anyone regain control over their finances.

> Budgeting helps you learn more about your expenditure habits and understand how to regain control over your finances and any overspending.

It is a helpful learning experience, allowing you to notice progress in your savings journey and money management skills. Budgeting is an important tool to help you positively impact your life and financial situation. It is a continuous process; despite the challenging task, you must be consistent in your savings activity. You also have to track your expenses regularly and identify any areas of financial limitations.

The person who doesn't know where his next dollar is coming
from usually doesn't know where his last dollar went.
Unknown

4.1. Budgeting process

This is the process of using a financial plan and future income for tracking your returns and expenses to manage your spending and identify areas of overspending. It is a cost-effective approach that you can use to raise your awareness of how to monitor and manage your income and expenses. You use budgeting to identify unnecessary expenditures, adjust your lifestyle in terms of your expenses, and turn your deficit, if any, into a surplus. Reducing the amount of your money spent on non-essential goods and/or services by finding better deals and shifting to less costly options is important. However, this can be achieved without compromising quality and making it harder to function daily. This is crucial to get your spending behaviour back under control, keep expenses on track, and, most importantly, stick to your budget. Be aware that budgeting does not necessarily mean always selecting the lowest price, and the price does not reflect quality. Budgeting can help you to monitor your finances and support the implementation of your financial plan. In a nutshell, budgeting can help you to:

- monitor and control your financial situation;
- support your savings plan;
- track your financial transactions;
- identify areas of financial problems such as overspending and unpaid debts;
- identify cost-effective sources and suppliers for your goods and services;
- plan your financial actions, including future investment;
- improve your financial skills.

As a powerful tool, budgeting is a continuous process that will help you improve your financial knowledge and achieve your goals. You will use budgeting to spend your income listed in the cash flow statement and expense categories. This is to avoid overspending on certain shopping items or expense categories unless they are justified: for instance, due to unexpected circumstances such as medical emergencies or necessary travel, urgent debt repayments, etc. Budgeting is about self-discipline, pushing yourself to the limit, and the ability to adapt, otherwise you will never make it. Ultimately, the aim is to minimise expenses, avoid overspending, save as

Reducing the amount of your money spent on non-essential goods and/or services by finding better deals and shifting to less costly options is important.

Budgeting is about self-discipline, pushing yourself to the limit, and the ability to adapt, otherwise you will never make it.

much money as possible, and create long-term wealth. If you want to meet your financial and budgeting plans, then you have to:

- develop a cash flow statement;
- record your income from all sources;
- keep track of each expense item;
- record those expenses in your cash flow spreadsheet;
- allocate a specific budget to each expense category.

Developing a cash flow statement is a crucial part of the budgeting process to record all sources of net income and different types of spending and expenses. Your bank statements and cash payment receipts should help you prepare your cash flow statement. In your cash flow statement, categorising your expenses with clear headings for each category is helpful, as shown in the following sub-sections and examples. Do not worry if your income and expenses are irregular; you should be fine if you record them weekly or monthly on the cash flow statement. Recording your income and expenses is repetitive, so once you master it, it will be straightforward. You can use any spreadsheet tool to develop your cash flow statement; many are available online for free. Figure 4.4 summarises the main steps of the budgeting process. Remember that the main aim of budgeting is to help you monitor the inflow and outflow of your money, get your spending under control, and plan for the future.

> Developing a cash flow statement is a crucial part of the budgeting process to record all sources of net income and different types of spending and expenses.

> You can use any spreadsheet tool to develop your cash flow statement; many are available online for free.

Figure 4.4 The budgeting process

4.2. Family budgeting

Budgeting is helpful for single-person and multi-person households to deal with financial issues and budgetary implications and manage their finances. It is often cheaper living with others than living alone because you can spread the costs among yourselves and share them, such as utility bills, transport, council tax, etc., and pay less overall due to economies of scale in consumption. Multi-person households and living in HMOs (Houses of

> It is often cheaper living with others than living alone because you can spread the costs among yourselves and share them, such as utility bills, transport, council tax, etc., and pay less overall due to economies of scale in consumption.

Multiple Occupations) help efficiently use goods and services. They can save money and are becoming a good option for many individuals. The following scenario introduces the concept of the household equivalence scale and equivalised income, which is about adjusting the incomes of households when they live together and share their cost of living.

The equivalised scale is used to identify how much more or less money a multi-person family would spend to maintain the same level of living as singles using their original income. Due to economies of scale, for example, the consumption needs for four people living together sharing a single property space and its bills will not be the same as for four individuals living separately. The Organisation for Economic Co-operation and Development (OECD) developed a scale known as the "OECD-modified equivalence scale" to calculate the annual equivalised income of each household adult and child, as shown in Table 4.1.

Table 4.1 OECD-modified equivalence scale with example

Household	OECD-modified equivalence scale
One adult (household head)	1
Additional adult	0.5
Each child (13 or under)	0.3
Example: Three adults and two children	$1 + (0.5 \times 2) + (0.3 \times 2) = 2.6$

If you are part of a family, you might need to deal with various financial challenges in managing expenses, earnings, and living costs. Managing family finances raises many questions about whether or not there is an agreement on how earnings are shared among family members living together. The family members need to agree on who is in charge of what and how financial resources available to them and incomes are managed. They must agree upon how financial decisions are made, by whom, how financial resources are allocated, and who controls how money is spent. It is essential to agree upon all those matters to maintain good relationships and avoid unnecessary arguments and disagreements, regardless of who has the most financial skills or earns more. It is also essential to have common grounds for plans in terms of budgeting and decision-making about financial matters.

Family members often help each other financially, even when it comes to borrowing, and use their relationships to arrange flexible private lending arrangements. Many people turn to family members for financial help during hardship and because of unexpected events. However, not all people have extended family to turn to for help and financial support. Therefore, their only option is mainstream credit, such as unsecured personal loans or using their credit cards despite the higher costs. How families manage their income tends to be complicated, especially if all or some of the family members are involved in a family business that provides income and financial support.

The family members need to agree on who is in charge of what and how financial resources available to them and incomes are managed.

Family members often help each other financially, even when it comes to borrowing, and use their relationships to arrange flexible private lending arrangements.

Money management systems used by families are different and depend on many social and cultural factors. Often, the family members who bring more income to the table are likely to have more control over how the family business is run, how the money is spent, and who can receive what income. However, the family business members can still agree upon how the business profits are spent, how a budget is allocated, and how much needs to be saved and reinvested if there is a surplus. They need to discuss and agree on how the decisions are made and how the business revenue is managed.

> Family business members can still agree upon how the business profits are spent, how a budget is allocated, and how much needs to be saved and reinvested if there is a surplus.

4.2.1. Equivalised income and budgeting

Let us assume that you live in Manchester, earning £24,260 a year after deductions for tax, National Insurance, and pension contributions. You are about to move into a flat with your partner, who has a young child, Anzar, aged three. Your partner is a teacher and earns £23,000 a year after tax and National Insurance. They also receive £21.80 a week in child benefits. Neither of you has any other source of income.

The annual equivalised net income of your and your partner's new household is £26,255.56 each.

Your household earnings on your net income are £24,260, and your partner's net income of £23,000. Your partner also receives £1,133.60 (£21.80 x 52) a year in child benefits. You have an equivalence scale of 1 + 0.5 + 0.3 = 1.8, meaning your equivalised income is £26,255.56. So, there has been an increase in the living standard of your household. Your household would be better off due to your generated equivalised income.

4.2.2. Budgeting scenario

Table 4.2 shows the average monthly cash flow statement, including your and your partner's income and expenditure information.

Table 4.2 Cash flow statement

Your and your partner's cashflow statement		
Income and Expenses	Cash flow	Average monthly cash flow
Disposable income		
Your salary	24,260 per year	2,021.67
Your partner's salary	23,000 per year	1,916.67
Child benefit	21.80 per week	94.47
Total income		4,032.81
Expenses		
Rent	1550	1550
Council tax	2400 per year	200
Food	650	650
Utility bills	390	390
Car finance	300	300
Clothes	195	195
Internet and Phone	95	95
Leisure	3000 per year	250
Other	300	300
Total spending		3930
Surplus (+) / Deficit (-)		102.81

Let us assume that you and your partner wanted to save up, borrow, or invest in funding to fit a new gazebo in your garden at the back of your house next year. This new gazebo will require £3,000 to be fitted. However, you don't have the money to pay the total amount upfront, so we are looking at three options, as follows:

Option A: reduce your spending on leisure and other expenses.
The above cash flow statement shows a surplus of £102.81 at the bottom under the average monthly cash flow column. The statement indicates that your current spending is sustainable. However, the surplus cannot be used to meet your goal of fitting a new gazebo in a year. The estimated cost of fitting the gazebo is £3,000. To achieve your goal, you must consider adjusting your cash flow to save £3,000. Therefore, you develop a plan to achieve your goal and have to get your spending under control.

You will have to cut down the amount you spend on some items such as leisure and other expenses. To achieve these cuts in spending, consider cheaper leisure events for a while and keep other expenses as minimal as possible. The suggested budget is for you to spend £200 monthly for leisure instead of £250 and reduce other expenses to £200. This will leave you with a surplus of £252.81 each month instead of £102.81, i.e., £3,033.72 a year, which is needed for the new gazebo, as shown in the budget column in the last column in Table 4.3.

Table 4.3 Cash flow statement with the budget figures

Your and your partner's cashflow statement			
Income and Expenses	**Cashflow**	**Average monthly cash flow**	**Budget**
Disposable income			
Your salary	24,260 per year	2,021.67	2,021.67
Your partner's salary	23,000 per year	1,916.67	1,916.67
Child benefit	21.80 per week	94.47	94.47
Total income		4,032.81	4,032.81
Expenses			
Rent	1550	1550	1550
Council tax	2400 per year	200	200
Food	650	650	650
Utility bills	390	390	390
Car finance	300	300	300
Clothes	195	195	195
Internet and Phone	95	95	95
Leisure	3000 per year	250	200
Other	300	300	200
Total spending		3930	3780
Surplus (+) / Deficit (-)		102.81	252.81

It's not how much money you make, but how much money you keep, how hard it works for you, and how many generations you keep it for.
Robert Kiyosaki

Your efforts to save can have a positive impact if there is a sharp rise in interest rates, which might cause a fall in gazebos' prices. This is because of the increase in the cost of borrowing for the producers and consumers, which implies an increase in their monthly loan payments.

Option B: use the credit deal offered by the retailer you are using to provide the gazebo. The offer has an APR (annual percentage rate) of 19.75% and enables you to pay in monthly instalments of £150, spreading the cost over two years, as shown in Table 4.4.

The APR is the total cost of borrowing, including standard fees and interest that you must pay each year. Because of the way interest is calculated, your monthly repayments will be the same. However, the amounts of your interest and loan balance paid monthly at the beginning of the loan term differ from those towards the end.

Option C: buy the gazebo partly on your credit card, which has an APR of 24.72 %. You don't have outstanding credit on your card and can borrow up to £3,000. You would aim to pay off the credit card by paying £95 per month, as shown in Table 4.3.

Table 4.4 The borrowing options B and C

	Repayment period (years)	Monthly payment (£)	APR	Total interest (£)
Option B	2	150	19.75	600
Option C	4	95	24.72	1560

Option D: You have noticed that stock market shares in a particular REIT (Real Estate Investment Trust) company have given a 20% return each year over the past three years. You are considering using all your savings of £1,500 to buy shares in this REIT company.

Option E: You received an offer to obtain a rate of return on your savings that will enable you to reach your target amount of £3,000 if you commit to a savings plan that runs for three years rather than one year of budget plan based on Table 4.3.

There is a sharp rise in interest rates which causes a fall in house prices.

4.2.3. Budgeting options analysis

Let us discuss what could be the advantages and disadvantages of each of the introduced scenarios in Table 4.5.

Table 4.5 Advantages and disadvantages of all options

Option	Advantages	Disadvantages
A	1. This option allows you to adjust your spending and develop a cash flow plan to save the £3,000. 2. You don't need to borrow to raise funds to buy and fit a new gazebo. 3. A sharp rise in interest rates implies an increase in the interest on your savings. This will positively impact your efforts to save the required amount in a shorter period.	You have to take unpleasant measures of cutting spending on leisure activities and maybe other essential activities which might have a knock-on effect on the family's joy in the shared experience.
B	1. This option offers a cheaper deal that provides a lower APR. 2. It provides a lower repayment period with lower total interest to be paid.	This option has a higher monthly repayment.
C	1. Using credit cards offers a lower monthly repayment, paid slowly with less financial stress. 2. It is a flexible option that allows you to increase the repayments if your budget improves in the future and pay off the balance more quickly than expected.	This option has a higher total interest of £960 that is charged for a longer term.

Option	Advantages	Disadvantages
D	Investing in high-risk stock shares such as REITs could produce a high reward.	1. Putting all your savings of £1,500 into this company's shares might not be the optimum strategy. If the company's share prices fall, it could lead to losing most of your invested money – better avoid putting all your eggs in one basket. 2. Investing your money for three years is quite a short period and may not help you achieve your goal in terms of capital gains.
E	Less pressure to save the target amount of £3,000.	1. The price of gazebos might increase due to increased demand. 2. Your savings might lose some power due to inflation during the extra three years.

5. BALANCE SHEET AND FINANCIAL RATIOS

In 2022, you moved to a new property, and your mortgage adviser helped you select the right option. Your adviser would have discussed the available mortgages with you and talked you through interest-only and repayment mortgages. You used your savings for the deposit and chose a repayment mortgage with an outstanding balance of £350,000. The purchase price was £450,000.

By January 2023, you managed to save an amount of £1,500 cash and bought gold worth £1,750 from your net annual income of £24,260, as indicated on your cash flow statement. You owe £1,500 on a credit card and took a loan of £5,000 last year to buy new furniture and do some refurbishment work. The loan is now down to £4,000, and you have an overdraft on your current account of £1,000. To review your current finances in January 2023, you developed your balance sheet and financial ratios, as shown in Tables 4.6 and 4.7, respectively. Your net worth, current asset ratio, and leverage are calculated as follows:

Net worth / Wealth = Total Assets – Total Liabilities
Current asset ratio = Total liquid assets
÷ Total short-term liabilities
Leverage (%) = (Total liabilities ÷ Total assets) x 100

The current asset ratio indicates liquidity, which is the ability to turn assets into actual money. Leverage means solvency, which shows the ability to repay all debts (Shipman, 2019).

Table 4.6 Balance sheet in January 2023

Your Balance Sheet in January 2023	
Assets	
Liquid assets	
Cash	£1,500.00
Gold	£1,750.00
Total	£3,250.00
Non-Liquid assets	
Residential property value	£450,000.00
Total Assets	£453,250.00
Liabilities	
Short-term Liabilities	
Credit card debts	£1,500.00
Overdraft	£1,000.00
Total	£2,500.00
Long-term Liabilities	
Mortgage	£350,000.00
Car finance	£19,500.00
Personal loans	£4,000.00
Total	£373,500.00
Total Liabilities	£376,000.00
Net worth / Wealth	£77,250.00

Table 4.7 Financial ratios in January 2023

Financial Ratios in January 2023	
Net worth / Wealth	77250.00
Current asset ratio	1.30
Leverage ratio	82.96

In terms of your mortgage, the factors that you might have considered in choosing a repayment mortgage over an interest-only mortgage are as follows (Stone and Fribbance, 2019; Base, 2022).

- Pay off the whole principal and own your home at the end of the mortgage term.
- Pay less interest as the mortgage amount owed decreases.
- Pay regularly throughout the life of the mortgage towards repaying your loan or into an investment scheme with the assumption that the investment would grow at a rate to produce enough amount to repay the principal in full at the end of the mortgage term.

Let us assume that Table 4.8 shows your financial ratios, including your net worth in 2022.

Table 4.8 Your financial ratios in January 2022

Financial Ratios in January 2022	
Net worth / Wealth	45500.00
Asset ratio	1.10
Leverage ratio	86.00

Your financial situation in January 2023 looks better than in January 2022, as described in Table 4.8. Table 4.9 compares both of your financial situations in 2022 and 2023.

Table 4.9 Comparison of financial situations between January 2022 and January 2023

Ratios	Comparison
Net worth/wealth	Your net worth in January 2022 was lower than in January 2023. This is due to higher total assets and lower total liabilities in 2023 compared to January 2022.
Current asset ratio	The current asset ratio in January 2023 was higher than in January 2022. This is due to decreased short-term liabilities and could be more saved cash in January 2023.
Leverage ratio	The leverage ratio in January 2023 was less in comparison to January 2022. This is because of the higher total liabilities and lower total assets in 2022 compared to January 2023.

Understanding the financial ratios helps identify the actions that need to be taken to improve the shape of your balance sheet and develop a financial plan to take for the future. For example, financial planning for future funds would be required to support the necessary adjustment to the balance sheet and cash flow statement.

For you to improve the financial situation in terms of increasing your net worth and current asset ratio you need to:

- Reduce your short-term liabilities by cutting expenses in terms of using overdrafts and credit cards.
- Grow your liquid assets by increasing the instant access savings and the cash in your current account.

Understanding the financial ratios helps identify the actions that need to be taken to improve the shape of your balance sheet and develop a financial plan to take for the future.

6. SUMMARY

Saving is a helpful tool to support your financial plans regarding spending and managing expenses. Accumulating part of the income is helpful for necessary future consumption and unexpected circumstances. Budgeting is also useful for monitoring your cash flow, setting financial goals and controlling finances. Many people feel they need to be more comfortable using saving and budgeting tools to manage their money and reduce over-spending in buying unnecessary products or services. This chapter discusses the main concepts and principles of saving and budgeting and their roles in managing our spending and planning for the future. It covered the influences and motivations of saving and introduced the benefits of budgeting to build your cash assets. Some practical, real-life scenarios of saving and budgeting and financial tools such as balance sheets and financial ratios have been presented to help you develop your financial plans and improve your financial skills.

Sometimes, we unnecessarily overpay for expensive products, services, or leisure. However, out-of-control spending could lead to stressful financial situations and unhealthy habits. Therefore, we must learn to monitor our expenditures and debts and develop a proper financial plan. The next chapter discusses some exciting ideas on managing your expenses and avoiding compulsive spending behaviour supported with numerical examples. Access to capital in the form of loans offered by creditors can be accessible to people with a good credit history. However, unmanageable debt could also lead to unpleasant situations, financial pressure, and mental health problems. Successful investors use good debt to fund investment deals, build asset portfolios, and create wealth. In the following chapter, we discuss the difference between good debt and bad debt, issues related to consumption and overspending problems practised by individuals with modest incomes. The principles of managing mortgage debts and ensuring that debt is under control, the impact of inflation on debt, and issues related to credit referencing are also covered in the next chapter.

Budgeting is also useful for monitoring your cash flow, setting financial goals and controlling finances.

Sometimes, we unnecessarily overpay for expensive products, services, or leisure. However, out-of-control spending could lead to stressful financial situations and unhealthy habits.

Successful investors use good debt to fund investment deals, build asset portfolios, and create wealth.

EXPENDITURE AND MANAGING DEBT

5

*Don't tell me where your priorities are. Show me where
you spend your money and I'll tell you what they are.*
James W. Frick

We tend to spend more sometimes to pay for specific products or services or to cover the expenses for unexpected circumstances. However, out-of-control spending, for example, on unnecessary, ridiculously expensive products, could lead to unpleasant situations and unmanageable habits. Therefore, we must be careful and do our best to avoid consistently overspending for unnecessary expenses and spending more money than we bring in. Furthermore, monitoring our expenditures, debts, and cash flow and having a financial plan are essential. Developing a financial plan is a challenging task many avoid because they either need to learn how or feel uncomfortable doing it. This chapter introduces some ideas on managing your expenses and avoiding compulsive spending behaviour, especially for those with limited resources.

Individuals with good credit history have access to capital inaccessible through their regular earnings. They often use this as loans to pay for products or services when they cannot do so using their steady income. However, overborrowing could also lead to financial stress and mental health issues. People often get into unhealthy habits because of social influences and marketing pressures. Successful investors use their creative abilities to increase their income even during difficult economic times and avoid stressful financial situations. They use good debt, which they only use to fund their investment deals, build their asset portfolios, and create wealth. In this chapter, we introduce the issues related to consumption and spending habits practised by individuals with modest incomes and successful investors.

Banks have procedures to check individuals' credit reports and history and assess their financial status and affordability. This ensures the borrower can pay their monthly mortgage payments during the entire mortgage term and keep the lending risk as minimal as possible. This chapter covers the principles of managing mortgage debts, ensuring that the associated costs with mortgages are controlled, and the impact of inflation on debt. This minimises losses and keeps the risk of failure as low as possible. This

> Out-of-control spending, for example, on unnecessary, ridiculously expensive products, could lead to unpleasant situations and unmanageable habits.

> People often get into unhealthy habits because of social influences and marketing pressures. Successful investors use their creative abilities to increase their income even during difficult economic times and avoid stressful financial situations.

chapter introduces the issue of credit referencing, credit reports, and using credit cards.

1. MANAGING EXPENDITURE

Managing your expenses is essential for implementing your financial plans and achieving your goals. People spend their money on different products and services from those who can afford them. This is to cover their needs and essentials of life as well as entertainment and leisure activities. However, spending without control and living beyond your means could lead to unmanageable and unpleasant situations. The level of expenditure is impacted by various economic factors such as cost of living, income, and demand and supply of goods and services. However, social influences and pressures also play a role in spending, using our money, and making financial decisions. Especially in consumer societies, people tend to judge and give opinions about others based on their consumption level and assets.

> *Too many people spend money they earned to buy things they don't want to impress people that they don't like.*
>
> Will Rogers

People spend more as their pay rises and at certain times, especially during festive times and summer holidays when many products and services are advertised. They use the extra income to buy more expensive goods and services and sometimes unaffordable luxuries, non-essential items, or unhealthier options. This often happens due to a lack of financial knowledge, financial planning, and money management skills, which are necessary for everyone. When income increases, most people ignore the importance of saving and do not use the opportunity to develop a financial plan to buy assets or prepare for future investment projects. The situation worsens when prices fall, known as deflation; people tend to postpone spending and purchase assets to get them cheaper if they wait longer (Lowe and Higginson, 2019).

1.1. Expenditure and marketing

The products and services offered to people often have valuable functions and can help them make informed choices. However, intelligent marketing strategies and tactics are used by corporations to convince people about the quality and features of those offered products and services. Those in charge of marketing use innovative advertising techniques and exciting ideas via symbolic images and video advertising to target potential customers relentlessly in order to evoke their emotions toward their products and services. Imaginative adverts are used as a persuasion tool to attract attention, convey information, and reach wider communities and audiences to sell the marketers' products and services. Consumers are willing to spend money to acquire those products and services that suit them and satisfy their needs.

The level of expenditure is impacted by various economic factors such as cost of living, income, and demand and supply of goods and services.

When income increases, most people ignore the importance of saving and do not use the opportunity to develop a financial plan to buy assets or prepare for future investment projects.

People value money differently, which is why cash is distributed differently between people, resulting in inequality. Those who like to spend and value expenditure, but value money less, make it easy for money to move to those who value it more. Regardless of what governments and rulers throughout history have tried to invent regarding regulations, rules, taxation, etc., to redistribute their countries' wealth equally, it will always return to its natural situation. Tax is essential, and the more we earn, the more we should expect to pay as tax, and there is nothing wrong with that. This is to help a government to manage the country's wealth and ensure the proper delivery of essential services, such as education, healthcare, etc., to their citizens. Governments can use taxes to support those in need, but not to redistribute wealth equally among a country's citizens.

Various media channels and online social networks monitor users' behaviours and browsing history to collect data about their shopping interests and habits. This categorises people based on economic and demographic factors such as income, age, ethnicity, and address. When people use the internet and browse the World Wide Web, they give away a lot of important data about themselves that is collected by search engines and social network platforms, which they then sell to corporations. The marketers in those corporations use this data to target potential consumers with customised and personalised products and services that they often browse and buy regularly. Marketers aim to help people make decisions and encourage them to spend more money than they worked hard to earn to buy those advertised products and services.

Those serious about improving their lives have to consider savings, cutting unnecessary spending, and avoiding non-essential goods and services by being wise about their expenditure. It is helpful to know how much you receive as gross income and what is actually transferred to your bank account as a net income for you to spend. You shouldn't be easily influenced by marketing adverts and manipulated emotionally to spend your money. It is also good to have a cash flow statement that you produce each month or quarter and check to know whether or not you are living within your means and to help you plan for the future. The difference between your monthly net income and the total amount spent during the month would determine whether or not a surplus is left at the end of that period. Having a surplus will determine how much you should be able to save every month and how much you can invest in the future.

If you cannot control your emotions, you cannot control your money.
Warren Buffett

1.2. Spending and conspicuous consumption

As a consumer, you play a role in the economy and the country's GDP when you decide how much money you spend and the kind of products and services you consume. The GDP is a tool used to measure the performance of a country's economy over some time. Spending money in one area of the economy becomes an income for other areas. Money often keeps moving from one area to another until it returns to the starting point to be spent

---

People value money differently, which is why cash is distributed differently between people, resulting in inequality.

Tax is essential, and the more we earn, the more we should expect to pay as tax, and there is nothing wrong with that.

You shouldn't be easily influenced by marketing adverts and manipulated emotionally to spend your money. It is also good to have a cash flow statement that you produce each month or quarter and check to know whether or not you are living within your means and to help you plan for the future.

Money often keeps moving from one area to another until it returns to the starting point to be spent again.

again. For example, when you spend money on specific services, this would increase the profits of the service provider. The cash flows into privately owned or state-owned firms, which then positively impacts the amount of money, i.e., tax, received by the government. This money comes back to you as self-employment income, employment income, benefits, investment returns, etc., from the government.

While countries with strong economies, such as the G7, have higher status levels among the international community, this is always the case with wealthier people with higher incomes who can publicly display their wealth and carry high social status. Unfortunately, this tends to motivate those who are not rich and with modest gains to spend on expensive goods unnecessarily, go into debt, and live beyond their means. They do this to seek temporary pleasure and fulfil a temporary desire, which could lead to various problems and negatively impact their lives.

According to the economist Thorstein Veblen (Wikipedia), individuals who buy expensive goods and spend lots of money to acquire quality luxurious commodities tend to display economic power and be seen as wealthy in their societies. In 1899, Veblen introduced the concept of 'Conspicuous consumption', which describes how wealthy individuals publicly display accumulated assets. This shows their ability to spend money on costly items to indulge themselves and demonstrate ownership of those luxurious products. These individuals aim to maintain social prestige and status. Such behaviour might encourage those with limited resources and assets to borrow money to act as if they are also rich. This shows that they can apparently afford those luxurious goods and expensive commodities and they get into compulsive spending habits. Veblen's theory and idea about individuals' spending behaviour can help us understand why people spend money in specific ways.

Individuals with modest incomes are generally more likely to suffer financial stress and exclusion than other households, such as couples. Being part of a couple can positively impact managing expenses, sharing financial burdens, and budgeting, as living together is cheaper than living alone due to the economies of scale. Individuals in highly skilled occupations are much better paid than those in less professional careers. They have an advantage over their contemporaries for promotions at work, and the ability to save and to invest. However, despite receiving a high income, they need more money management skills and often need to learn how to develop a financial plan and spend their money wisely.

> *Everyone wants to ride with you in the limo, but what you want is someone who will take the bus with you when the limo breaks down.*
> Oprah Winfrey

People often adjust their living expenses and lifestyle to their income, so, when they receive a pay rise or increase their income through part-time jobs, they tend to raise their expenditure instead of improving their savings. This makes it challenging to improve their financial situation and develop a financial plan to:

Sidebar notes:

According to the economist Thorstein Veblen (Wikipedia), individuals who buy expensive goods and spend lots of money to acquire quality luxurious commodities tend to display economic power and be seen as wealthy in their societies.

Individuals with modest incomes are generally more likely to suffer financial stress and exclusion than other households, such as couples.

- know how much they need to spend monthly;
- avoid overspending;
- develop an action plan to manage their expenses;
- design a budget;
- plan and manage finances.

2. YOUR INCOME AND EXPENDITURE

We covered how income received from a job may fluctuate during a lifetime. Income profiles vary significantly between individuals in respect of abilities and priorities, and circumstances change frequently. Although earnings and spending habits tend to be influenced by different situations, life experiences, and skills and qualifications gained, some patterns apply to most people, as discussed previously in Chapter 3. Figure 5.1 shows a generic curve that depicts approximate patterns of an individual's income and expenditure in each stage of their life as they get older, assuming they lived all their working life as an employee in a job, stuck in the hamster wheel.

Figure 5.1 captures how individuals may begin their working life as low earners and then move to better income levels and, finally, the curve turns down as they age and retire. Of course, people's life experiences and earnings are different and will have different patterns and fluctuations of income and spending due to varying circumstances. In general, people start their early life with more spending due to limited earnings, and as income improves they can save for future consumption and retirement. However, most retired people who worked for many years often suffer financially after just a few years of their retirement. Their pension income and savings might not be enough to cover extra costs associated with the life expenses of the elderly. This is often due to inflation, which would have eroded their pension income and savings.

People's life experiences and earnings are different and will have different patterns and fluctuations of income and spending due to varying circumstances.

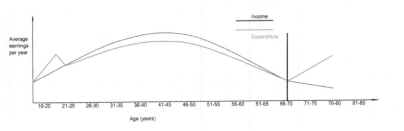

Figure 5.1 An individual's income and expenditure

Figure 5.2 shows an updated diagram of an investor's income also covered previously (see Chapter 3). It shows what I estimate to be successful investor curves that depict how their income and expenditure changes and how they relate to each other over the years. The diagram shows that their income continuously increases, even after their early retirement. If they have a proper legacy plan, it will probably continue despite inflation and after their death. If you want, you can draw your own income and spending curves and see your patterns over the past years since you started earning an income, and then try to predict your future income and spending to see how they will change over the rest of your life. Such curves are helpful for planning, identifying future risks, and exploring any potential action to take, such as savings, investing, or budgeting required to minimise those risks. This is to avoid financial problems that might arise in the future (thus mitigating stress) and allow you to manage your money correctly.

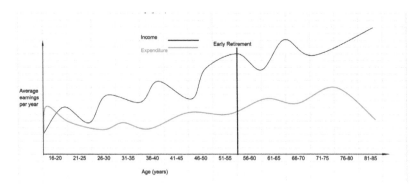

Figure 5.2 A successful investor's income and expenditure

3. BORROWING AND DEBT

Debt enables people to have access to capital and raise funds that are inaccessible through their regular earnings. Borrowers have to repay the money they borrowed out of the money they get from their future income. For instance, real estate investors often borrow large interest-only loans/mortgages to fund their buy-to-let properties. They let future inflation, especially if it is higher than the interest rate, erode the capital borrowed, which must be repaid at the end of the loan term. That is why banks try to keep the interest rate they charge borrowers higher than the rate of inflation to minimise risk.

Good debt is desirable and used by investors to fund their investment deals, build their businesses, and create wealth, as shown in Figure 5.3. Interest is the cost of debt offered as a percentage of the money borrowed from the bank. The interest rate decided by the lender determines the monthly payments that have to be paid by the borrower and the total cost of borrowing. Banks are often obliged to provide a standard measure of lending cost, which includes any charges associated with the borrowed money, such as administration fees. This common measure is known as APR (annual percentage rate).

> Good debt is desirable and used by investors to fund their investment deals, build their businesses, and create wealth.

> Banks are often obliged to provide a standard measure of lending cost, which includes any charges associated with the borrowed money, such as administration fees.

Figure 5.3 Good debt versus bad debt

Borrowing is useful and opens up opportunities, but it requires proper management skills; therefore, you must have a clear financial plan to repay the money you borrowed to the lender. You must be sure how you will repay the borrowed money on time and ensure there will be enough income to cover the necessary repayments in order to avoid any unpleasant surprises and unexpected financial hardship. When you want to borrow money, you had better compare the loan cost offered by multiple lenders. They might offer different annual interest rates and often use two types of loans, as follows:

> You must be sure how you will repay the borrowed money on time and ensure there will be enough income to cover the necessary repayments in order to avoid any unpleasant surprises and unexpected financial hardship.

- Secured loan: this type of loan is offered when the lender wants to keep the risk as minimal as possible by securing the debt against a particular asset you have. If you received a secured loan to buy a residential property, the lender would have secured the loan against your purchased house. If you fail to pay your monthly commitments/instalments or to repay the loan at the end of the term, the lender can enforce the sale of your asset to get their money back and pay you the remaining amount, if anything is left.
- Unsecured loan: this loan is not protected and, therefore, not backed by any of your assets; however, this kind of loan has a higher interest rate than secured loans. For example, if you borrowed an amount of £20,000 as an unsecured loan with an interest rate of 4% to be repaid in a single lump sum at the end of one year, then you have to pay £800 (£20,000 x 0.04) at the end of the year. The £800 represents the charges you must pay for receiving the loan, i.e., the cost of borrowing.

Keeping the debt and its associated costs always under control and well-managed is crucial. Therefore, the next section presents various aspects of debt management to minimise risk. Banks check borrowers' affordability and credit history to minimise losses by ensuring that they can cover their financial commitments. This section covers credit referencing and discusses how banks use credit reports to gather information and assess the financial status of potential borrowers. Credit reference agencies play a significant role in compiling credit reports. Credit cards help perform financial transactions and minimise the risk of fraudulent transactions. The following section will discuss the issues of credit referencing, credit reports, and using credit cards by borrowers.

> Banks check borrowers' affordability and credit history to minimise losses by ensuring that they can cover their financial commitments.

4. MANAGING DEBT

Debt often puts people
in unpleasant situations
or could even lead
to chaotic financial
problems and stressful
and sleepless nights.

Investors use good debt
to fund their investment
projects and leverage
but make sure that
they pay it back within
a certain period. Banks
are willing to lend to
investors by offering
different rates of
interest on various loan
products to fund their
investment projects.

The amount of your debt could be used to measure your ability to manage money and whether or not you are good at dealing with debt. Debt often puts people in unpleasant situations or could even lead to chaotic financial problems and stressful and sleepless nights. Owing to the easy access to credit offered by lenders, some people might use their credit cards to spend excessively on non-essential goods, which can lead to their becoming habituated to acquiring material possessions. However, investors use good debt to fund their investment projects and leverage but make sure that they pay it back within a certain period. Banks are willing to lend to investors by offering different rates of interest on various loan products to fund their investment projects.

Many households in the UK use loans whenever possible to pay for different kinds of goods and services. According to the Office of National Statistics (ONS):

Increases in total household property debt and total household financial debt in the latest period were driven by a combination of both an increase in the number of households with debt and increasing levels of debt.

Office of National Statistics (ONS)

Table 5.1 shows the household debt in billions in the UK between July 2010 and June 2016 and April 2014 and March 2020. The table shows two types of debt: property debt, which is associated with mortgages, and financial debt, which is related to household unsecured loans, overdrafts, credit cards, household bills, and student loans. Both types of debt are increasing yearly, showing the massive demand for credit in the UK. The figures only include households with every kind of debt. According to ONS, recently, total household financial debt increased by £12 billion (11%), from £107 billion from April 2014 to March 2016, due to increased hire purchase debt (up by £6 billion) and student loans from the Student Loans Company (up by£7 billion).

Table 5.1 Household debt in Great Britain 2010–2018. Source: https://www. ons.gov.uk/peoplepopulationandcommunity/personalandhouseholdfinances/ incomeandwealth/datasets/householddebtwealthingreatbritain

	July 2010 to June 2012	July 2012 to June 2014	July 2014 to June 2016	April 2014 to March 2016	April 2016 to March 2018	April 2018 to March 2020
	Billion (£)					
Property Debt	1,012	1,029	1,110	1,099	1,164	1,234
Financial Debt	100	94	107	104	119	125
Total Debt	1,112	1,123	1,217	1,203	1,283	1,360

Overspending and borrowing money to buy expensive items and luxurious goods just to maintain social status is unwise behaviour by those with limited resources and modest incomes. Such people need to pay more attention to the importance of saving and cutting unnecessary spending in order to use the opportunity to buy assets when prices fall during economic downturns or to plan for their future. Unnecessary spending makes it hard for them to repay the borrowed money, get out of debt, and improve their financial situation. Recording all your loans and debt, including credit card(s) debt, direct debits, unpaid balances, etc., in a spreadsheet will help you understand your financial commitments and monitor your total debt. Watching your debt is a significant step towards

- knowing exactly how much your debt is;
- specifying how much you have to repay to which debt category;
- developing an action plan to manage your debt;
- freeing yourself from your debt burden;
- managing your money.

> Recording all your loans and debt, including credit card(s) debt, direct debits, unpaid balances, etc., in a spreadsheet will help you understand your financial commitments and monitor your total debt.

As part of your debt management, you can use your debt spreadsheet to rank your debts based on their interest rate in descending order regardless of the debt amount. This is to use your extra funds to prioritise paying the debt with the highest interest rate first on top of the regular payments. You have to go back to the income and budgeting sections to figure out how to manage your finances and repay your debt. Intelligent borrowers know how to manage their debt and investments, control their debt, and avoid bankruptcy. Bankruptcy is a declaration by an individual or company that they cannot meet their financial commitments and debt repayment. This would have a negative effect on the borrower's reputation, credit rating, future lending, and investment projects. To avoid such issues, borrowers must ensure their monthly loan repayments are lower than what they receive as income.

> Intelligent borrowers know how to manage their debt and investments, control their debt, and avoid bankruptcy.

4.1. Impact of inflation on debt

As I have pointed out, not all debt is bad and has a negative impact; borrowers benefit when inflation increases despite its negative effect on lenders, savers, and people's living standards. Inflation erodes the value of money, making it suitable for borrowers as inflation also erodes their debt. For instance, during inflation, property prices increase, which benefits property investors and landlords who have borrowed money from banks to fund the purchase of properties. Because property prices increase during inflation, the LTV (loan-to-value), which represents the percentage of the borrowed loan to the property price, decreases. This means that the value of the borrowed loan and paid interest is eroded, consequently benefiting landlords. Increasing property prices allows landlords to raise funds through remortgaging their properties, buying more properties, and growing their portfolios. However, landlords need to increase the rent to meet the banks' requirement of what is known as the stress test.

> Inflation erodes the value of money, making it suitable for borrowers as inflation also erodes their debt.

Let us assume that you invested in buying three buy-to-let properties, each house costs £100,000 (£100,000 x 3 = £300,000 total) and you borrowed 75% of the value all three properties (£75,000 x 3 = £225,000) for a five-year term. Assuming the property prices increased 50% during those five years, the property prices will become £300,000 x (1 + inflation rate = 1.5) = £450,000. The nominal value of the borrowed loan is £225,000; however, the real value of the loan will be as follows:

$$Real\ loan\ value = nominal\ loan\ value -$$
$$(nominal\ loan\ value \times inflation)$$
$$= £225,000 - (225,000 \times 0.5) = £112,500$$

The borrowed loan has been eroded by 50% due to inflation. This means that you will be paying back the bank in real terms the £225,000 multiplied by 50%. It will remain the same after five years, i.e., £225,000, but the real value will be less due to inflation. Assuming the annual interest you were charged by the bank was 4% yearly, this means you pay (4% x 5 = 20%) interest rate at the end of the fifth year, i.e., £225,000 x 20% = £45,000 at the end of the loan term. However, we can examine the impact of inflation on the interest rate as well, as follows:

$$Real\ interest\ rate = nominal\ interest\ rate - inflation\ rate$$
$$= 20\% - 50\%$$
$$= -30\%$$

The nominal value is the cash value of the money as it stands every time in any period.

The interest adds 20% over the five years to the loan, but in real terms, inflation reduces the cost by 50%, which is more than the interest itself. Regarding the real loan value and its associated interest cost, we have to consider the cost of the real value of the interest. Therefore, the real loan value and associated interest cost, which are paid at the end of the term, are as follows:

$$Real\ loan\ value\ and\ interest = nominal\ loan\ value - (nominal\ loan$$
$$value \times inflation) \times (1 + real\ interest\ rate)$$
$$Real\ loan\ value\ and\ interest = £112,500 \times (1 + (-30\%))$$
$$= £78,750$$

If inflation were the same as the interest rate, then the value of the charged interest would disappear, i.e., inflation will erode the interest altogether.

Although the nominal value of the loan you borrowed was £225,000, the real loan value and interest paid by you are less than what you took out as a loan. This is because the loan value and interest have been eroded by the 50% inflation over the five years. If inflation were the same as the interest rate, then the value of the charged interest would disappear, i.e., inflation will erode the interest altogether. However, if the inflation rate went higher than the interest rate, in this case, the banks are effectively losing money, as if they were paying the borrowers for taking out their loans. That is why banks are often careful about the interest they charge the borrowers and ensure it is above the inflation rate.

Acquiring the necessary financial knowledge and having a proper financial plan should help you manage your debt and its stress.

Acquiring the necessary financial knowledge and having a proper financial plan should help you manage your debt and its stress. There are many valuable online resources that you can access to help you with your financial situation, such as the UK's government website https://www.gov.uk/options-for-paying-off-your-debts and UK Citizens' Advice https://www.citizensadvice.org.uk/debt-and-money/help-with-debt/ These websites contain lots of useful information and resources for educational purposes.

You can refer to them to help you deal with your financial challenges and debt issues and understand your credit reports. Many not-for-profit organisations provide financial counselling services and valuable information. These organisations offer support and help with personal finances for the general public and consumers seeking solutions to their financial problems.

4.2. Banks and lending

Banks borrow money from the central banks in the countries they operate in and pay interest on that borrowed money. Central banks set the interest rate (known as the base rate in the UK) they charge for the money they lend. Banks use the base rate as a benchmark for setting the interest rate they charge borrowers. The interest rate set by banks is always higher than the base rate to earn some profit. Banks tend to increase their interest rate for those unlikely to repay the borrowed money due to unpredictable income and high risk. That is why banks assess each loan applicant individually and check whether or not they are creditworthy, then decide what the interest rate should be.

In the UK, traditional banks are regulated by the Financial Conduct Authority (FCA) and must be stringent about their funding and lending criteria. Non-bank financial institutions (NBFIs) do not have a full banking licence. The FCA does not regulate NBFIs; they offer various banking services such as money transfer, financial consulting, and investment. However, they are not allowed to accept deposits from the public. NBFIs serve as competitors to traditional banks. NBFIs are more flexible regarding lending criteria to investors or businesses and sometimes offer better products. Examples of NBFIs include:

- Insurance firms: they offer insurance products to provide financial protection for future hazardous events for premiums subject to the level of risk – they are regulated by the PRA (Prudential Regulation Authority).
- Peer-to-peer lenders: these are online platforms that bring together private lenders, who are individual investors, with potential entrepreneurs and business investors who want to borrow money for investment purposes. These platforms offer competitive interest rates to both borrowers and private lenders. The lenders can use the same credit referencing tools the banks use to assess the risk they are taking.
- Crowdfunding: internet-based systems used to raise capital to fund investment projects from cash assets accumulated by individuals.
- Commercial loan providers: provide business loans designed to meet companies' needs and finance their commercial projects.

All banks are required to carry out checks on investors' financial ability and their financial history. This is to ensure that they can provide a deposit that is a percentage of the property price and that they can pay their monthly mortgage commitments. Banks often use two main criteria to carry out their checks, as follows:

Affordability: To check the investor's income, financial commitments, and the house-price-to-earnings ratio

Many not-for-profit organisations provide financial counselling services and valuable information. These organisations offer support and help with personal finances for the general public and consumers seeking solutions to their financial problems.

Central banks set the interest rate (known as the base rate in the UK) they charge for the money they lend. Banks use the base rate as a benchmark for setting the interest rate they charge borrowers.

NBFIs are more flexible regarding lending criteria to investors or businesses and sometimes offer better products.

All banks are required to carry out checks on investors' financial ability and their financial history.

Credit history: To check the investor's credit card(s) activity, financial transactions, and history using some credit referencing tools

To measure financial performance regarding your ability to pay a debt and keep up repayments, we use the debt-to-income (DTI) ratio, which banks use to measure lending risk. DTI is an indicator that measures your affordability of meeting debt repayments while maintaining your necessary spending. The lower the DTI ratio, the more likely you are to pass the banks' affordability checks, making them more confident about your ability to repay your debt using your current income. Banks are often willing to lend if your DTI is approximately equal to or below 35%, which means less than 35% of your monthly gross income is spent on your debt repayments, which is okay. The DTI can be calculated using the following formula.

> Banks are often willing to lend if your DTI is approximately equal to or below 35%, which means less than 35% of your monthly gross income is spent on your debt repayments.

$$DTI\ ratio = Debt\ repayments\ per\ month\ /$$
$$Gross\ income\ per\ month$$

Assuming that you want to apply for a personal loan and would like to calculate your DTI ratio, first, you have to list all your monthly debt and income as follows:

- Gross income: £5450
- Monthly debt:
    - Mortgage payment: £750
    - Personal loans: £630
    - Car finance: £320
    - Credit cards: £220

$$DTI\ ratio = (750 + 630 + 320 + 220)\ /\ 5450$$
$$DTI\ ratio = 35\%$$

Your DTI of 35% is acceptable for most banks, but you must ensure you spend less than you receive as income. Consequently, you can avoid any financial difficulty and borrowing restrictions in future.

Financing your deficit is an option, but it could lead to a decline in assets and a rise in liabilities. If your monthly income exceeds your spending, you can use the surplus to repay your debts. Saving part of your monthly income is essential to avoid incurring debt. It opens up good opportunities for receiving investment funds and achieving financial goals.

> Saving part of your monthly income is essential to avoid incurring debt. It opens up good opportunities for receiving investment funds and achieving financial goals.

Be aware that interest rates play a significant role in monthly debt repayments, i.e., the higher the interest rate, the greater the monthly repayments. This means that the bank would take a higher proportion of your income, which could have a knock-on effect on your expenditure. That is why national banks are cautious when deciding to raise interest rates. Such decisions could impact people's finances, the countries' GDP, and the economy as a whole.

> Be aware that interest rates play a significant role in monthly debt repayments, i.e., the higher the interest rate, the greater the monthly repayments.

In the UK, high street banks don't lend when an investor's property portfolio reaches a certain level. Property investors with about six to ten properties will face difficulty in getting funding from high street banks for their next property investment. However, non-high street banks such as Precise, Aldermore, The Mortgage Works, LendInvest, Paragon, etc., are often valuable options for funding investment projects. As mentioned earlier,

NBFIs are more flexible in their lending criteria. Regardless of the number of mortgages someone has, banks use stress testing plus other measures to check whether or not the borrower meets their standard and to ensure their affordability. Investors only need to look for the best mortgage deal; often, their mortgage adviser should be able to offer them a few options, and then they can select the best one(s).

It is essential to look for mortgages with the lowest interest rates, but investors need to check if any other fees are set by the lender(s). Mortgages with low interest rates tend to incorporate higher costs and vice versa. Bridge loans tend to offer high interest rates and are used to purchase properties at the auction, but investors can only get them from specialist lenders. The interest rates offered by commercial banks are strongly dependent on the base rate decided by the central bank, which, in turn, depends on the cyclical phase of the economy. The interest rate is the price paid by the property buyer for the offered mortgage by the bank/lender. Mortgage interest rates affect the property market and prices.

Whether or not lenders offer cheap or expensive mortgages, they would expect an investor to contribute to the property price. Moreover, lenders want to ensure the property produces an excellent net cash flow. In other words, the rental income paid by tenants should cover the monthly mortgage payment by around 1.3 debt coverage, i.e., the monthly rental income is 1.3 times more than the monthly mortgage payment. Investors must ensure that the property they buy meets this vital requirement. Low interest rates encourage first-time buyers or investors to purchase properties, increasing demand and property prices.

Property developers should respond to the opportunity of cheaper access to credit. The lower interest rates lenders offer and the increased demand for properties will encourage developers to improve the property supply. However, it often takes time for development projects to complete and for newly developed properties to become available. Making proper use of good debt can make a difference in property investment. When capital and mortgages are used wisely, they can increase the annual income and return on investment (ROI). The debt used to invest in real estate is often secured against the property an investor is buying. However, using debt increases the risk of their investment as well.

4.3. Credit referencing

One of the assessment tools banks use for loan applicants is the credit score, a measure used to reflect an individual's financial situation. Credit referencing refers to gathering information about an individual's financial status, including their credit score and past track record with credit. The higher the credit score for an individual, the lower the risk and the interest rate the banks offer. Banks use a credit rating system to assess the ability of potential borrowers to meet their financial obligations. They use the borrower's credit report to decide whether or not to lend to them, how much, and on what terms. An individual's credit report is compiled by companies known as credit reference agencies (CRAs). CRAs specialise in gathering financial data and creditworthiness status about individuals based on current and historical data using different technologies such as Big Data and AI (artificial intelligence). There are three main CRAs in the UK:

The interest rates offered by commercial banks are strongly dependent on the base rate decided by the central bank, which, in turn, depends on the cyclical phase of the economy.

The debt used to invest in real estate is often secured against the property an investor is buying. However, using debt increases the risk of their investment as well.

Credit referencing refers to gathering information about an individual's financial status, including their credit score and past track record with credit.

An individual's credit report is compiled by companies known as credit reference agencies (CRAs).

- Experian;
- Equifax;
- TransUnion.

A bank is a place that will lend you money
if you can prove you don't need it.

Bob Hope

CRAs create and keep hold of people's credit reports and collect information about their current financial status and credit history. Each agency holds different information about individuals and produces a credit report that includes their credit score based on the data collected. Banks tend to ask one or more CRAs for information about individuals before accepting their request for funds. Banks tend to check borrowers' reports for any existing loans, unpaid or late credit card transactions, mortgage payments, or any unclear transactions affecting their credit rating. CRAs collect credit information about people and calculate a credit score based on various algorithms and methodologies using the following information:

Banks tend to ask one or more CRAs for information about individuals before accepting their request for funds.

- history of late or missed payments;
- number of credit applications during a specific period;
- joint accounts;
- credit cards usage;
- current status of your debt;
- amount of debt;
- type of debt;
- length of your credit history;
- bankruptcies;
- whether or not you are on the electoral roll.

If you plan to get a new credit card or buy a house, you must ensure you have an excellent credit history and report.

All CRAs rely on the same sources to gather your credit information; however, they may have different credit scores for you. But if one CRA gives you an 'Excellent' score, the others are likely to do the same. If you plan to get a new credit card or buy a house, you must ensure you have an excellent credit history and report. Your credit report will provide financial information to the lenders and how likely it is that you will be able to pay back any borrowed money. Your financial report will help the banks to measure the risk of lending you the requested amount, predict your future behaviour toward the borrowed money, and then make an informed decision. Banks are aware that people differ in their management of money and their financial abilities, so they cannot treat them equally.

Your financial report will help the banks to measure the risk of lending you the requested amount, predict your future behaviour toward the borrowed money, and then make an informed decision.

Borrowers must check their credit history and score regularly and take all required measures to improve their credit rating if necessary. Various useful tools, web applications, and mobile apps can help individuals monitor their credit scores and get advice on improving their reports. Credit Karma is one of the mobile apps that provides individuals with free access to their credit scores and reports from TransUnion and Equifax. It offers updates on credit reports regularly and allows individuals to track their credit history changes and scores over time.

Various useful tools, web applications, and mobile apps can help individuals monitor their credit scores and get advice on improving their reports.

Your credit score and report are important for the banks you plan to borrow money from and any service provider company. They are also essential for future business partners or individuals with whom you might consider a joint venture. They might also be interested in accessing your credit information and knowing more about your financial behaviour. Therefore, it is in your interest and that of all the parties involved that you have a high credit score, preferably excellent, i.e., the higher your score, the higher the chance of getting a good rate loan or securing a joint venture deal. Table 5.2 shows what 'Fair', 'Good', or 'Excellent' credit scores look like from Experian and Equifax CRAs. Figure 5.4 shows a map of the average credit score for the age range 31–35 years in the UK, which does not look encouraging for this particular age group. The map is generated from the Experian website to allow people to compare their credit scores with different age groups in various regions throughout the UK.

Table 5.2 Credit scores from Experian and Equifax CRAs

Credit Score	Experian	Equifax
Fair	721-880	380-419
Good	881-960	420-465
Excellent	961-999	466-700

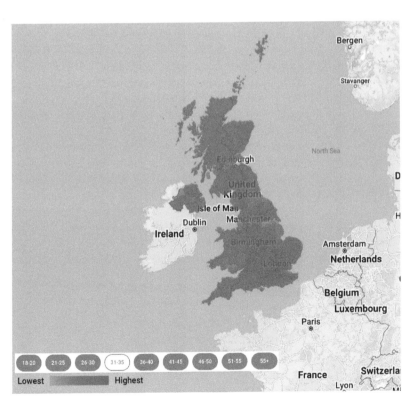

Figure 5.4 Experian map of the average credit score for the age range 31–35 years in the UK. Source: https://www.experian.co.uk/consumer/credit-score-map-uk/ (accessed: 24th January 2024

Checkmyfile.com is an online multi-agency credit report provider that can gather information from all four CRAs. Checkmyfile.com allows individuals to see their information from the CRA agencies and view individual's credit scores. All those tools provide useful information and tips to improve credit scores:

- make all payments on time;
- check that they are on the electoral register at their current address;
- keep their credit accounts active;
- avoid credit overutilisation and multiple credit applications in a short space of time;
- manage debt and all accounts, including credit cards, mortgages, loans, etc.

5. IMPROVING YOUR CREDIT SCORE

Your payment history and the amount of debt play a significant role in calculating your credit score by the CRAs.

Having a good credit report is one thing that helps banks to accept your loan application happily. Therefore, ensure you know what can hurt your credit rating and what can be done to improve your scores. CRAs want to see you using your credit cards regularly, making timely payments, and managing your accounts properly. Your payment history and the amount of debt play a significant role in calculating your credit score by the CRAs. Delaying your credit card payments is a red flag for many lenders and shows a lack of financial responsibility. Your ability to manage your credit and reliably service your debt reflects the kind of financial management and skills that your lenders would like to notice about you.

Your ability to manage your credit and reliably service your debt reflects the kind of financial management and skills that your lenders would like to notice about you.

It is a good practice to monitor your credit scores and reports regularly. Make sure to contact your CRA in case you find any error in your report and discuss any issues you notice. This is to avoid false credit scores and information published in your credit report. If your scores are not up to the level, then there are a few things you need to do to raise your credit scores, such as paying your credit debt and utility bills on time. You should always remember your financial commitments and not have any excuse for delaying the payments of your bills and not paying on time. The costs associated with postponing payments are often expensive. In summary, you must stay on top of things; therefore, to improve your credit score, you have to make sure that you

You should always remember your financial commitments and not have any excuse for delaying the payments of your bills and not paying on time.

- stay within your credit limit;
- do not withdraw cash from your credit card;
- make credit payments on time each month;
- are careful of links with someone else's credit history;
- pay your utility bills and outstanding County Court Judgments (CCJs), if any, on time.

A good debt is what you use to invest, produce extra income, and gain a financial benefit.

What is important now is that you must know the difference between good debt and bad debt. If the debt is used or invested correctly, it is likely to lead to valuable outcomes. A good debt is what you use to invest, produce extra income, and gain a financial benefit. A loan you use to set up a new business or expand a running business, or a mortgage to purchase a buy-to-let property is an example of good debt. To aim for a good loan deal with a low interest rate from the lender, you must ensure a high credit score. The higher your credit score, for example, between 961 and 999 Experian scores, the better the deal and the lower the loan payments, and the higher the profit margins achieved from your business.

You have to understand the reasons behind any low credit scores and should develop a plan to increase your scores. You must be aware of any financial difficulties and unpleasant situations and their causes, whether these are due to a lack of financial knowledge, mental health, psychological issues, etc. You only need to worry about the bad debt accumulated from unwise spending or irresistible purchases. You must avoid financial mistakes and learn to manage your overspending behaviour to achieve your financial objectives. No one else can do that for you, and no one is to blame. You are the only one who is responsible for your financial issues and behaviour.

It has been recognised that money is a standard measure of value for goods and services provided and is used for financial transactions. Anyone seeking creative finance skills must understand the difference between money, currency, and credit as part of their money management and investment journey and how banks can influence their investment decisions.

6. Summary

Overspending on unnecessary, expensive products could lead to various problems and unpleasant financial situations. Spending on ridiculously expensive products or services is not normal for someone with limited financial resources. Therefore, we must be careful of our income, monitor our expenditures and debt, and avoid spending more money than we bring in. We must learn how to develop a financial plan and feel comfortable doing so. This helps us manage our money correctly and avoid financial problems and stressful situations. By now, you have learnt how to manage your expenses and avoid compulsive spending behaviour and unhealthy financial habits, especially during difficult economic times. You should have understood how to monitor your credit history and review your credit reports. This will enhance your affordability and allow you to access credit from many lenders/banks to pay for specific products or services, apply for a mortgage, or invest in the future.

This chapter covered the principles of debt management regarding loan payments and monthly mortgage commitments. This is to avoid financial losses, damage to your credit history and to keep the risk of failure as minimal as possible. Learning from successful investors how to use your creative mind and abilities to apply creative finance techniques, such as using good debt to increase your income, is essential. Creative finance is a smart way of managing your finances and structuring investment deals legally to grow your asset portfolio. The next chapter will teach you about creative finance and discuss using good debt to build your assets portfolio, even during an economic downturn. Creative finance can help you understand how to raise capital, gain financial skills, and manage good debts. Another useful skill you will learn is producing financial statements, including income statements (or profit and loss statements) and balance sheets.

You must be aware of any financial difficulties and unpleasant situations and their causes, whether these are due to a lack of financial knowledge, mental health, psychological issues, etc.

You must avoid financial mistakes and learn to manage your overspending behaviour to achieve your financial objectives.

Anyone seeking creative finance skills must understand the difference between money, currency, and credit as part of their money management and investment journey and how banks can influence their investment decisions.

The next chapter will introduce my wealth generation engine, which can be used as a financial strategy to support your passive income generation and investment journey. It will discuss the strengths of active entrepreneurs and investors and their abilities to deal with their business challenges. Furthermore, the main phases of building a successful investment portfolio using creative finance will be presented with valuable examples of income-generating property investments. The chapter will cover the other issues related to evaluating a property deal in terms of cash flow, ROI, and rental yield.

CREATIVE FINANCE

6

Happiness is not in the mere possession of money; it lies in
the joy of achievement, in the thrill of creative effort.
Franklin D. Roosevelt

Creative finance is an intelligent way of structuring investment deals to build wealth and accumulate valuable possessions legally, such as in a portfolio of income-producing properties. Creative financing can be considered a financial model for arranging a deal to purchase or finance a property using capital from a third-party institution or OPM (other people's money).

However, financial management is crucial to planning and controlling all the creative financial activities and business financial resources. Creative financing mainly allows investors to use financial techniques such as leveraging to expand their portfolios. For example, third-party creative financing can help investors avoid using too much capital to invest in real estate.

The *Cambridge English Dictionary* defines creative financing as 'new or unusual ways of legally getting money to finance something such as a home, project, or business'.

This chapter introduces a wealth generation engine model to help you develop your financial and multi-stream income strategy. Owing to accessible funds and reasonable interest rates, investors properly use this opportunity to fund their investment projects. The issues of developing income-generating portfolios and building wealth using creative finance are introduced at the start of the chapter. This chapter covers the main concepts of creative finance and property finance, including profits from rental income and capital growth and the costs associated with a property business. It highlights the importance of understanding the financial statements, including the income statement and balance sheets.

Active entrepreneurs are often willing to take the risk of setting up new businesses and investing in learning new skills to deal with business challenges. Those who built investment portfolios, tech companies, or other successful businesses often differ from the rest, especially in areas such as creativity, decision-making, and risk-taking. This chapter covers the main phases of building a successful investment portfolio using creative finance. Some examples of creative financing for property deals are also presented. Proper use of creative finance can help investors benefit from the market regardless of the economic situation and property price fluctuations. This chapter ends with examples of evaluating deals regarding produced cash flow, ROI (return on investment), and achieved rental yield.

> Creative financing mainly allows investors to use financial techniques such as leveraging to expand their portfolios.

> Owing to accessible funds and reasonable interest rates, investors properly use this opportunity to fund their investment projects.

> Those who built investment portfolios, tech companies, or other successful businesses often differ from the rest, especially in areas such as creativity, decision-making, and risk-taking.

Formal education will make you a living; self-education will make you a fortune.

Jim Rohn

1. MANAGING PERSONAL FINANCE

Wealth can be considered in terms of valuable possessions, such as a portfolio of income-generating real estate accumulated over time using creative finance and strategy. To achieve that, investors need to monitor the markets closely, update their knowledge regularly, and ensure they are updated regarding skills and news. According to cnbc.com's 2019 report22, most billionaires worldwide were self-made, without much cash and funding available to many of them. Individual investors, or groups of businesses, set their financial goals and develop and establish their investment plans and projects using creative financial strategies to build up their assets and wealth. Figure 6.1 shows my model of the wealth generator engine of a creative financial plan. In the real estate business, creative finance is used by business-minded individuals as follows:

> Individual investors, or groups of businesses, set their financial goals and develop and establish their investment plans and projects using creative financial strategies to build up their assets and wealth.

- buy what could make an income-generating property using as little of their money as possible to pay for a deposit;
- add value to the property; and then
- refinance the property after it has increased in value to release equity, pay off debts, or reinvest.

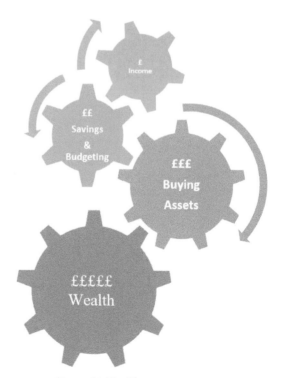

Figure 6.1 Wealth generator engine

For individuals, the two main types of income are as listed below.

- Active income: earning from delivering a service for an employer or customer, i.e., exchanging income for work in which an individual is actively involved, e.g., a job.
- Passive income: earning without participating or with little effort, where an individual is not actively involved, e.g., rental income or as a result of capital growth. Such an income requires some work and extra attention at the beginning to set it up.

Multiple sources of income do help to ensure regular savings. However, whether it is an active or passive income or a combination of both, keeping expenses lower than income, having a spending plan, managing after-tax income savings regularly, monitoring the budget, and investing carefully are all significant steps to creating wealth. Assets are any accessible cash from active or passive income, savings, and personal assets such as properties, gold, or items that are convertible to cash. Liabilities represent debts, regular financial commitments, and sometimes unnecessary expenses or fees. They often result from unwise financial decisions, which add an extra burden to individuals.

> Assets are any accessible cash from active or passive income, savings, and personal assets such as properties, gold, or items that are convertible to cash. Liabilities represent debts, regular financial commitments, and sometimes unnecessary expenses or fees.

2. FINANCIAL STATEMENTS

Maintaining healthy financial accounts is very important if you want to live a peaceful life. Financial statements are used as a record of your financial information and status to show the performance of your financial activities. There are two important financial statements for any type of business or investment: the income statement (or profit and loss statements if the income is generated from a business) and the balance sheet. The income statement includes your salary and income from other jobs and/or the revenues from a particular company. It also includes your living expenses and expenses incurred to keep the business running.

> Financial statements are used as a record of your financial information and status to show the performance of your financial activities.

The income statement is produced during a certain period, often each month or at the end of the tax year. This statement shows whether you can save money and the business's ability to produce a profit. The balance sheet includes the assets and liabilities at a specific point in time. It reveals what an individual or business owns and owes and its equity. The liabilities refer to debt, i.e., what you owe to other entities, such as banks. Assets represent what you own and items that produce income or financial benefits, such as a house, savings, gold, rented properties, etc.

2.1. Income statement and balance sheet

Tables 6.1 and 6.2 show a simplified version of both financial statements, the income statement and the balance sheet. You have to make sure that your assets are worth more than your liabilities to avoid solvency problems and financial stress and be able to use assets to pay off a debt if necessary. A solvency problem happens when your liabilities exceed your assets due to poor debt management or investment losses. Insolvent means that you have an unhealthy balance sheet with a lower value of assets to liabilities and,

> You have to make sure that your assets are worth more than your liabilities to avoid solvency problems and financial stress and be able to use assets to pay off a debt if necessary.

hence, a negative net worth but not necessarily with a liquidity problem. Net worth or wealth represents the total net worth on the balance sheet at any given time, as follows:

$$Wealth\ (net\ worth) = Assets - Liabilities$$

Table 6.1 Income statement

Income Statement	
Company Name	
Period	
Revenue	
Rental income	
Dividends	
Royalties	
Gross profit	
Expenses	
Mortgage payments	
Interest	
Legal and Professional Fees	
Insurance	
Marketing	
Rent	
Repairs and Maintenance	
Supplies	
Internet	
Travel	
Salaries	
Total Expenses	
Net Income	

Table 6.2 Balance sheet

Balance Sheet	
Company Name	
Date	
Assets	
Residential properties value	
Commercial properties value	
REITs stock shares value	
Gold	
Cash	
Total assets	
Liabilities	
Mortgages	
Credit card debts	
Car finance	
Loans	
Total Liabilities	
Total Equity (Net worth)	

The balance sheet determines someone's wealth, so lenders are often interested in checking the balance sheet to determine how much an individual is worth. It can help them assess their financial status and make a decision on whether or not to lend them money. In his book *Rich Dad Poor Dad*, Robert Kiyosaki discussed the importance of understanding the income statement and balance sheet and the relationship and cash flow between them.

2.2. Assessing your balance sheet

The best way to build wealth is through investment and reinvestment to generate revenues and accumulate income-producing assets. Successful investors tend to reinvest the generated income and funds from remortgages to create wealth and leverage. Leverage is an investment strategy of using borrowed capital to increase earnings. It provides a measure of the total debt using the overall liabilities and assets as follows:

$$Leverage\ (\%) = (Liabilities\ /\ Assets) \times 100$$

You must keep leveraging at less than 100% to avoid solvency problems, but not very low because it is not a viable business strategy. You want to use good debt to fund investment projects, buy more assets, and grow wealth. However, you must measure your investment risk and make informed decisions before taking action. As mentioned earlier, you must keep your assets worth more than your liabilities to maintain a positive net worth and avoid financial problems such as being unable to pay off debt. Table 6.3 shows the balance sheet presented differently with two adjacent columns, the assets listed in the left column and the liabilities listed in the right column. As part of assets management, you must ensure enough liquid assets that exceed short-term liabilities. Liquid assets can be turned into cash to clear short-term debts that must be repaid immediately, such as a monthly mortgage or unsecured loan payments.

Table 6.3 Liquidity problem

Balance Sheet	
Date	DD/MM/YYYY
Assets	**Liabilities**
Liquid assets	Short-term liabilities
A1	
A2	L1
A3	L2
A4	L3
:	:
:	:
:	:
:	:
:	:
An	Ln
Total Assets = Liquid assets + (A1-An)	Total Liabilities = Short-term Liabilities + (L1-Ln)
Total Equity (Net worth) =	Total Assets - Total Liabilities

A liquidity problem occurs when you cannot repay your debt on time as agreed with the lender.

In emergencies, such as a sudden income loss, you always have enough liquid assets, such as savings, to meet those commitments.

Having short-term liabilities that exceed the value of liquid assets reflects an unhealthy financial situation and could lead to a liquidity problem, as shown in Table 6.3. A liquidity problem occurs when you cannot repay your debt on time as agreed with the lender. Even though you have lots of assets and an excellent credit report, liquid assets are necessary to avoid getting into financial difficulties. Therefore, you must ensure you meet your financial commitments regarding repaying short-term debts. In emergencies, such as a sudden income loss, you always have enough liquid assets, such as savings, to meet those commitments. To deal with such financial difficulties, you might consider the following:

- Developing a short-term budget.
- Saving on unnecessary costs.
- Cutting your expenses.
- Reviewing your assets to reassess their liquidity.

The person who doesn't know where his next dollar is coming from usually doesn't know where his last dollar went.

Unknown

To assess the financial status of a balance sheet and check whether or not it has a risk of developing liquidity or solvency difficulties, we use the current asset ratio formula as follows:

Current asset ratio = Liquid assets / Short-term liabilities

Current asset ratio and leverage are valuable indicators of your financial performance and ability to deal with debt and unexpected financial circumstances during economic downturns such as inflation and increased interest rates.

As long as the current asset ratio is more than 1, preferably 3 or more, you will have a healthy balance sheet, you can pay off your short-term debt, and do not suffer from any liability difficulties. Current asset ratio and leverage are valuable indicators of your financial performance and ability to deal with debt and unexpected financial circumstances during economic downturns such as inflation and increased interest rates.

3. PHASES OF INVESTMENT

Investors focus on growing their assets column using the profits from their business revenues and increasing their profits from their asset portfolios vice versa. This helps them to reinvest and build their wealth. Also, investors manage their liabilities and expenses effectively to reduce financial risk and continue investing in more assets. However, the majority, particularly the middle class, focus on acquiring liabilities instead of assets, which implies more expenses. For most people, getting more money or a pay rise often won't solve their problems, and they end up struggling financially. This is because of the following reasons:

- they rely only on their salary;
- they spend everything they earn on liabilities;

- their assets are always less than their liabilities;
- they lack financial knowledge.

In the real estate business, properties appreciate, often at a reasonable rate over time. Real estate investment generates income regularly. If this income plus savings are reinvested in more properties rather than spent on unnecessary things, the portfolio and wealth will grow in the long term. The earlier people start, the more flexibility there will be to gain the necessary skills and knowledge, the more time they will have to recover from losses, and the more likely they will be to succeed.

> The earlier people start, the more flexibility there will be to gain the necessary skills and knowledge, the more time they will have to recover from losses, and the more likely they will be to succeed.

The wealth, or net worth figure, is used as an indicator by financial institutions to determine an investor's financial situation at a certain point in time and decide whether to fund their investment. Net worth figures tend to change frequently, depending on the level of investment activities, amount of financial transactions, and projects carried out. Figure 6.2 shows the three main phases of investment for building wealth used by investors:

- Phase one – Save and Build: in the beginning, you can use your savings to build the business and start producing income.
- Phase two – Monitor and Reinvest: monitor the market regularly and reinvest received earnings.
- Phase three – Develop and Leverage: finally, develop the business using the appropriate investment strategy to maximise returns and grow wealth.

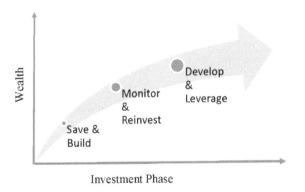

Figure 6.2 Investment phases for building wealth

Investors ensure that their investment business is adequately managed, generating profits with minimal expenditure. Any capital gains from their portfolio are reinvested in buying more properties to generate extra rental income and capital gains. This is called compounding. It is challenging for a beginner to set up a real estate business, starting from scratch to develop a successful investment company and build wealth, but that is the case with every start. That is why successful investors tend to invest in themselves by learning from experienced investors and attending relevant property investment and finance training. As businessman and philanthropist Warren Buffett said, 'The best investment you'll ever make is in yourself.'

> That is why successful investors tend to invest in themselves by learning from experienced investors and attending relevant property investment and finance training.

4. INVESTING AND ENTREPRENEURSHIP

Successful investors can conduct a detailed entrepreneurial business analysis of their targeted area for investment or business strategy.

Many successful investors are entrepreneurs, but not all entrepreneurs understand investing. Successful investors can conduct a detailed entrepreneurial business analysis of their targeted area for investment or business strategy. The outcome of their research and analysis, whether it is supply and demand, ROI, yield, etc., should help them identify the strengths and limitations or positives and negatives of the potential business strategy before making their investment decisions. For example, the supply of properties in the market tends to take time to complete, and it requires a longer time to adapt to an increase in demand effectively. Unlike other businesses, property investment is a long-term business with a long economic life, requiring long-term vision, large amounts of capital, and access to funds. Therefore, active investors involved in entrepreneurial operations are willing to take risks, explore new systems and processes to improve the quality of their products or services, and make informed decisions.

According to the *Cambridge English Dictionary*, an investor is 'a person who puts money into something to make a profit or get an advantage', and an entrepreneur is 'someone who starts their own business, especially when this involves seeing a new opportunity'.

Successful investors are often creative and proactive, know how to offer solutions to real-life problems, manage wealth and money, value it most, and understand how and where to spend it.

Successful investors are often creative and proactive, know how to offer solutions to real-life problems, manage wealth and money, value it most, and understand how and where to spend it. They would refrain from spending money on liabilities, unnecessary consumables, or depreciables. This makes money flow towards these people because of the products and services they offer, as well as their understanding of money, managing and valuing it with full respect. In the UK, according to the ONS, wealth is unevenly distributed among individuals, with the top 10% of wealthy British estimated to own around 50% of all wealth in the UK, mainly in private pensions and property. The super-rich know how to

- use the money to solve business problems;
- invest in new business strategies or assets;
- acquire new businesses;
- set up and manage companies;
- grow multi-stream income portfolios;
- build professional teams and business networks, etc.

Never depend on single income. Make investment to create a second source.
Warren Buffet

Active entrepreneurs take the risk of starting up their companies, investing time to gain the 'know-how' to deal with various entities such as banks, solicitors, local authorities, insurers, etc.

Active entrepreneurs take the risk of starting up their companies, investing time to gain the 'know-how' to deal with various entities such as banks, solicitors, local authorities, insurers, etc. They are willing to interact with all the stakeholders and deal with all aspects of the business in terms of marketing, sales, technology, economics, finance, accounting, operations management, strategic planning, etc. Most successful entrepreneurs who have managed to build quality companies invested time and effort in attracting talent to their companies. All these activities are essential to businesses and require certain qualities and skills to build a successful investment business. That is why successful investors and entrepreneurs are risk-takers, which makes them different from the majority based on the 80/20 rule, also known as the Pareto principle, as shown in Figure 6.3.

I don't pay good wages because I have a lot of money;
I have a lot of money because I pay good wages
Robert Bosch

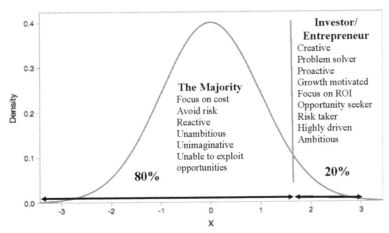

Figure 6.3 Investors and the majority. Adapted from the Pareto Principle (80/20 Rule)

Money is multiplied in practical value depending on the
number of W's you control in your life: what you do, when
you do it, where you do it, and with whom you do it.
Tim Ferriss

This 80/20 principle states that about 80% of a population are the consumers of the products or services of the 20% of people who put effort into providing those products or services. As long as the 20% keep creating jobs, producing and offering their services, and there is demand for the jobs they create and what they provide in products or services, consumers will keep spending and consuming those products and services. The 20% tend to be responsible when it comes to spending money; they know their priorities and how to meet them. However, when that 80% receive a pay rise or inheritance or win the lottery, they will most likely think about where to spend their money rather than investing it. Countless products and services are offered daily and fairly to the public, who are happy to spend their money on those

This 80/20 principle states that about 80% of a population are the consumers of the products or services of the 20% of people who put effort into providing those products or services.

Countless products and services are offered daily and fairly to the public, who are happy to spend their money on those services and products and consume them.

services and products and consume them. Are you ready to be part of that 20% who offer those products and services or the 80% who just consume? If that 20% made it, anyone can, regardless of background, culture, religion, or ethnicity. Making money is a skill like any other skill that people can learn and master.

Starting entrepreneurs need help at the beginning because they often need a lot of cash in the early days of their projects. However, experienced investors and traders use their expertise and financial skills to properly use good debt to grow their asset portfolios and revenues regardless of the economic situation and marketplace. Therefore, using the following strategies, you should consider changing your mindset and belief about money to build healthy bank accounts and meet your financial goals.

- Develop a financial plan: to manage income and savings and start investing.
- Manage debt: to control outgoings and avoid bad debts and financial stress.
- Monitor your spending behaviour: to control shopping habits and avoid unnecessary expenditure.
- Develop a saving strategy: to avoid overspending and raise funds for future investments.
- Develop budgets: to manage and control your spending.

George Soros is a famously wealthy man well-known for a single-day gain of $1 billion in 1992. He is a leading philanthropist who has donated more than $30 billion of his wealth to charitable causes. Successful investors learn how to invest, when and where to get good deals, and how to fund them. They would be expected to deal with high street and non-high street banks to get lending and fund their investment projects. For instance, in the property business, lenders offer various mortgage options, fixed and variable rates using mortgage terms, often two, three, or five years. If an investor decides to pay their mortgage in full through remortgaging before the end of their mortgage term, they would expect to pay an early payment penalty, also known as an early redemption fee. Investors may decide to do so when refinancing any of their properties before the end of the mortgage term. This usually occurs after the investor has added value to a property and is confident the refinance will be successful. This enables the investor to access extra funds despite the unpleasant cost of early payment penalties, which are part of business costs. However, any property investor needs to focus on the profits in capital gains earned and not on business costs. To achieve that, investors have to ensure that they invest in properties located in good areas with the potential for capital growth and increased demand.

Sometimes it is possible to get a mortgage without early payment penalties, but such mortgages are not always available. As part of the earlier discussion with the mortgage advisers about refinancing, it is always worth asking them if such an option is available. Bridging loans, often expensive compared to 'normal' mortgages, could also be an option. Bridging mortgages are helpful for short-term borrowing: for example, to buy derelict properties from auctions to renovate, add value, and then rent or sell. Bridging mortgages are also helpful for properties with legal or technical problems; these are often sold BMV (below market value), so getting 'normal' mortgages for such properties can be difficult. Unlike active investors willing to invest in

> Successful investors learn how to invest, when and where to get good deals, and how to fund them. They would be expected to deal with high street and non-high street banks to get lending and fund their investment projects.

> Bridging loans, often expensive compared to 'normal' mortgages, could also be an option. Bridging mortgages are helpful for short-term borrowing.

properties with problems and during uncertain market conditions, banks are often reluctant to offer funds regardless of how minor the issues are. This makes bridging mortgages an accessible option for investors to fund investment projects.

During the COVID-19 pandemic period in 2020, income-producing properties continued to work for their owners with few problems. However, due to the challenging situation and uncertainty, banks were reluctant to approve mortgages or refinance applications. They applied stringent lending requirements that impacted property businesses during the pandemic. However, the business bounce-back loans introduced by the UK government made the refinance delays less painful for many real estate investment companies.

5. PROPERTY FINANCE

Property investment is becoming popular among investors worldwide due to the low interest rates banks offer and the good yields achieved. However, various expenses are associated with the property business, such as maintenance, insurance, mortgage costs, management time, etc., which require proper financial operations. Owing to limited capital, investors often rely on banks to fund investment projects. However, investors with sufficient capital still go for the option of getting extra funds from banks. This allows them to invest in more properties and leverage to magnify their returns. Different factors attract investors to the property business. The three major factors are as follows:

Owing to limited capital, investors often rely on banks to fund investment projects. However, investors with sufficient capital still go for the option of getting extra funds from banks.

1. Return on investment (ROI): Investors use ROI to evaluate the efficiency of their capital investment and measure the amount of return relative to the cost of the investment. It is an indicator used to measure the return on a particular real estate investment.
   The basic formula for ROI is:

Investors use ROI to evaluate the efficiency of their capital investment and measure the amount of return relative to the cost of the investment.

$$ROI = (Annual\ rental\ cash\ flow\ /\ Initial\ investment) \times 100$$
$$Annual\ rental\ cash\ flow = Rental\ income - Running\ costs$$
$$Initial\ investment = Cost\ of\ investment\ (e.g.,\ Deposit) +$$
$$SDLT + Refurbs + Legal\ fees$$
$$SDLT = Stamp\ Duty,\ Land\ Tax$$
$$Number\ of\ years\ to\ get\ back\ initial\ investment = 1\ /\ ROI$$

2. Rental yield: Owing to the limited supply of properties, the anticipated demand for renting will be sufficient to expect a good yield and profits. Rental yield is a percentage figure used to calculate the return an investor is likely to achieve on a property through rental income. The higher the yield, the more cash flows should be expected. We can calculate the yield as follows:

Rental yield is a percentage figure used to calculate the return an investor is likely to achieve on a property through rental income.

$$Yield = (Annual\ rental\ income\ /\ Total\ amount\ of\ investment) \times 100$$
$$The\ total\ amount\ of\ investment$$
$$= House\ price + SDLT + Refurbs\ cost + Legal\ fees$$

3. Capital gain/appreciation: Investors often expect capital appreciation over a particular period from the income-generating property.
Any future inflation in the market would contribute to the investor's
capital gain.

After calculating the yield, investors may find it helpful to determine
the maximum offer price for a property, which they can provide to the
estate agent or the vendor as follows:

$$\textit{Maximum offer = Expected monthly rental income x}$$
$$\textit{12 / Required yield}$$

Sometimes, investors get a deal that compounds both rental return and
capital growth. Table 6.4 shows the main differences between rental yield
and capital gain.

Table 6.4 Main differences between rental yield and capital gain

RENTAL YIELD	CAPITAL GAIN
• Short-term return • Consistent income stream or rental return • Immediate return on an investment	• Long-term growth • Increase in property value • Investors benefit when selling the property or refinancing • Based on historical market data

6. CREATIVE FINANCE SCENARIO

Let us assume that an investor with a capital of £100,000 of their own in
their bank account wants to invest in a buy-to-let business. They have two
options to select from. The first option is to buy one two-bedroom house
using their capital of £100,000 cash, which can achieve a 10% annual yield.
Since they are purchasing this property with cash, they do not need to get
a loan, so it is a debt-free purchase. The second option is to buy four properties using one mortgage with a 75% loan-to-value for each one. So, their
£100,000 will be split over the four properties to pay for their deposits, i.e.,
£25,000 deposit for each property.

Let us compare the achieved income of both purchase options, knowing
that the investor is using the same amount of capital for the investment,
which is £100,000. For option 1, they can aim for a rental income of £10,000
per year, i.e., 10% yield. For option 2, they should be able to aim for a gross
rental income of £10,000 x 4, which is £40,000. However, they must pay
their monthly mortgage cost (or interest, about 3% of the mortgage amount)
for each of the four properties. This means that their annual income from
those four properties will be as follows:

$$\textit{10\% Yield – (3\% interest rate of four mortgage loans) =}$$
$$\textit{(£10,000 x 4) – 3\% x (£75,000 x 4) =}$$
$$\textit{£40,000 – £9,000 = £31,000}$$

So, the income generated from the capital investment of buying four properties, i.e., using option 2, is £31,000. Using good debt/a mortgage to buy the four properties results in a higher annual income, about three times the income from investing all cash in one property. In terms of capital gain, the value of the first option property will be £105,000 at the end of the year. However, if the investor selects the second option of buying four properties instead, the value of the four properties combined will become £420,000 after one year. Therefore, they can make £20,000 on the second option and a gain of only £5,000 on the first purchase. Table 6.5 compares a cash buyer investment and using a mortgage to buy four income-producing properties.

Table 6.5 Comparison between a cash purchase and using a mortgage

Option 1 – cash buyer		Comparison Items		Option 2 – using mortgage	
	Cash	Purchase	Mortgage (75%)		
	£100,000	Price	£100,000 x 4 = £400,000		
	£0	Loan Amount	£75,000 x 4 = £300,000		
	£100,000	Capital	£100,000		
	10% (£10,000)	Achieved annual cashflow	£31,000		
	5% (£5,000)	Capital gain	5% (£5,000 x 4 = £20,000)		

The investor should be able to aim for 20% as a return on capital investment of their £100,000 using option 2. Using good debt/a mortgage to buy more properties results in a higher annual income and a ROI. The achieved annual income and ROI from investing in the four properties is £31,000 + £20,000 = £51,000, which comes from what is known as financial leverage. So, even if the investor does not achieve a good capital gain of 5%, they can still produce £31,000 from rental income, which is an excellent achievement.

Leverage refers to the funds received from a lender, i.e., debt financing relative to the part financed by equity and measured using the loan-to-value (LTV) ratio. The LTV ratio is defined by how much the lender is willing to fund the investment property purchase. Lenders are often reluctant to increase the LTV above a certain level to keep risk under control. Despite the increasing returns from leverage, a direct relationship exists between an investor's leverage and risk. Therefore, property investors should trade off the risk brought by leveraging with the increased returns achieved by extra lending.

7. SUMMARY

The main idea of
creative finance is for
investors to arrange
a business deal using
funds from a third-
party entity to build
an income-producing
portfolio and accumu-
late valuable assets.

Active investors use creative finance to benefit from certain market conditions, make the right investment decisions, and generate high revenues
and capital growth. The main idea of creative finance is for investors to
arrange a business deal using funds from a third-party entity to build an
income-producing portfolio and accumulate valuable assets. There is no
excuse for you not to learn those skills, using online educational resources
and training programmes. You should have learnt so far how investors
use intelligent financial techniques to carry out investment activities and
leveraging to expand their portfolios without using much of their capital.
Moreover, practical examples of how investors can leverage and expand
their income-producing property portfolios have been introduced. A model
of the wealth generation engine has been presented to help you understand
how to develop a financial strategy and plan; furthermore, the principles
of building asset portfolios and growing income-generating businesses have
been discussed.

You should have learnt
so far how investors
use intelligent financial
techniques to carry out
investment activities
and leveraging to
expand their portfolios
without using much of
their capital.

The way investors raise funds using capital lenders through mortgage/
remortgage products with appropriate LTV has been presented. However,
using creative finance requires attention and skills in understanding the costs
associated with mortgages and debt management. This chapter covered
the financial statements, mainly the income statement and balance sheet,
which are helpful tools for financial management. Risk-taking, fast decision-making, and creativity are among other skills often mastered by active
entrepreneurs and investors who manage to build successful businesses. In
this chapter, the main strengths of active entrepreneurs and investors and
how they are different from the rest have been discussed. The main phases
of building a successful investment portfolio, supported with examples of
creative financing for property deals, have been introduced. Also, examples
of evaluating investment deals using cash flows, ROI, and rental yield have
been presented.

Risk-taking, fast
decision-making, and
creativity are among
other skills often
mastered by active
entrepreneurs and
investors who manage
to build successful
businesses.

Creative finance can help your investment skills and financial situation
and help you achieve your plans, but you must select the right time for
investing. Investing is a challenging task requiring patience and research
skills to make informed decisions, not emotional ones. The next chapter
introduces a 5-step investing process to help you develop your investment
knowledge and asset portfolio. You will learn about market situations such
as real estate, equities, etc., dealing with inflation, and long-term investment to achieve higher capital appreciation and returns. Investing requires
assessing the markets of different asset classes, knowing your ROI and taking
a risk; therefore, the next chapter will discuss real-life investment scenarios
supported with numerical examples. You must understand the principles
and concepts of investing and improve your financial skills and abilities to
manage risk. The next chapter will introduce issues about risk and return
and risk management.

Investing is a chal-
lenging task requiring
patience and research
skills to make informed
decisions, not
emotional ones.

PRINCIPLES OF INVESTMENT

7

*Before you speak, listen. Before you write, think. Before
you spend, earn. Before you invest, investigate. Before
you criticize, wait. Before you pray, forgive. Before you
quit, try. Before you retire, save. Before you die, give.*

William A. Ward

Investing can help you improve your financial situation, increase your income and achieve your financial goals. However, it is challenging and requires a good understanding of the principles of finance, accounting, economics, and using the right resources. It is essential to know the best time for investing and using future opportunities when the prices of commodities, stock shares, precious metals, or properties are appropriate. Investing needs a lot of focus, patience, and proper information-gathering techniques to help make informed decisions. You should avoid speculating and making emotional decisions and invest more time learning and educating yourself about investing and making intelligent investment decisions.

This chapter covers a 5-step investing process, representing the guidelines for investors to build multi-stream income and asset portfolios. You will need such a process to develop your knowledge about investing, remain focused, and achieve your goals. Keeping money in your savings accounts without making it work for you could lead to losing value and purchasing power due to inflation. Therefore, we need a solid investment portfolio that brings good returns and helps us beat inflation. Investing is a long-term game; the longer you invest, the more likely it is that you will achieve higher capital appreciation and returns. This applies to most markets such as real estate, equities or stock shares, gold, etc. However, your real investment return would consider inflation; for example, if your investment return is 12% and the inflation is 8%, then your real investment return would be 4%.

This chapter covers risk and return and the ROI, a metric used to evaluate and measure the performance of an investment. It will cover real-life investment scenarios and numerical examples to help you explore different investment cases. Investing is about thinking long term and seeking opportunities for better investment returns. However, investing requires a professional work attitude, discipline, and willingness to take risks. Different asset classes have different risk levels and there are no riskless investments. Therefore, your knowledge of, and ability to manage, risk should help you develop your financial strategies and improve your money management

Investing can help you improve your financial situation, increase your income and achieve your financial goals. However, it is challenging and requires a good understanding of the principles of finance, accounting, economics, and using the right resources.

You should avoid speculating and making emotional decisions and invest more time learning and educating yourself about investing and making intelligent investment decisions.

Keeping money in your savings accounts without making it work for you could lead to losing value and purchasing power due to inflation.

Investing is about thinking long-term and seeking opportunities for better investment returns. However, investing requires a professional work attitude, discipline, and willingness to take risks.

skills. The issues of risk and return and risk management are discussed at the end of this chapter.

1. INVESTING YOUR MONEY

Investing time and money to build wealth and achieve financial aims is necessary. When good savings have been built up, it is the right time to consider investing and working on your financial plans. There should be different options for investment vehicles, such as stocks and real estate, commodities, etc. Investing in multiple stream income assets long term can help you build wealth and minimise risk. It is challenging, but getting the proper knowledge and using the right resources will help you achieve your financial aims, objectives, and investment journey. Individuals often think there are no investment opportunities when the markets are distressed and tend to avoid taking risks.

During an economic downturn, there are often many opportunities for investing in real estate and getting BMV (below market value) properties offered for sale. However, getting into real estate investment requires understanding property market fluctuations to help you know how much you should pay and whether it is time to invest, refinance, or sell (Stone and Fribbance, 2019). Various economic factors that affect the property market determine property prices and rent charges. It often requires a lot of time and effort to supply real estate's market needs and meet the demand. Property development projects take time, due to the development requirements and strict building regulations.

Real estate investment could help produce a healthy passive income. Figure 7.1 shows an example of a four-bedroom house my company, Anzar Property Investors Limited, bought from an online auction through Pugh Auctions in December 2022 for £200,000. It was a good deal for what was considered a BMV property and was bought when the UK was in a recession during the cost-of-living crisis. We spent about £18,000 on refurbishment works and then rented it for £1,550 per month just after completing all the work. When writing this book, just two months after receiving the keys to this property and renting it, this house was valued at £265,000 and remortgaged based on this figure. The raised funds covered most of the purchase costs and will be used to invest in another buy-to-let property. The average house prices and residential property sales in the UK have been accelerating recently. However, changes in real estate investment strategies and regulations by the government can have an impact on property investors, and tenants as well.

The average house prices and residential property sales in the UK have been accelerating recently. However, changes in real estate investment strategies and regulations by the government can have an impact on property investors, and tenants as well.

It's not the employer who pays the wages. Employers only handle the money. It's the customer who pays the wages.
Henry Ford

Figure 7.1 A property bought from an auction. Image courtesy of Pugh Auctions: https://www.pugh-auctions.com/

I will tell you the secret to getting rich on Wall Street.
You try to be greedy when others are fearful. And
you try to be fearful when others are greedy.

Warren Buffett

Property prices play a significant role in people's finances regarding their ability to save and budget for the future. Property prices and rents depend on the law of supply and demand in a free-market economy. The demand for housing represents the number of residential properties buyers are willing to purchase at a specific price. The supply represents the construction and flow of residential properties at a particular price. The market determines the property price, based on comparable neighbouring properties and the ability of property developers, investors, and the need to supply enough properties.

> The demand for housing represents the number of residential properties buyers are willing to purchase at a specific price. The supply represents the construction and flow of residential properties at a particular price.

An investor is 'a person who puts money into something
in order to make a profit or get an advantage'.

Cambridge English Dictionary

> Understanding the basic economic principles can help investors decide the best time to invest.

Understanding the basic economic principles can help investors decide the best time to invest. For instance, proactive investors can use the opportunity when property prices are either low or high. During an economic downturn, property prices tend to decrease, making it a good time for investors to buy and grow their portfolios. When property prices are high, investors can remortgage or refinance their properties to release equity, get funds to reinvest, and enlarge their portfolio again. Investing does require patience and focus, as making quick moves from one investment opportunity to another is not helpful and will never lead to positive results. It is essential

> Investing does require patience and focus, as making quick moves from one investment opportunity to another is not helpful and will never lead to positive results.

that you carefully manage your emotions and avoid non-rational decisions when investing, as listed below.

- Monitor and control your emotions when investing.
- Avoid intense feelings about money and upsetting situations.
- Keep your cool during unpleasant market situations.
- Become self-aware of your behaviour towards money and emotions.
- Be aware of your limitations and try to deal with them.
- Avoid speculation and assumptions when making investment decisions.
- Be proactive rather than reactive to market changes.
- Avoid financial stress and worries.
- Be patient when investing and always expect some unpleasant results.
- Do your due diligence and research.
- Manage your investment risk carefully and be long-term orientated.
- Keep fit and take care of your mental health.
- Find a balance between excessive emotions and no emotions at all.
- Consider professional support whenever needed.

Those who speculate tend to gamble and look for short-term gains and profits without investing time for studying, understanding, and assessing the market. Therefore, we must make informed decisions before we invest, not speculate to make quick profits. This ensures that our saved money is appropriately invested and we make intelligent investment decisions.

> *It always seems impossible until it is done.*
> Nelson Mandela

2. 5-STEP INVESTMENT PROCESS

Investing money follows a 5-step process that outlines the main actions in creating an asset portfolio, as shown in Figure 7.2. Those five steps represent the guidelines for investors to support them during their investment journey and to allow them to remain focused on building their portfolios and achieving their investment goals. The investment process involves a sequence of activities with the aim of acquiring assets and receiving returns in the future, as is shown below.

- Identify the investment strategy and objectives.
- Analyse multiple options for investment vehicles.
- Select the asset class(es) that helps you achieve your investment objectives, i.e., investing in equity, commodities, real estate, etc.
- Start building the selected asset class.
- Evaluate the performance of your investment portfolio to determine whether or not you achieved your objectives, review consistently, and adjust accordingly.

Those who speculate tend to gamble and look for short-term gains and profits without investing time for studying, understanding, and assessing the market.

The investment process involves a sequence of activities with the aim of acquiring assets and receiving returns in the future.

Figure 7.2 5-step investment process

It is essential to diversify your portfolio by assembling diverse assets spanning various classes to keep your risk as minimal as possible. If you decide to invest in equity, you must choose whether to understand how the stock market operates, the trading process, and portfolio management or keep it simple: do not get involved in the investment game. Without a good understanding of the portfolio construction and investment process, it is not enough to just appoint an experienced investment adviser or agent to manage your portfolio. Deciding on which asset class to invest in will depend on factors such as expected returns, required funds, market conditions, etc.

> *Success is not the result of making money; earning money is the result of success – and success is in direct proportion to our service.*
> Earl Nightingale

3. INVESTING AND INFLATION

To start your investment journey, you must save enough money to raise the funds necessary for your investment projects. Be aware that keeping money saved for a long time without making it work for you could have a negative impact on its value and purchasing power due to inflation. Therefore, to beat inflation and its corrosive effect on your money, you need to have a solid investment that brings good returns on a monthly or annual basis.

It is essential to diversify your portfolio by assembling diverse assets spanning various classes to keep your risk as minimal as possible.

Deciding on which asset class to invest in will depend on factors such as expected returns, required funds, market conditions, etc.

To start your investment journey, you must save enough money to raise the funds necessary for your investment projects.

To beat inflation and its corrosive effect on your money, you need to have a solid investment that brings good returns on a monthly or annual basis.

Many people take no care of their money till they come nearly
to the end of it, and others do just the same with their time.
Johann Wolfgang von Goethe

The cost-of-living
problem led to many
demonstrations by
people and employees,
such as junior doctors
and nurses, railway
employees, and royal
mail workers in many
cities in the UK.

You should not spend
your life thinking about
money and living
with barely enough,
struggling to make ends
meet, unable to deal
with your debts and
inflation or provide for
yourself and your family.

There is nothing wrong
with joining a university,
but if you can master
learning martial arts,
football, basketball,
or anything else, you
should be able to learn
how to make money.

Investing is a learnable
skill; for instance, investors must master money
management, finances,
and risk management
and seek knowledge in
other related areas.

You have to consider
inflation when you
invest your money and
predict your returns
because it reduces the
purchasing power of
your capital.

In October 2022, inflation hit a 41-year high of 11.1%, and the estimated annual inflation rate was 11.2% in 2022, according to the ONS. The cost-of-living crisis in 2022 affected many households in the UK, as indicated and published by the BBC News and a number of other mass media platforms. The cost-of-living problem led to many demonstrations by people and employees, such as junior doctors and nurses, railway employees, and royal mail workers in many cities in the UK.

You should not spend your life thinking about money and living with barely enough, struggling to make ends meet, unable to deal with your debts and inflation or provide for yourself and your family. You have to have a positive relationship with money, and it is not impossible for you to make a lot of it without compromising your relationships or beliefs or losing the connection with any of your family members or friends. There is a difference between an inability to make money and lacking the skills to make it. You have to know your limitations and strengths, but do not need to spend years at university to learn how to make money. There is nothing wrong with joining a university, but if you can master learning martial arts, football, basketball, or anything else, you should be able to learn how to make money. I used to be a university lecturer and I had intelligent colleagues teaching economics and finance, but they were financially struggling. Unfortunately, teaching economic theories and financial models and knowing how to solve complicated mathematical formulae alone helps only a little when learning how to make money.

Many valuable tools and systems are accessible and available to you freely, and you can utilise them to improve your skills and achieve your financial goals, many of which are covered in this book. Investing is a learnable skill; for instance, investors must master money management, finances, and risk management and seek knowledge in other related areas. Investing is a long-term business, i.e., the longer they invest, the more likely it is that they achieve higher capital appreciation and rental returns. This applies to stock markets that require investment for extended periods (ten years or more) and earn good returns (7–10%). These figures are similar to what you can achieve in real estate investment; however, due to the impact of inflation, your real investment return must take inflation into account and can be calculated as follows:

$$Real\ investment\ return = Investment\ return - inflation$$

So, if your investment return is 10% and inflation is 5%, your real investment return is just 5%. You have to consider inflation when you invest your money and predict your returns because it reduces the purchasing power of your capital. Many research studies in which financial analysts and experienced investors present interesting results and predictions of different financial markets are published. They conduct analysis and valuation activities and report the market trends and long-term returns investors can expect when investing in real estate and equity markets. Many of those reports are available online, which you can access freely.

4. RETURN ON INVESTMENT (ROI)

A factor that you need to be aware of when you invest your money is the ROI, a well-known metric used to measure the performance of a particular investment using a mathematical formula. It is used to evaluate the returned initial investment during a period. For example, it should take about ten years to produce an initial investment at 7.2% ROI with an inflation of 0%. However, investors should aim for a higher ROI to double their money in less than ten years, as shown in Table 7.1 below.

Table 7.1 ROI calculations

Annualised ROI	No of years to return initial investment
2.8%	25
3.5%	20
4.7%	15
7.2%	10
10.4%	7
14.9%	5

We can compute the annual percentage ROI using the following formula:

$$\textbf{\textit{Annualised ROI = ((Principal + Gained Value) / Principal)}}$$
$$\textbf{\textit{1/n − 1 x 100}}$$

ROI must keep up with the inflation rate to improve the buying and investment power. For example, an inflation rate of 3% after an investment return of 2.8% will not produce a positive return (2.8% − 3% = −0.2%). Inflation can reduce the returns of an investment, which is why understanding inflation is essential. Diversifying an investment business, for example, with exposure to Buy-to-let, HMO, or REITs may help investors protect their investment returns against inflation.

It is helpful to determine how much money can grow using the power of compound interest compared to ROI. Compounding interest includes the accumulated interest from several years on an investment or savings. It increases faster than simple interest, boosts investment returns, and significantly affects the initial investment over the long term, as shown in Table 7.2. Figure 7.3 below shows approximate figures for how much an initial saving will grow for different scenarios. It highlights the results of doubling the initial investment of $10,000 in savings using interest of 10.4% in seven years. Be aware that inflation compounds in the same way that interest does.

ROI must keep up with the inflation rate to improve the buying and investment power.

Inflation can reduce the returns of an investment, which is why understanding inflation is essential.

Table 7.2 Compound interest over many years

Interest rate per year	No of years to return initial investment
2.8%	25
3.5%	20
4.7%	15
7.2%	10
10.4%	7
14.9%	5

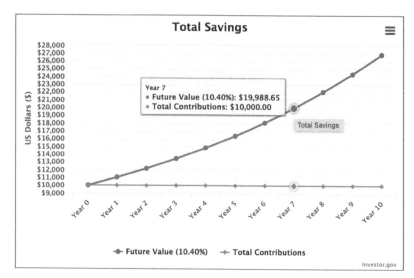

Figure 7.3 Doubling initial investment of $10,000 savings in seven years using 10.4% compound interest. Adapted from https://www.investor.gov/financial-tools-calculators/calculators/compound-interest-calculator

The compound interest can be calculated using the following formula:

$$= P [(1 + i)n - 1]$$

where P = initial principal or initial investment or saving amount,
i = nominal annual interest rate, and
n = number of compounding periods

Compound interest is the eighth wonder of the world. He who understands it earns it ... he who doesn't pays it

Albert Einstein

5. INVESTING IN EQUITIES

Investing in equities or shares allows you to have a stake or part-ownership of a business or company. It is about owning small shares in a public company's stock and aiming for them to grow in value and create future financial gains. The prices of stock shares tend to fluctuate frequently and are considered high risk, but have the potential for increased profits. Investing in stock shares is a high risk because of market changes and fluctuations and deliberate mis-selling of those financial products and scams. Such incidents could lead to unpleasant consequences such as an investor losing the original invested capital. However, as an investor, you could expect a financial gain either from capital gains after selling your shares at a higher price than you originally paid for them or from dividends from the profits generated by the company whose shares you invested in.

By using online platforms to buy stock shares for a public company, investors could profit if they decide to sell them. Many valuable resources for beginners provide helpful information about using such opportunities. Before investing real money in online stock markets, beginners can use stock market simulators. The following list shows the main steps for investing in the stock market.

1. Decide on an investment strategy and how to invest.
2. Decide whether or not you want brokerage support. If yes, then
   a. evaluate and assess a few brokers based on their investment options, costs, etc.;
   b. select an investing brokerage account.
3. If you decided to do it yourself, then choose either to
   a. do it with an ETF (exchange traded fund): to buy multiple stocks in a single transaction to diversify your portfolio, or
   b. invest in an individual stock market business: purchase shares for a specific company.
4. Allocate a budget for your investment.
5. Transfer money to an online investment account of your choice.
6. Manage your portfolio and costs.

6. INVESTMENT SCENARIOS

This section will cover some investment examples to help you explore different real-life investment cases.

6.1 Investment scenario 1 – Savings, investment, and inflation

If you placed $1,000 in a safe in 1980 and left it there untouched, it would still be $1,000 in 2018 but would have lost about 65% of its value. However, according to CNBC, an investor who invested $1,000 in Apple stock in 1980 could have sold it in 2018 for around $340,000. If you invested your savings in a buy-to-let property with an annual yield of 8% but at the end of the year, annual inflation was 5%, in this case, the real rental yield would be 3%. The real yield is calculated as follows:

Investing in equities or shares allows you to have a stake or part-ownership of a business or company.

Investing in stock shares is a high risk because of market changes and fluctuations and deliberate mis-selling of those financial products and scams.

Before investing real money in online stock markets, beginners can use stock market simulators.

Real Rental Yield = Yield 8% − Inflation 5% = 3%

So, if you save your money and do nothing, then inflation will decrease your money's purchasing power. To beat annual inflation of 5%, you have to earn an investment return of at least 5% to break even at the end of the year.

6.2 Investment scenario 2 – Managing expenses

When you start managing your expenses, you will find items that have significant savings potential.

When you start managing your expenses, you will find items that have significant savings potential. Let us assume a smoker spends £150 on his cigarettes every month. If he saves this amount of money and puts it into savings, that is £1,800 a year and £18,000 in ten years. So, instead of spending his money on harmful cigarettes, he could save £18,000 in ten years and invest such an amount if he wanted to. If he decided to turn that £150 spent per month into contributions to an investment account that offers an 8% annual return for ten years, the £18,000 he made in contributions to the investment would grow to approximately £27,624.

This amount of £27,624 is known as the future value of his investment, and the total investment return is about £9,624. This is the amount of return that he would have achieved if he had made regular contributions of £150 throughout the ten years. A small amount of £150 that is saved and invested monthly can grow to become a significant fund for a business project or a deposit for a buy-to-let investment property. Having an income-generating property is very helpful for someone planning to retire early. Unfortunately, most people do not understand the power of saving consistently, even in small amounts, and managing their expenses is the basis for building wealth. I support focusing on increasing our income to the maximum to achieve financial freedom instead of concentrating on savings. Still, regular savings are of significant importance to those starting their FI journey.

Unfortunately, most people do not understand the power of saving consistently, even in small amounts, and managing their expenses is the basis for building wealth. I support focusing on increasing our income to the maximum to achieve financial freedom instead of concentrating on savings.

6.3 Investment scenario 3 – Gold and Bitcoin

This is to build up your savings and use the available resources to fund potential investment projects when they become available. If you had a proper savings plan and managed to save £7,500 in 2005 and contributed to an investment in a gold bullion vault for 17 years, your £7,500 investment would have grown to £46,593 in 2022, as shown in Figure 7.4. However, if you invested £215.20 in Bitcoin in November 2015, you could have sold it in February 2022 for £30,752 or £13,684 in December 2022, as shown in Figure 7.5.

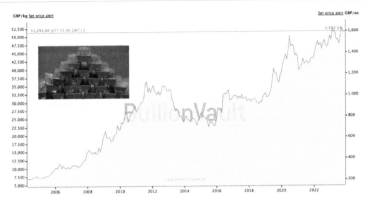

Figure 7.4 Gold price chart (2003–2022). Chart courtesy of
BullionVault: https://www.bullionvault.com/gold-price-chart.do

Figure 7.5 Price changes for Bitcoin 2006–2022. Chart courtesy
of Google Finance: https://www.google.com/finance/quote/
BTC-GBP. Google Finance is a trademark of Google LLC. This
book is not endorsed by or affiliated with Google in any way.

If you are planning to invest in stocks, choosing a company whose services
or products you use might be a good idea. Companies also publish their
investor presentation on their websites, which contains helpful information
about the financial situation.

Many professional investors freely share their knowledge in different
areas such as finances, equity investment, real estate investment, tax, etc.,
and what they think about other assets and capital markets. They are a
significant source of vital investing information and financial intelligence.
Those investors are helpful resources and share their expertise and thoughts
with the public using various online platforms such as YouTube, Facebook,
and other social media. Some investors manage large companies; others
have built massive portfolios and wealth. Listening to such successful

Many professional
investors freely share
their knowledge in
different areas such
as finances, equity
investment, real estate
investment, tax, etc.,
and what they think
about other assets and
capital markets.

investors with incredible records and outstanding performance will help you develop your investment plans and become successful.

Many valuable resources and publications, financial magazines, and online resources can help you develop your investment strategies, such as *The Economist*, investopedia.com, cnbc.com, and uk.finance.yahoo.com. Following such resources will provide you with the necessary information to:

- improve your financial knowledge;
- get up-to-date information about the stock market and major companies;
- learn what successful investors invest in;
- find out which are the popular stocks;
- learn about investment and capital markets; and
- develop your investment strategies.

Money grows on the tree of persistence.
Japanese proverb

7. RISK AND RETURN

Thinking long term, searching for opportunities, and taking risks is essential for anyone seeking incredible success and financial rewards. Such a positive attitude would give you a significant competitive advantage over your competitors and peers. For instance, successful entrepreneurs tend to be disciplined, avoid unnecessary distractions, behave themselves, and have a professional work attitude. They are prepared to go the extra mile to achieve their business goals and grow their earnings quickly. Despite entrepreneurs having expertise and know-how in particular fields, they often need more financial knowledge and money management skills. Therefore, being an expert in your business field and knowing how to manage finances is an unbeatable combination.

If you aim to build your multi-asset class portfolio and future wealth, you may start putting money aside consistently, and the higher the amount you save and invest, the more likely it is that you will achieve your aims. Different asset classes have different levels of risk, but there is no riskless investment, and the higher the expected return, the higher the risk attached. Therefore, risk management is vital for any investor to reduce any potential losses and maximise the likelihood of positive outcomes. Investors should acquire the necessary skills to manage and keep the risk of failure as minimal as possible. They must know the risk of losing out if their business fails to achieve its predicted profits. This could be due to unexpected changes in the market or economic circumstances. That is why many successful young entrepreneurs have built successful businesses, made a fortune, and become financially free. Working smart with a clear vision and persistence can give your life a new direction.

Your ability to manage risk should allow you to enhance your financial skills and capabilities, improve your money management abilities, and

---

Margin notes:

Many valuable resources and publications, financial magazines, and online resources can help you develop your investment strategies, such as *The Economist*, investopedia.com, cnbc.com, and uk.finance.yahoo.com.

Thinking long term, searching for opportunities, and taking risks is essential for anyone seeking incredible success and financial rewards.

Different asset classes have different levels of risk, but there is no riskless investment, and the higher the expected return, the higher the risk attached.

Working smart with a clear vision and persistence can give your life a new direction.

Your ability to manage risk should allow you to enhance your financial skills and capabilities, improve your money management abilities, and make the most of funds available for investment.

make the most of funds available for investment. Consider the following two strategies to keep your investment risks as minimal as possible and avoid the impact of market fluctuations.

- Lengthening your investment time: Part of the risk assessment is the time you intend to invest, so the longer you plan to invest in stock shares without selling, the less volatile the investment and the higher the risk you can tolerate. Long-term investments can allow you to handle more risk. The capital gains on stock shares from long-term investment also tend to show positive outcomes that outperform income generated from savings and interest and above inflation. However, you may need to consider the fees of an asset management company dealing with your portfolio on your behalf, if you choose that option, as well as transaction charges (Stone, 2019).

- Diversifying your investment: Diversification is essential to long-term investment and financial plans and strategies. It is about investing in different asset classes, such as stocks and real estate investments, and spreading your risk and funds over multiple investments in various sectors, industries, and countries. A diversified portfolio would allow you to minimise risk, keep losses as minimal as possible, and build a robust long-term portfolio. Diversification is about risk management and tolerance and is a way to properly manage your money in case of unpleasant events and market downturns.

> Long-term investments can allow you to handle more risk.

> A diversified portfolio would allow you to minimise risk, keep losses as minimal as possible, and build a robust long-term portfolio.

Both strategies should help you manage your risk and develop a diversified portfolio of asset classes. The more financially able you are, the more likely you are to take on more risk and invest in multiple asset classes without affecting your living expenses and lifestyle.

8. SUMMARY

This chapter introduced the principles of investment and its importance in modern life. Understanding the main concepts of investing is becoming essential if you are serious about improving your financial situation and achieving your goals. There are many investment opportunities occurring every day, whether in the stock market, real estate, cryptocurrency, etc., but people without knowledge are unlikely to see or recognise them. You need to seek knowledge and learn from the experts, and you cannot rely on speculation to make financial decisions. In this chapter, I introduced the 5-step investing process, which includes the main guidelines to develop your knowledge and help you build your asset portfolio. You cannot afford to lose your saved money's value and purchasing power because of inflation. Some real-life examples showing the impact of inflation on savings have been introduced. To assess and measure the performance of an investment, we use the ROI. This chapter presented some investment and ROI scenarios supported with numerical examples to help you improve your knowledge using practical investment cases.

There is no riskless investment; therefore, you must be prepared financially and psychologically to take risks. Asset diversification is an approach that active investors use to invest in multiple business strategies to improve

> There is no riskless investment; therefore, you must be prepared financially and psychologically to take risks.

Investing in different asset classes can offer multiple income streams and the ability to establish resilient investments.

Seeking opportunities such as lower interest rate green mortgages can bring various benefits as well as financial and social benefits.

earnings and minimise risk. They invest long term in multiple asset classes to tolerate more risk, but lower-risk investments tend to have lower returns. Investing in different asset classes can offer multiple income streams and the ability to establish resilient investments. The next chapter discusses the importance of having a diverse investment portfolio and how investors can reassess their portfolios. For example, real estate investment diversification presents new challenges and opportunities to build healthy portfolios. Seeking opportunities such as lower interest rate green mortgages can bring various benefits as well as financial and social benefits. Using a mixture of investment strategies can help investors to achieve better profits and respond to different market conditions.

INVESTMENT DIVERSIFICATION

8

Asset diversification is about investing in multiple business strategies to improve earnings and minimise risk, i.e., not putting all your eggs in one basket. Long-term investments can help you tolerate more risk, and the longer you intend to invest, the less risky the investment is. However, investing in high-risk strategies can produce higher returns, and those lower-risk investments tend to have lower returns. Using various investment strategies entails putting capital into income-producing assets using numerous classes such as equities, rental income, properties for capital gains, or dividends from REIT(s) shares. Therefore, investing in different asset classes can offer multiple income streams or capital gains and the ability to respond to challenging market conditions. Examples of a diversified portfolio containing different asset classes and expected returns from each asset class are presented in this chapter. Asset diversification should help investors invest in multiple asset classes to improve revenues and establish resilient investments.

This chapter discusses the importance of having a diverse investment portfolio and how investors can reassess their portfolios. It introduces the real estate market expansion grid, the difference between passive and negative investing, REITs markets, and examples of publicly listed REITs. Investing in multiple strategies, such as sustainable REITs, can benefit investors; therefore, this chapter introduces the benefits of portfolio diversification and the main asset classes. Using a mixture of investment strategies can help investors to achieve better profits and respond to different market conditions. Real estate investment diversification presents new challenges and opportunities to build healthy portfolios. Furthermore, investing in multiple asset classes and seeking opportunities such as lower interest rate green mortgages can bring various benefits to investors and tenants, as well as financial and social benefits.

1. INVESTING AND RISK MANAGEMENT

All sorts of investments come with certain returns, and the returns you would expect from any investment would depend on the levels of risk you take. Investment returns correlate with risks, i.e., the lower the expected rate of return is, the less risky investment is. Investment returns are never guaranteed, and it is impossible in any investment to be sure about the returns you think you will earn. You expect an average return of 7–10% annually in a long-term investment. Be aware that guaranteed returns on investment do

Asset diversification is about investing in multiple business strategies to improve earnings and minimise risk, i.e., not putting all your eggs in one basket.

Investing in different asset classes can offer multiple income streams or capital gains and the ability to respond to challenging market conditions.

Investment returns are never guaranteed, and it is impossible in any investment to be sure about the returns you think you will earn.

Be aware that guaranteed returns on investment do not exist – investment is a long-term business.

not exist – investment is a long-term business. Low-risk investments, such as bank savings, often provide minimum income.

Figure 8.1 shows the relationship between risk and return. High-risk investments tend to have higher returns, and those with lower risks are likely to generate lower returns. The figure highlights the three levels of invest-ment risks and returns. The bottom left side of the graph shows the savings accounts representing the foundation of your investment and wealth gener-ation. This is because savings are less volatile and have the lowest return and risk. As you move toward the top right side of the graph, you will see other assets that provide more returns and higher potential risks. The three primary levels of investment kinds with different levels of risk are the stock market, real estate, and savings accounts, as follows:

- Equities/Stock shares: Most of the investment literature indicates that investing in equities or stock markets is risky, especially for begin-ners, but provides an attractive return potential over the long term. Companies issue stock shares sold to traders or investors in order to raise funds for reinvestment.
- Real estate: Real estate investment has a moderate level of risk. It provides long-term growth and consistent cash flow. Having an income-generating property investment provides security and regular returns.
- Cash savings: With the inflation rate at the time of writing being over 11% per annum, cash is being eroded as banks offer no or very low returns on an individual's cash savings.

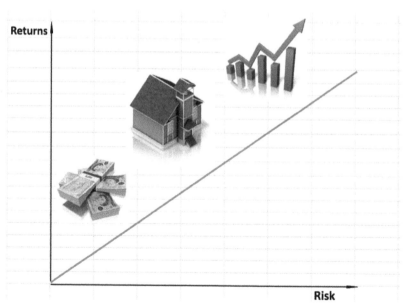

Figure 8.1 Risk versus returns

Risk comes from not knowing what you are doing.
Warren Buffett

Whether to save or invest in real estate or equities will depend on the trade-off between risk and return, the risk you are willing to take, and your financial objectives. Risk-averse people tend to go only for products promising good returns, which makes them different from high-risk-taking investors. Stock markets are more volatile than real estate because the share prices tend to fluctuate consistently. However, for most successful companies, the trend is upward in the long term, as shown in Figure 8.2. The figure illustrates the volatility of the share prices and the trend of the S&P500 from December 1984 to December 2022, reflecting the performance of the S&P500 index stocks. The index contains the leading 500 US companies and is tracked by many ETFs (exchange-traded funds). The figure shows that the average prices of those 500 companies' shares increased massively from US$181.18 in Dec 1984 to US$3,839.50 in December 2022.

> Risk-averse people tend to go only for products promising good returns, which makes them different from high-risk-taking investors.

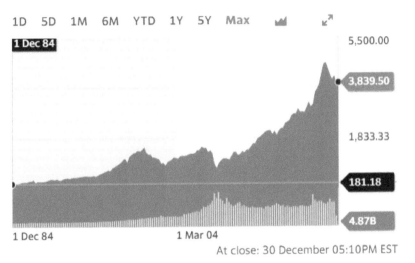

1D   5D   1M   6M   YTD   1Y   5Y   Max

1 Dec 84

5,500.00

3,839.50

1,833.33

181.18

4.87B

1 Dec 84   1 Mar 04

At close: 30 December 05:10PM EST

Figure 8.2 S&P500 Index (Dec 1984–Dec 2022). Source: Yahoo Finance 2023

Investing in stocks could earn you tens of per cent of your invested capital quickly, but you could also lose all your money. Therefore, avoiding speculating when investing in stocks and acquiring the proper knowledge and skills is vital, especially if you seek to build long-term wealth without unpleasant financial stress and worry. Financial risk management is an important subject to learn before investing in stocks. It is concerned with identifying the types of factors and price fluctuation that have the most significant impact on business value. Fear of failure never helps and could lead to major problems, not only financially but socially as well. You must consider the following two business strategies to minimise the risk of investment failure and deal with unexpected market circumstances.

> Avoiding speculating when investing in stocks and acquiring the proper knowledge and skills is vital, especially if you seek to build long-term wealth without unpleasant financial stress and worry.

> Fear of failure never helps and could lead to major problems, not only financially but socially as well.

- Lengthening your investment time.
- Diversifying your investment.

It is helpful to consider both strategies when you start investing, so let us get into the details of each strategy.

1.1. Long-term investments

Investing in the long term can allow you to tolerate more risk, and the longer you intend to invest without selling, the less volatile the investment is. For instance, the capital gains on stock shares from long-term investment often show positive outcomes. However, you may need to consider the management costs of your assets, relevant fees to deal with your portfolio on your behalf, and transaction charges (Stone, 2019).

As discussed earlier, investing in high-risk business strategies tends to have higher returns, and those with lower risks have lower returns. Buy-to-let (Buy-to-let) properties are less risky than HMOs, holiday lets, SAs (serviced accommodation), hotels, and REITs stock markets. This is because SAs, holiday lets, hotels, and REITs stock shares are volatile and seasonal kinds of accommodation services. For instance, demand for holiday lets and hotels is at its peak only during summer, between June and August. Investing in REITs equities is risky but provides an attractive return potential to raise funds for reinvestment and retirement over the long term.

Investing in real estate, whether building assets or equities, is long term. Strategies such as holiday lets and hotels are labour-intensive and time-consuming businesses requiring attention and commitment. The risk–return straight diagonal line shown in Figure 8.3 can represent the spectrum of different income-producing real estate investment strategies/ assets. However, the expected returns from those different strategies will vary depending on location and level of demand. For instance, SAs tend to produce better income when located closer to city centres and business parks but are at high risk if situated in remote rural areas where holiday lets can perform very well. The higher and more frequent customer payments a strategy brings, the higher the risk is the strategy.

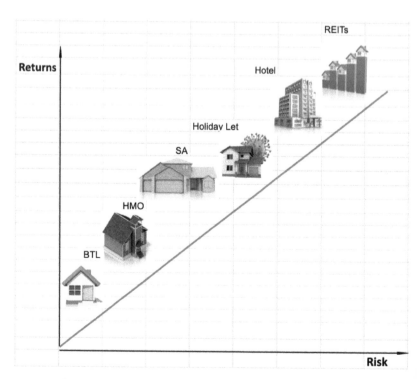

Figure 8.3 Real estate strategies placed on the risk–return line

The trade-off between risk and return is essential in deciding which real estate business to select and is determined by a personal view of risk: how much risk individuals are willing to take, and why they are doing it. Long-term investments such as real estate assets or equities should help you avoid the impact of market fluctuations and obtain excellent returns. However, focusing on single company shares is highly likely to be risky, even over a long period. This leads us to our next topic, investment diversification, which is about building a portfolio of various assets from different industries, such as stock shares and real estate.

The trade-off between risk and return is essential in deciding which real estate business to select and is determined by a personal view of risk: how much risk individuals are willing to take, and why they are doing it.

1.2. Diversifying your investment

Diversification is about investing in different asset classes, such as stocks and real estate investments and spreading the risk over some investments in various industries. To keep risk as minimal as possible, consider building a diversified portfolio that would allow you to build a robust long-term portfolio. Figure 8.4 shows an example of a diversified portfolio containing different asset classes. Diversification is about managing risk and properly managing your money in case of an unpleasant situation and market downturns. The rule is that when investing, you should avoid putting all your eggs in one basket, thus depending 100% on a single asset class in your portfolio. If this single asset doesn't perform well, for whatever reason, you will not be able to deal with such a problem due to a lack of investment options and assets in your portfolio. However, if you have spread your funds over some asset classes, then a drop in returns of one asset class will have less impact on the performance of your total portfolio.

To keep risk as minimal as possible, consider building a diversified portfolio that would allow you to build a robust long-term portfolio.

The rule is that when investing, you should avoid putting all your eggs in one basket, thus depending 100% on a single asset class in your portfolio.

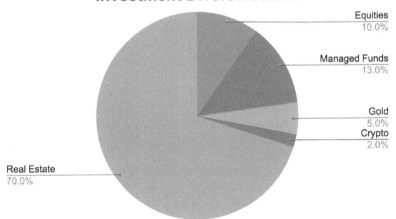

Investment Diversification

Equities 10.0%

Managed Funds 13.0%

Gold 5.0%

Crypto 2.0%

Real Estate 70.0%

Figure 8.4 An example of a diversified portfolio

*Only buy something that you'd be perfectly happy to
hold if the market shuts down for ten years.*

Warren Buffett

The more diversified
your investments and
asset classes you have
in your portfolio, the
less vulnerable is your
portfolio, the less risk
is in your investments,
and the better position
you are in for managing
your risk.

The more diversified investments and asset classes you have in your portfolio, the less vulnerable is your portfolio, the less risk is in your investments, and the better position you are in for managing your risk. So, suppose you are investing in the real estate business; your portfolio should include different real estate asset classes such as buy-to-let, SAs, HMOs, or REITs such as Realty Income's stock. Realty Income is a well-performing REITs stock company listed as a public company in 1994. At the time of writing this book, the Realty Income website has the following paragraph on its main page. (NYSE: O is a symbol assigned to reality income. It represents 'O' company as a REIT for its public listing on the New York Stock Exchange, 'NYSE'.)

Realty Income, The Monthly Dividend Company®, is an S&P 500 company and member of the S&P 500 Dividend Aristocrats® index. For more than five decades, we have invested in people and places to deliver dependable monthly dividends that increase over time. The company is structured as a REIT, and its monthly dividends are supported by the cash flow from over 11,700 real estate properties owned under long-term net lease agreements with commercial clients. To date, the company has declared 629 consecutive common stock monthly dividends throughout its 53-year operating history and increased the dividend 117 times since Realty Income's public listing in 1994.

(NYSE: O)

However, suppose you are one of those investors who prefer to invest in different assets like stocks, commodities, real estate, etc. Because your portfolio is diversified, consider a simple, time-efficient, and hands-off investment strategy. For example, in terms of the stocks portfolio, you might consider ETFs, which operate in a way that tracks an index, commodity, sector, or other assets to provide a return. They cover various asset classes in specific markets and use various investment strategies. Your age plays a role in the asset classes you select to invest in and the level of risk to take. Furthermore, different asset portfolios suit different investors; therefore, you should regularly review your asset allocation and portfolio and adjust according to your circumstances and needs.

Your age plays a role in
the asset classes you
select to invest in and
the level of risk to take.

As an investor, you can decide how your portfolio is managed, actively or passively. Active portfolio management is about regularly managing and reviewing your assets, conducting market research, and making decisions. You are highly involved in the trading process and may take professional help to seek short-term investments and higher returns. As an active investor, you may outsource your investment activities to an active fund manager who can manage your portfolio on your behalf. Fund managers are professional money specialists who offer their services for an expensive fee. They decide which stock companies to invest in and which have the potential to perform well. Fund managers are often accused of lower performance and the inability to outperform the market in the long term and produce competitive returns.

As an investor, you
can decide how your
portfolio is managed,
actively or passively.

Fund managers are
often accused of lower
performance and the
inability to outperform
the market in the long
term and produce
competitive returns.

If you prefer a hands-free investment option, you may choose passive management using a buy-and-hold investment strategy. You allocate your investment activities and assets to an ETF that can track the performance of a particular stock index and aims to match the performance of the market rather than trying to beat it. ETFs such as Vanguard's S&P500 tend to be cost-effective with a much lower expense ratio than fund managers. ETFs are low-cost for busy investors aiming to build portfolios and long-term wealth. Table 8.1 provides a summary of the main difference between active and passive investment management.

Table 8.1 Active and passive investing

The difference between active and passive investing		
Feature	**Active investing**	**Passive investing**
Strategy	The manager selects researched stocks carefully and makes decisions based on market trends. It involves frequent buy-and-sell	Less involvement and limited decision-making by the investor. It uses a buy-and-hold approach
Costs	More expensive due to higher fees charged by fund managers	Low-cost operating expenses and cost-effective option for investment
Risk	High risk – limited abilities for fund managers to always beat the market and market risk	Only market risk so lower risk
Flexibility	Flexible due to the ability to select which stocks to invest in and make decisions	Inflexible due to limited ability to choose and make decisions
Returns	Potential for above-market returns (high risk, high returns)	Always in line with the index (low risk, low returns)
Transparency	Less transparent	Reasonably transparent, easy to monitor and understand
Tax	Tax-inefficient	Tax-efficient

During recession times and weak market activities, investors prefer investing in less risky stock companies such as healthcare, telecoms, and

We must keep an eye on our assets portfolio that we spent time, effort, and money to develop and build over the years and ensure that it is well protected against downside risks.

Investors with a diversified portfolio can aim for better business resilience because real estate asset classes respond differently to the same market conditions and during difficult economic times.

Spreading your investment risk in various asset classes over multiple income streams using different strategies can help you achieve your investment goals.

You should adopt an asset allocation strategy to balance risk with returns by assessing the expected return percentage from each asset class.

utilities. Companies can perform well even during downturns due to stable demand for their services. A diversified assets portfolio that includes such stock companies is highly likely to withstand turbulent economic times and perform well with minimum risk. We must keep an eye on our assets portfolio that we spent time, effort, and money to develop and build over the years and ensure that it is well protected against downside risks.

Considering having a diverse investment portfolio in the real estate business is essential. Investors should reassess their diversified portfolio regularly and their real estate business in general. A diversified real estate investment is a portfolio of different types of assets with a mixture of strategies such as income-producing properties, properties for capital gain, or shares in REITs. Investors with a diversified portfolio can aim for better business resilience because real estate asset classes respond differently to the same market conditions and during difficult economic times.

2. PORTFOLIO DIVERSIFICATION

Diversifying your portfolio helps manage risk by investing in asset classes such as properties and equities (or stock shares). Spreading your investment risk in various asset classes over multiple income streams using different strategies can help you achieve your investment goals. Keeping risk as minimal as possible in case of economic downturn or market fluctuation is vital for any business and investment. Portfolio diversification should help your investments by spreading the risk in different asset classes and sectors. You should adopt an asset allocation strategy to balance risk with returns by assessing the expected return percentage from each asset class. Figure 8.5 illustrates an example of a diversified portfolio, expected returns from each asset class, and the investor's expected return from each asset class. In this example, the investor put 55% of their portfolio in real estate, producing a 12% return (or yield), which makes an expected return of 6.6% (55% x 12%).

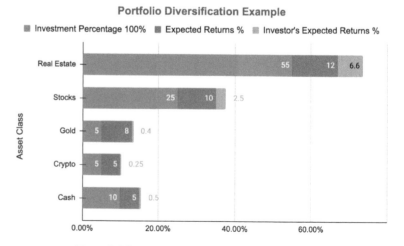

Figure 8.5 Diversified portfolio and allocated assets

This investment example is expected to provide an average return of 8% from all asset classes, and the expected total investment return is 10.25% (6.6% + 2.5% + 0.4% + 0.25% + 0.5%). Such an investment model would allow you to predict the overall returns of the whole asset portfolio. The more financially able you are, the more likely you are to take on more risk and invest in multiple asset classes, such as equities, properties, gold, etc., without affecting your living expenses and lifestyle.

Real estate investors need to monitor their market and develop strategies for growth and expansion. Business diversification is about entering a new market or providing a unique service due to a new strategy. Table 8.2 shows a modified version of the Ansoff Matrix. It indicates four strategies real estate investors can use to grow their investment as part of their business strategy and risk analysis. The four strategies are:

> Business diversification is about entering a new market or providing a unique service due to a new strategy.

1. **Market Penetration:** This strategy focuses on expanding the current portfolio, e.g., increasing the number of existing income-producing properties in an existing rental market.
2. **Service Development:** This strategy introduces new housing services such as HMOs or SAs (serviced accommodation) to an existing market.
3. **Market Development:** This strategy focuses on entering a new market, e.g., starting a real estate business in a different city or country using existing housing service(s).
4. **Diversification:** This strategy focuses on entering a new market by introducing new housing service(s), e.g., investing in a new asset class in a different market or country.

Table 8.2 Real estate market expansion grid. Adapted from Ansoff Matrix

		SERVICES	
		EXISTING SERVICE	NEW SERVICES
MARKETS	EXISTING MARKETS	Market Penetration	Service Development
	NEW MARKETS	Market Development	**Diversification**

There is no doubt that there are benefits to real estate investment and asset diversification. Diversification can bring new opportunities, such as entering new markets, delivering new services, accessing funds, interacting with new clients, dealing with new tools and technologies, etc. Real estate is one of the most diversified businesses and a highly profitable income-generating asset.

Asset allocation is about setting a percentage of each asset class in a portfolio, such as Buy-to-let rental properties, capital gains properties, and shares in REITs. The allocation of assets can be set up according to an

> Diversification can bring new opportunities, such as entering new markets, delivering new services, accessing funds, interacting with new clients, dealing with new tools and technologies, etc.

> The allocation of assets can be set up according to an investor's preference and investment plans.

investor's preference and investment plans. Figure 8.6 shows the three main real estate asset classes. Investors need to know which type of investment to select to earn a return. The well-performing assets could offset losses from a poorly performing asset class in their portfolio. However, this requires regular monitoring of the business portfolio and the performance of the asset classes.

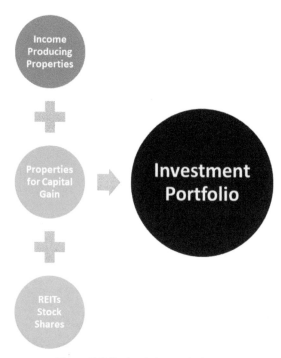

Figure 8.6 Real estate asset classes

> An efficient and optimal portfolio provides the highest investment returns and minimum risk.

> The optimal portfolio uses statistical techniques to quantify and adjust asset diversification according to the investor's plans. This is to help investors achieve their goals of balancing returns and risk.

Investors use various indicators to track the performance of REITs. However, NAV (net asset value) and AFFO (adjusted funds from operations) are the most commonly used indicators to monitor the performance of REITs' operations and their financial position. Getting into higher levels of risky real estate investment means investors should expect higher returns and vice versa. However, investors should be wise in their investments and risk-taking and aim to build an optimal portfolio. An efficient and optimal portfolio provides the highest investment returns and minimum risk. This allows investors to limit the likelihood of incurring income losses because of taking specific financial risk(s). The optimal portfolio uses statistical techniques to quantify and adjust asset diversification according to the investor's plans. This is to help investors achieve their goals of balancing returns and risk.

3. DIRECT AND INDIRECT INVESTMENT

There are many different investment types by which investors can invest in real estate. However, the two main types of real estate investments are as follows:

- **Direct:** Investors gain exposure to the real estate business by directly purchasing a property. They have complete control over the property's purchase and ownership and decide which properties to buy.
- **Indirect:** Investors gain exposure to real estate business without directly purchasing a property, such as via REITs stocks. They have less control over the properties purchased and rely on experts to decide which properties to buy.

Direct investment might provide higher returns than indirect investment, but achieving those higher returns would require more effort and time from the investor. In a direct real estate investment, investors can select their investment strategy and choose the properties and locations they like. As a property owner, the investor is responsible for checking the property's structural stability. They can decide the capital structure and amount of upfront investment. They are responsible for paying capital gains tax and rental income tax. Also, investors can manage their portfolios themselves, appoint someone, or arrange an agreement with a letting agent to do the work for them. They need to check and negotiate the terms and conditions of the tenancy agreement if necessary.

> Direct investment might provide higher returns than indirect investment, but achieving those higher returns would require more effort and time from the investor.

In indirect real estate investment, investors cannot choose the properties bought by the REIT or influence the investment strategy. Such matters are left to the experts operating the REIT to decide upon. The investment structure is determined by the experts as well. Investors do not own the properties and cannot manage or influence their management procedures. Tenancy agreements are arranged by the REIT or their appointed agents directly with their tenants. Investors do not have a say in such crucial decisions and management processes. Indirect investments use market shares traded at specific prices for REITs and can be executed efficiently and easily.

Investors should consider diversifying their investment portfolio to minimise risk and maximise returns. Investing in one asset class could have a negative impact on their returns if that asset class unexpectedly fails to perform as well as investors had anticipated. Therefore, spreading the risk over multiple asset classes can give investors good asset allocation options, better business resilience, and more confidence. An asset class represents a specific investment category; therefore, investors need to know how much investment or budget they must allocate to each category.

> Investing in one asset class could have a negative impact on their returns if that asset class unexpectedly fails to perform as well as investors had anticipated.

The issue of sustainable real estate and the contribution of real estate to greenhouse emissions, which could lead to various environmental problems, has attracted the attention of many entities such as policymakers, NGOs, international organisations, etc. Investing in sustainable real estate should help investors access new opportunities, such as financial and social benefits. For instance, property investors have access to the UK government incentives supported by green policies such as green mortgages to develop sustainable buildings, reduce greenhouse emissions, and bring financial and social benefits.

> Investing in sustainable real estate should help investors access new opportunities, such as financial and social benefits.

4. REITs (Real Estate Investment Trusts)

As indirect real estate investment, REITs allow property investors to invest in income-generating asset portfolios. The REIT industry has become popular in many countries and has experienced significant growth around the globe. Many property investors have become aware of REIT investment as a useful option for asset diversification. REITs operate in various property investment activities such as mortgage services and real estate financing, commercial buildings, property development and construction, land and real estate acquisition, etc. Despite the lack of control over which properties are selected, REITs provide a flexible option for investors. REIT experts take care of choosing which properties to invest in. REITs rely on investors to raise additional funds and expand their business; therefore, investors are expected to benefit from REIT returns and to get paid dividends regularly. Investors assess the performance of REITs based on the following factors:

- higher yields;
- larger dividend rates;
- long-term capital appreciation;
- larger portfolio;
- produced profits and balance sheets;
- experience and strong management.

REIT investors buy shares in a company, meaning they own part of its properties or portfolio. The share prices tend to fluctuate, and investors can buy and sell according to the business rules. In the UK, all REITs are publicly listed on the stock exchange. Each REIT has to meet certain requirements in an approval process in order to be accepted and listed. The company's share price becomes available for investors and trading. Like direct real estate investment, shares in REITs are sensitive to economic changes, interest rate fluctuations, and central banks' monetary policies and regulations.

REITs are set up as companies or trusts, and once they become active and start a business, they pay part of their earnings from rental income and capital gains as dividends to their shareholders.

Unlike other traditional stock markets, REITs are less volatile due to the relative stability of the real estate market. Investing in REIT stock shares can be a good option for investors to diversify their investment business, improve their investment portfolio, and make it more resilient. REITs are set up as companies or trusts, and once they become active and start a business, they pay part of their earnings from rental income and capital gains as dividends to their shareholders. The main five types of REITs are:

- **Residential REITs:** invest in apartment blocks and family renting market. They focus on large demand areas, higher occupancy rates, and good rental income.
- **Office REITs:** specialise in office buildings such as law firms, accountants, banks, etc., and often focus on CBD (central business district) areas due to large demand and higher rental income.
- **Retail REITs:** specialise in shopping centres and retail parks. They generate rental income from their tenants, i.e., the retailers. The retail business has been under pressure recently due to the shift to online shopping.
- **Mortgage REITs:** invest in mortgages, financing, and secured and unsecured loans. The interest rate changes influence their stock prices

and financing services. Historically, mortgage REITs are known for their relatively high dividends.

- **Healthcare REITs:** specialise in hospitals, retirement apartments, nursing homes, and healthcare services. It is a growing business due to increased demand for healthcare buildings and services. However, healthcare REITs are under pressure due to the recent challenges of COVID-19.

When REIT share prices increase, investors should benefit from capital growth and make a profit, but they may lose money if the share price of the REIT falls. Falling share prices of a REIT company can have a negative impact, not only on investors, but also on the company's reputation and future business. Successful REITs invest in a well-developed, financially robust, diverse real estate portfolio to mitigate risks or market volatility. The higher the value of the shares and stocks over time, the better is the dividends payout. Many REITs offer their shareholders dividend reinvestment plans in additional company shares. Investors can check if such an option is available before committing to an investment. REITs with such a feature can accelerate the compounding rate and achieve a higher rate of growth in comparison with those which do not offer reinvestment plans.

> Many REITs offer their shareholders dividend reinvestment plans in additional company shares. Investors can check if such an option is available before committing to an investment.

Investing in a diversified portfolio with a mixture of strategies can help investors use multiple asset classes in their business. This will improve revenues, develop resilient investment, and minimise risk during adverse market conditions. Investing in REITs shares in the stock market implies owning a percentage of REITs properties and receiving dividends annually. REIT investors would expect to receive regular reports about the generated earnings and capital gain portion. REITs are governed by local regulations and legislations of the jurisdiction in which they are set up and must meet their criteria to practise business. About 50 REITs listed on the London Stock Exchange invest in various asset classes such as office, residential, hotel, and retail. Figure 8.7 shows the London Stock Exchange FTSE 350 – Real Estate Investment Trusts REITs Streaming Chart from January 2011 to July 2020. Like many other stock markets, the REIT market has reacted unpredictably, with significant drops from March to June 2020 due to the COVID-19 pandemic. In the UK, REITs must meet the following main criteria and requirements to carry out business:

- Practise trading on an established and recognised stock market exchange. In the USA, REITs are not required to be listed on public stock markets.
- Pay at least 90% of rental income to shareholders each year. 75% of total earnings should be from real estate rental income.
- UK residents for tax purposes.
- Investors follow tax procedures and regulations.
- They are solely involved in the property investment business with at least three properties.

Figure 8.7 FTSE 350 REITs streaming chart (Jan 2011–July 2020). Chart courtesy of Investing.com: https://uk.investing.com/indices/ftse-350-reits-chart

REITs provide a useful option for portfolio diversification, and people can use various REIT platforms that offer different returns for potential investments.

As a source of pollution, real estate contributes to carbon emissions, produces a large amount of waste, and adversely impacts energy consumption and the climate.

Sustainable REITs can bring enormous benefits to both property investors and tenants.

The Investment Property website https://investmentproperty.co.uk/ provides valuable information on the UK REITs market and business. It gives helpful guidance to real estate investors who are seeking investment opportunities in the UK's REITs. Nareit's website https://www.reit.com/ is a helpful resource and presents publicly traded real estate companies in the US market to the global investment community. As an investor, I prioritise direct real estate investment because I like to have complete control of my properties, self-manage the business through my property business company anzar.co.uk, and have flexibility in selecting which type of properties to invest in. This does not mean direct investment is better, but each investor has preferences and business priorities. REITs provide a useful option for portfolio diversification, and people can use various REIT platforms that offer different returns for potential investments.

REIT investors and stakeholders increasingly recognise buildings as large energy consumers and major pollution contributors. As a source of pollution, real estate contributes to carbon emissions, produces a large amount of waste, and adversely impacts energy consumption and the climate. Investing in multiple strategies, such as sustainable REITs, is more crucial than ever. Sustainable REITs can bring enormous benefits to both property investors and tenants. Investors who are considering sustainable REITs will be better positioned for the risks and opportunities in terms of cost-saving, increased revenues, energy-efficient performance, tenants' well-being, and building resilience against climate change.

5. SUMMARY

Real estate investment diversification is helpful for investors to improve their revenues and develop resilient portfolios. Investors should consider reassessing their portfolios regularly and investing in multiple asset classes to seek opportunities and minimise risk. This chapter introduced the principles of investment diversification, the main types of asset classes, and their benefits to investors. As an investment asset class, REIT implies owning REITs shares as a percentage of properties and receiving dividends annually. Using a mixture of investment strategies, including sustainability and investing in sustainable markets of stocks, commodities, real estate, REITs, etc., can help investors achieve better profits and respond to adverse market conditions. However, investors must be aware of how to assess the markets to understand them and their challenges and opportunities and make proper investment decisions. The next chapter focuses on one particular market, real estate, and provides helpful information about the principles of property market assessment.

Individuals interested in the real estate business must gain the necessary skills to carry out their investment activities. Therefore, some skills and knowledge that investors require to establish a successful real investment, such as selecting suitable properties, are discussed in the next chapter. The subject of real estate investment, which entails putting capital into an income-producing asset using one or more classes and a modified version of Porter's Five Forces model, is presented. This model can help investors in their market assessment and evaluation before implementing their investment strategies. Real estate business philosophy and how the UK government deals with this industry are discussed, including rules and regulation development and their implications. The next chapter highlights the importance of choosing the right property location and area in real estate investment. For instance, factors such as proximity to a CBD, local services, and amenities that investors need to consider when choosing their deals are covered.

> Investors should consider reassessing their portfolios regularly and investing in multiple asset classes to seek opportunities and minimise risk.

> Individuals interested in the real estate business must gain the necessary skills to carry out their investment activities.

REAL ESTATE INVESTMENTS

9

Investors need to understand how to assess the property market to gain a good understanding of it as well as its challenges and opportunities and make proper investment decisions. This chapter provides useful information, including the general concepts and principles of property market assessment, which can help investors to gain the necessary skills to carry out their investment activities. Therefore, this chapter presents some skills and knowledge that investors require to establish a successful real estate investment, such as selecting suitable properties in an attractive place. This chapter introduces the subject of real estate investment, which entails putting capital into an income-producing asset using one or more classes, such as rental income or capital gains. A modified version of Porter's Five Forces model is presented to support investors in their market assessment and evaluation. This chapter also introduces the four main methods of information gathering that investors need to identify useful resources. These will help them to not only identify publishing organisations and content producers, but also to implement their own investment strategies.

This chapter introduces real estate investment and how investors can put their capital into income-producing properties. It also describes the different asset classes that can offer multiple income streams or capital gains. Investors need to follow a particular business philosophy to lead to a successful investment. Therefore, real estate business philosophy and how the UK government deals with this industry are discussed, such as rules and regulation development and their implications. We discuss the importance of choosing the right property location in real estate investment. Because property location depends on different factors, such as proximity to a CBD (central business district), local services, and amenities, investors must consider such issues when selecting their best deals. Investing in an income-producing property in the right area can generate substantial revenue. The importance of property locations lies in the fact that properties in a good neighbourhood can produce significant revenues and high rental profits. Selecting the right residential and commercial real estate in a good location and with the potential to add value should make a worthwhile investment. Investors should know how to select the right property location, how it can affect prices, and how to diversify their investments and assets.

Investors need to understand how to assess the property market to gain a good understanding of it as well as its challenges and opportunities and make proper investment decisions.

A modified version of Porter's Five Forces model is presented to support investors in their market assessment and evaluation.

Selecting the right residential and commercial real estate in a good location and with the potential to add value should make a worthwhile investment.

Property is 'a building or area of land, or both together'.
Cambridge English Dictionary

1. ASSESSING THE MARKET

Investors dedicate time to conducting market analysis and assessments before making investment decisions. This is necessary to understand the market, analyse data, and check as to whether or not the market is suitable for investment. Investors must ensure that the market provides opportunities and that their investment will succeed. A broader market understanding can illuminate certain opportunities and help plan good business strategies. Also, it can help you develop an overall picture of the market and to check if resources and business abilities can meet the market challenges and requirements. Figure 9.1 shows a modified version of Porter's Five Forces model of Business Competition Analysis, developed by Michael Porter of Harvard Business School in 1987.

> A broader market understanding can illuminate certain opportunities and help plan good business strategies.

Figure 9.1 Real estate market assessment model.
Adapted from Porter's Five Forces

Porter's model is a simple market assessment and evaluation solution that a business organisation or investor can use. The model was introduced to identify the five main competitive forces that can help businesses understand the factors affecting profitability. The model has been modified to help business investors to determine the market challenges and the dynamic/changing characteristics of the real estate industry. Porter's Five Forces model is used to understand and analyse the level of competition within the property market and develop a competitive strategy. I updated Porter's Five Forces model as follows:

> Porter's Five Forces model is used to understand and analyse the level of competition within the property market and develop a competitive strategy.

1. **Power of property suppliers:** To assess how easily property developers or estate agents can raise prices. This depends on the level of property supply in terms of its size, the cost of new developments, the price of land, and the number of properties for sale offered by

estate agents or motivated sellers. The higher the number of property-for-sale options available to investors, the easier it is to find good deals.

2. **Power of tenants or buyers:** To assess how easy it is for tenants and property buyers to find alternatives and drive prices down. Investors should be able to determine how powerful they are depending on the number of properties available for rent or sale, the demand intensity, and how flexible they can be in their service. They may consider targeting a specific type of tenant, e.g., professionals or communities, or changing strategy.

3. **The threat of new entrants:** To assess the extent to which new entrant investors are attracted to the property market and the extent to which new competitors surround experienced investors. The property market is tightly regulated and needs large amounts of investment capital with high financial risk. This makes it a challenging and competitive market for new starters, copycat businesses, and low-profile investors.

4. **The threat of substitutes:** To assess the ability of substitute accommodation service providers to introduce housing options to the market and how easy it is for renters to find an alternative to a property investor's service. This allows tenants and buyers to find alternatives in response to increased rents or property prices. This will have an effect on investors' income and/or profitability. Therefore, they may consider improving service quality, offering a new service, changing strategy, or targeting a different market.

5. **Competition in the industry:** To assess the market's number and capabilities of investors, estate agents, and property developers. The more capable competitors are chasing property deals and competing amongst one another; the less attractive the market is, the less power investors will have to stay competitive. In this case, they may identify the strengths and limitations of their competitors and then develop a new strategy to remain resilient or become more competitive.

A proper market assessment should help investors find answers to the questions introduced in Porter's model and make better investment decisions. Evaluating the supply and demand should help investors ensure that the demand for their accommodation service or strategy type is real. Understanding the target customers' specific needs is crucial in the investment business. Assessing the market, understanding the level of competition, and evaluating the level of service competitors provide is an endless game.

Not all property business opportunities and strategies are worth pursuing unless they meet market conditions and customer needs. Selecting business options with the highest growth potential would be likely to lead to a successful investment. Identifying the main market environment factors that can positively impact strategic investment planning, business operations development, and competitive intelligence is valuable. The following list introduces the main market environment factors, which include, but are not limited to:

- employability rate;
- local authority regulations;
- infrastructure;

The higher the number of property-for-sale options available to investors, the easier it is to find good deals.

Investors should be able to determine how powerful they are depending on the number of properties available for rent or sale, the demand intensity, and how flexible they can be in their service.

A proper market assessment should help investors find answers to the questions introduced in Porter's model and make better investment decisions.

Understanding the target customers' specific needs is crucial in the investment business.

Identifying the main market environment factors that can positively impact strategic investment planning, business operations development, and competitive intelligence is valuable.

- transport links;
- local amenities;
- demographic shifts;
- economic indicators.

2. INFORMATION GATHERING

It is essential to be well-resourced, whether it is with skills, technology, or material that can bring about progress and effective development.

The more information is collected about the targeted area, the more likely it is that relevant and useful results will be obtained.

Information is a key factor in any real estate investment, which must begin with a clear understanding of the market assessment and needs. It is essential to be well-resourced, whether it is with skills, technology, or material that can bring about progress and effective development. Information gathering is an essential step in market research for quality data and information about the targeted investment area. The beginning stage of market assessment is where the investor carries out the necessary information intelligence. The more information is collected about the targeted area, the more likely it is that relevant and useful results will be obtained. It is an art that every investor should master to gain the necessary knowledge and experience.

The information-gathering strategy would evolve through the investor collecting the relevant information at each investment stage. An investor's strategy should focus on identifying the main resources and obtaining necessary information from valid and recognised sources. Various resources, techniques, and tools are available for investors and can help them to collect vital information. Undoubtedly, it is a necessary step because it is the crucial stage of market assessment. The type of information that investors may need to gather includes, but is not limited to:

- average property prices;
- predicted market growth;
- expected yield;
- expected ROI;
- level of demand and supply;
- market strengths and weaknesses;
- market opportunities and threats;
- the best strategy to use.

The information obtained will enable an investor to analyse well-defined facts and figures and observe a complete picture of how the market operates and the entities and data involved.

The information must be gathered from suitable sources to determine the requirements of an investment. The information obtained will enable an investor to analyse well-defined facts and figures and observe a complete picture of how the market operates and the entities and data involved. The type of information an investor is trying to obtain and the entities providing the information will determine which resources they should use. Many techniques can be employed when gathering information. Electronic data can be accessed online using the internet from any location or using other means of electronic communication. However, non-electronic information can only be accessed in person or through a face-to-face gathering at a specific location. The four methods of gathering real estate investment information, which are illustrated in Figure 9.2, are:

- Interviews with local estate agents and letting agents.
- Networking with peer investors during property network meetings, e.g., PIN (Property Investor Network) meetings, conferences, seminars, etc.
- Observation of the local market using local news and local authority online resources and published reports.
- A research study of the existing market and published documents such as online resources, property magazines, and reports.

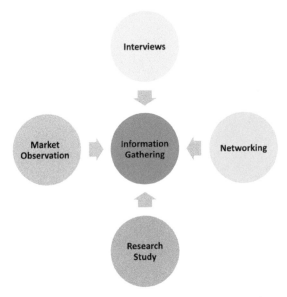

Figure 9.2 The main methods of information gathering

3. INFORMATION RESOURCES

Many reputable publishing organisations produce a variety of valuable information. Much useful material has been published to provide quality content and information to property investors. This material enables access to essential and relevant data and information that investors can use to analyse the market and make investment decisions. Property information flows through various organisations and content producers such as NRLA (National Residential Landlord Association), ONS (Office of National Statistics), and publications such as property magazines, reports, books, etc.

Collecting information on market analytical figures and reports is time-consuming and labour-intensive. This requires a lot of research skills and knowledge of information analysis. Many cost-effective resources are available for property investors to help them find the information they need to better assess the housing market. These resources help investors gain the necessary knowledge from recent reports and understand the business environment and current demand for, and supply of, property.

Rightmove is one of the largest property portals for advertising, searching, and researching properties. Their online property search platform provides information about properties for sale, prices, and locations. It is used by estate agents and letting agents to advertise their properties for sale and rent, respectively. Rightmove focuses on the UK property advertising market and seeks to reach UK property advertisers. Figure 9.3 shows search results of properties for sale for prices equal to, or more than, £350,000 in the greater Manchester area.

Figure 9.3 Search results of properties for sale. Source: rightmove.co.uk portal

It is crucial to evaluate the housing market in terms of average house prices, growth level, and supply and demand intensity and to check if there is room for growth. Investors need to ask themselves some of the following questions.

What is the current supply and demand?
What is the size of the market?
What is the likelihood of market growth?
What is the intensity of competition, and who are the current competitors?
What is the best strategy to use?
What are the main challenges and barriers to entry?
What are the main opportunities and threats?

4. REAL ESTATE BUSINESS AND PHILOSOPHY

Real estate investment is about putting capital into an asset to produce a return. This can include using asset classes that offer additional returns, such as monthly rental income, capital gains, or dividends from shares in REITs. However, before making an investment decision, investors must assess the market and their financial situation. This section aims to introduce the subject of real estate investment, cover aspects of real estate business and philosophy, and discuss how the UK government deals with this industry regarding regulations and financial implications. The main types of residential and commercial properties are also introduced, alongside general information about property prices in various regions in the UK.

The real estate business has attracted local and international investors to invest in the UK property market. Because of this, real estate investment has created billions of pounds worth of property transactions yearly by property investors. These investors have managed to build up a stock of profitable properties and create successful investment portfolios. Investors tend to think about their investment philosophy when determining their approach to investing. As an investor of many years' standing, my philosophy is to acquire assets of high demand, which produce high returns with manageable risks to meet my financial goals, as shown in Figure 9.4. In other words, to buy properties in good locations with a clear demand, generate passive income and high yield, and achieve FI.

Investors tend to think about their investment philosophy when determining their approach to investing.

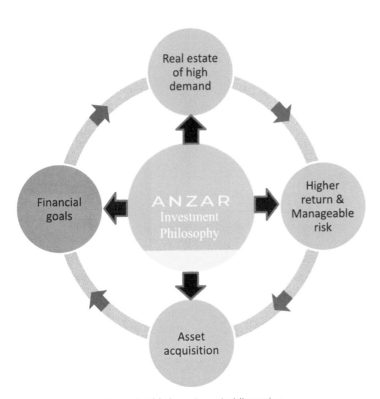

Figure 9.4 My investment philosophy

An investor's philosophy reflects their thinking about investment and their belief in their financial goals. However, their investment strategy is an activity that requires them to make effective decisions and utilise available resources to manage their investment operations. Before starting their real estate business journey and making decisions on their investment, investors need to understand the differences between the two main real estate types – residential and commercial. This allows them to narrow their investment options based on what they are interested in and what they are capable of.

An investor's philosophy reflects their thinking about investment and their belief in their financial goals.

Your time is limited, so don't waste it living someone else's life. Don't be trapped by dogma which is living with the results of other people's thinking. Don't let the noise of other's opinions drown out your own inner voice. And most important, have the courage to follow your heart and intuition. They somehow already know what you truly want to become. Everything else is secondary.

Steve Jobs

Each type of property investment has its characteristics, advantages, and drawbacks. Residential and commercial properties vary in almost every way in terms of occupancy, usage, design, leasing contracts, and funding.

Each type of property investment has its characteristics, advantages, and drawbacks. Residential and commercial properties vary in almost every way in terms of occupancy, usage, design, leasing contracts, and funding. While commercial properties will have broad functionality and are often developed for general use, the functionality of residential properties can be limited and developed for specific uses. Due to their extensive functionality, commercial properties require more focus and attention. There will be a need for certain services to be considered, such as security, lifts, lighting, storage, server rooms, etc. Also, commercial investment provides investors with a much more comprehensive range of potential opportunities, such as higher yield and more funding products and options.

5. REAL ESTATE INVESTMENT AND UK GOVERNMENT

Like many countries, the UK's economy relies heavily on the property market; tens of billions of overseas investments generate income for the government through a tax which helps to offset the country's deficit.

The UK government levies property taxes, such as stamp duty, capital gains tax, etc., to help and support its efforts to fund its national projects and resolve various economic problems. Like many countries, the UK's economy relies heavily on the property market; tens of billions of overseas investments generate income for the government through a tax which helps to offset the country's deficit. Property prices or tax changes might affect a property business's cash flows and investments, the country's economy, credit rating, and GDP. Recently, the UK government introduced property tax changes to MITR (mortgage interest tax relief), resulting in an increased tax bill for many Buy-to-let (buy-to-let) landlords and investors. The new tax measures introduced by the Conservative government are not intended to restrict Buy-to-let investments, because the property business plays a major role in the health of the UK economy. However, the recently introduced tax system aims to collect more essential taxes and minimise the losses due to unpaid tax from private landlords.

The recently introduced tax system aims to collect more essential taxes and minimise the losses due to unpaid tax from private landlords.

The UK government still needs to meet its targets of annual property supply since the 1990s. But the government is trying to slow down the growth of property prices, especially in London and the South East, and give first-time buyers a chance to get on the property ladder. Also, the reason behind the new tax system was to professionalise the Buy-to-let business and force low-profile landlords with just a few Buy-to-let properties to either become professional by setting up limited property companies or be replaced by those who are serious and are willing to incorporate. Limited companies pay only corporation tax on their annual profits. This recent tax system has forced many landlords to abandon the Buy-to-let business in favour of company owners. There are challenges and tax obligations involved in

Limited companies pay only corporation tax on their annual profits. This recent tax system has forced many landlords to abandon the Buy-to-let business in favour of company owners.

transferring ownership of Buy-to-let properties to a company, but there are legal ways to minimise such costs.

According to bid rent theory, rent price and demand for properties increase as the distance from the CBD decreases. However, sustainable buildings are expected to substantially increase rental prices in the future, primarily if they are located within the CBD. The UK government encourages the development of green buildings by offering various financial support schemes, such as property tax assessment incentives, environmental tax schemes, RHI (renewable heat incentive), and green financial products known as green mortgages. Therefore, investors are expected to achieve a higher net operating income due to lower operating expenses and cost-effective financial products. Something to seriously consider for future investments!

6. COMMERCIAL PROPERTIES

Commercial properties are buildings or premises that provide workspace and house businesses. They are business-focused and used by tenants to carry out commercial activities and to generate a profit, such as shops, supermarkets, banks, offices, shopping centres, etc. The performance of commercial properties in terms of their produced income, business activities, and occupancy rate plays a significant role in their valuation and price indices. As with residential properties, investors in commercial properties can aim for capital appreciation. The rental returns from commercial buildings are often higher than those from residential properties. Commercial properties are less sophisticated and provide better control over the lease terms. Also, commercial properties are less labour-intensive in managing tenants and building maintenance. They are traded publicly in REITs, which allow investors to invest indirectly in commercial real estate.

A proper market analysis is required to determine the area's supply and demand level to consider investing in real estate. Gathering information about the factors influencing supply and demand for specific areas and properties is helpful. Investors also need detailed information about the following:

- level of occupancy;
- current and new development projects;
- job markets;
- average household salaries;
- available infrastructure;
- local amenities;
- location;
- demographic changes;
- type of properties desired by local communities.

Another aspect that investors need to consider when investing in the UK market is that if they buy a freehold property, they own the land, so they won't pay ground rent. On the other hand, if they own a leasehold property, they must pay ground rent to the freeholder. It is all right if the lease period is a few hundred years. However, banks in the UK don't lend for properties

> The performance of commercial properties in terms of their produced income, business activities, and occupancy rate plays a significant role in their valuation and price indices.

> Commercial properties are less sophisticated and provide better control over the lease terms. Also, commercial properties are less labour-intensive in managing tenants and building maintenance.

It is possible to buy the freehold if the offered price by the freeholder is within the investor's budget and if it is worth the investment.

with a lease period of fewer than 70 years. It is possible to buy the freehold if the offered price by the freeholder is within the investor's budget and if it is worth the investment. In the UK, almost all flats are sold as leasehold.

7. REAL ESTATE LOCATION AND SELECTION

Property location relates to various factors such as distance to a CBD, and proximity to local services, amenities, and attractions.

In real estate investment, property location can determine whether the price is above or below the average. Property location relates to various factors such as distance to a CBD, and proximity to local services, amenities, and attractions. Property investors should be aware of the importance of investment location and how they select their best deals based not only on property location but also on the property situation and the seller's circumstances. Investing in residential or commercial properties located in good areas can generate substantial rental income, good profits, or promising capital gains. Property location matters and selection criteria are presented in the following subsections.

7.1. Property location

In some cases, edge cities have their subcentres, which attract firms and businesses and can drive prices up.

Cities develop because various economic factors drive major business decision-making by investors, commercial businesses, and local governments. Property location plays a significant role in its price; the closer it is to a CBD, i.e., a city centre, the higher the price. In some cases, edge cities have their subcentres, which attract firms and businesses and can drive prices up. An edge city is a mixed-use suburban area outside a CBD having a concentration of residential and business buildings. According to the land rent theory, rent price depends on land location and usage. Land rent theory states that as we move closer to CBDs we are more likely to pay more for real estate due to higher demand. CBDs often see population growth due to various economic factors such as land accessibility, good transport services, high employment rates, and affordable housing on the outskirts of the CBD.

CBDs often see population growth due to various economic factors such as land accessibility, good transport services, high employment rates, and affordable housing on the outskirts of the CBD.

Considering the level of services CBDs provide and their characteristics, city centres appear to be more attractive to firms and retailers than families and manufacturers, who are often pushed outside. Figure 9.5 shows the land rent curves representing a typical city's land usage pattern. As CBDs grow, more outskirt locations are being used, attracting increased development of high-rise buildings in CBDs, thus driving rent prices up.

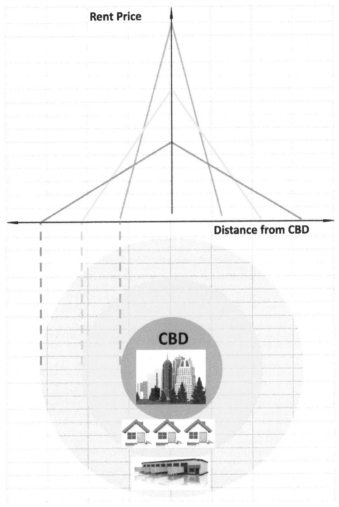

Figure 9.5 Land rent curves

Many CBDs have replaced manufacturing sites with commercial units attracting other services, businesses, and retail parks. Thriving cities reinvent themselves as service-driven economies with quality office space and high-rise buildings. They grow to create distinctive business areas and become exciting places for investment. Central locations attract higher real estate prices for the following reasons.

- Central locations are a hub for local, national, and international firms, providing quality hospitality services and transport links.
- Economic factors such as high employability rates and know-how centres tend to attract higher property prices.
- They provide the benefits of agglomeration economies, recruitment agencies, and access to skilled workers in heavily populated areas.
- Despite the higher costs, central locations provide access to quality office space, enhanced service delivery, and high-rise buildings.
- They attract individuals and couples because of job opportunities, access to information and quality services, and training and education opportunities.

Thriving cities reinvent themselves as service-driven economies with quality office space and high-rise buildings.

Central locations are a hub for local, national, and international firms, providing quality hospitality services and transport links.

7.2. Property location and rental market

Property rental rates are often determined by proximity to local services, amenities, and attractions. Another economic factor that is used to determine the rent charged to tenants is demand. Properties close to central places often attract potential tenants. Therefore, an investor would use a property's location and nearby services and attractions to their advantage and market it accordingly. The right location can be used as justification to charge higher rates than a competitor despite the similarity of properties in terms of their size, design, and structure. The pricing structure for rent depends not only on location but also on supply and demand, as well as market conditions.

> The right location can be used as justification to charge higher rates than a competitor despite the similarity of properties in terms of their size, design, and structure.

The area's occupancy levels and competitors' pricing behaviour will also affect the investor's rental rate decisions. Investors must regularly monitor and review local rental rates and price theirs accordingly. This is necessary to ensure business sustainability and avoid both under and overcharging their tenants. The principles of property business teach us that the more individuals who contact the investor about renting a property, the higher the rates an investor can charge, i.e., the more significant the demand, the higher the rental rates. There can be situations when investors need to drop their rents to compete with other rental rates in their local area, but they must never lose sight of profit margins. However, investors have to be practical and flexible with their rates to attract tenants; they also need to be aware of what their minimum rental rates should be. This will ensure that the property is remortgageable when prices increase soon.

> The principles of property business teach us that the more individuals who contact the investor about renting a property, the higher the rates an investor can charge, i.e., the more significant the demand, the higher the rental rates.

Investors must calculate monthly costs and overheads associated with their property and then add planned net cash flow to determine their charged rate. This ensures their property produces the proper profit and can pay for its management, monthly mortgage commitment, and maintenance costs. Failure to perform this step could result in barely enough rent to cover overheads despite achieving good occupancy rates. Finding the best locations, therefore, requires proper research and information-gathering processes. Before making any decisions, investors should collect information about the following:

> Finding the best locations, therefore, requires proper research and information-gathering processes.

- local government developments;
- transport infrastructure improvements;
- universities and schools;
- railway stations;
- hospitals;
- business parks;
- local parks;
- distance to the city centre;
- local amenities.

Property investors should know the importance of investment locations and how they appeal to certain communities. The demographic make-up of the population plays a role in specifying the market rent, the types of properties needed, and the level of demand. Certain communities tend to have specific property design requirements and prefer to cluster near locations that provide services they use often. For example, families with young children like easy access to facilities such as swimming pools, playgrounds, etc. Understanding the local communities' requirements can also help us to

> Understanding the local communities' requirements can also help us to understand why certain businesses and facilities enter and are set up in those areas.

understand why certain businesses and facilities enter and are set up in those areas. This is important when considering investment locations. The result of such investment decisions is delivering the required type of properties that appeal to certain customers and satisfy their needs. This market analysis process tends to help develop an investment strategy that maximises yields and revenues. Therefore, yield does vary by location, which significantly affects profitability. An investor needs to acquire the following skills and knowledge.

1. Study and analyse the property economics and local marketplace.
2. Know the competition and how the market operates.
3. Understand the levels of supply and demand.
4. Select the right location and business area.
5. Learn to deal with stakeholders such as banks, mortgage advisers, solicitors, estate agents, local authorities, planners, builders, etc.
6. Learn to deal with clients and customers.
7. Learn to deal with legal matters such as contracts and formal tenancy agreements.
8. Be aware of what constitutes a substantial renovation, maintenance works, associated costs, etc.

The key to successful property investment is finding deals, understanding the market, and gathering information. There are different places where investors can not only identify property location and the current market value of their potential investment but also find good deals. A system for gathering information, such as automated alerts about new properties on the market, is always helpful. By using the right resources, investors should also be able to identify the supply and demand and the average market rents in the area they are interested in. Property websites such as Rightmove or Zoopla can allow them to access current properties on offer and their historical data regarding previous sale prices and sale dates. Be aware that certain postcode areas sell well and others don't. Different regions might require different strategies, and there is a difference between a property's advertised sale price and its value. We looked at various resources that provide helpful information for property investors about the current market and property prices.

> The key to successful property investment is finding deals, understanding the market, and gathering information.

The best deals also come from distressed properties or motivated sellers where investors can aim for a BMV deal and add value to the property. Distressed properties do require quick flipping and marketing before selling or renting. Investors must ensure they have at least two exit strategy options, i.e., sell or rent. Working with a good mortgage broker is always useful to ensure they are paid well. A motivated seller is a person who might be dealing with any of the following cases:

> The best deals also come from distressed properties or motivated sellers where investors can aim for a BMV deal and add value to the property.

- retirement;
- divorce;
- equity release;
- repossession;
- family expansion;
- chain breaking;
- legal issues;
- refurbishment works;

- financial matters;
- inherited property.

8. SUMMARY

Assessing and analysing the property market provides an overall picture of the market regarding challenges and available opportunities.

Market assessment helps investors understand the real estate market before deciding and planning their strategies. Assessing and analysing the property market provides an overall picture of the market regarding challenges and available opportunities. I have developed a modified version of Porter's Five Forces model to help investors evaluate the dynamic real estate industry. This chapter introduced the concepts and principles of real estate market assessment methods and procedures. Market assessment depends on the quality of the information and resources gathered. The market assessment helps investors evaluate the housing market in terms of supply and demand and market growth. The issues surrounding the housing market in the UK and its development are presented at the end of the chapter. Property investors need to be aware of the various qualities and abilities they need to establish a successful real estate business; therefore, the primary skills and knowledge required to get into property investment are also presented at the end of this chapter.

Investors must gain the necessary skills of information gathering, research, and using the relevant technologies and tools to their advantage.

Investors must gain the necessary skills of information gathering, research, and using the relevant technologies and tools to their advantage. Therefore, this chapter presented the four main methods of information gathering: interviews, networking, market observations, and research. It also dedicated a section to information resources regarding publishing organisations and content producers. Investors need to identify valuable sources of information and material to help them correctly assess the market, its economic factors, and their potential investment opportunities. The next chapter covers how investing in property is influenced by different economic factors such as interest rates, local authorities' planning rules, government regulations, etc. These factors can cause shifts in supply and demand, thus influencing property investors' behaviour, prices, and market conditions.

Property prices increase and decrease cyclically due to various economic factors.

Property prices increase and decrease cyclically due to various economic factors. The next chapter presents the property cycle and its four phases: expansion, hyper-supply, recession, and recovery.

The increased demand, limited supply, and sometimes inflated prices represent economic challenges to the UK government and central bank. The relationship between supply and demand and their effects on real estate prices and the economy have been covered in this chapter. The next chapter covers the challenges to the shortage of housing and its implications, inflation, and the tools used by the UK government and central banks to deal with such challenges and to resolve them. Furthermore, the next chapter also discusses how investors can raise funds from available lending options to develop their investment projects and improve property supply and market conditions.

REAL ESTATE INVESTMENT AND ECONOMICS

10

The real estate market depends on the general economic situation and supply and demand. The property market's law of supply and demand is complicated and plays a significant role in a free-market economy. Economic factors such as property prices determine real estate investments and supply and demand. These economic factors and market conditions, including the role of elasticity in supply and demand, are presented in this chapter using a graphical model to monitor market prices. Property prices increase and decrease cyclically in four phases: expansion, hyper-supply, recession, and recovery. Various conditions and local, regional, and national regulations are responsible for price variations. This chapter discusses factors such as interest rates, local authorities' planning rules, government regulations, etc., which play a role in causing shifts in supply and demand and, thus, changes in the market. Understanding property economics helps investors make investment decisions.

> The property market's law of supply and demand is complicated and plays a significant role in a free-market economy.

> Property prices increase and decrease cyclically in four phases: expansion, hyper-supply, recession, and recovery.

1. PROPERTY ECONOMIC CYCLE

Property investment plays a major role in the economy of any society and in promoting its development. It is important in attracting foreign investment, supporting various industries, improving employment rates and production, and providing significant growth to local communities and the national economy. Therefore, we need to understand the relationship between real estate and all related industries, especially the interacting factors and linkages between them. The German economist Albert Hirschman introduced the term 'linkage' to describe the link between industries to emphasise the importance of connectivity between related industries. The expansion of real estate investment implies an increased demand for many industries and services to run and maintain those income-producing properties, creating an interesting network of interactions between all those industries. Real estate investment helps various industries to grow. For example, a real estate investment helps

> Property investment plays a major role in the economy of any society and in promoting its development.

> The expansion of real estate investment implies an increased demand for many industries and services to run and maintain those income-producing properties, creating an interesting network of interactions between all those industries.

- the insurance sector providing building insurance;
- the building supplies sector by developing refurbishment projects;
- local authorities, through the payment of council tax, ensuring that vacant properties become occupied;

- the government, through payment of capital gains tax, SDLT (stamp duty land tax), and income tax by real estate investors when buying, selling, and generating income from properties;
- certified electricians and plumbers by paying them to provide electric and gas safety checks and certificates, and so on.

In the UK, average house prices are accelerating, seeing growth in most regions, and residential property sales are continuing to grow. This includes the real estate development sector, which continues to rise. Changes in real estate investment strategies can affect property investors, tenants, and many sectors, such as building supplies, retailers, insurance, and banking.

The real estate investment sector significantly contributes to the financial and taxation industries. Besides their substantial lending schemes, banks consider real estate a guarantee for financing and growth. Alternative financing solutions from non-high street banks and crowdfunding have become more useful for investment projects.

Many events in our world recur naturally and repetitively during different periods, such as rain, winds, floods, etc. Similarly, due to various economic factors such as GDP, interest rates, population change, employment rates, etc., property prices also go up and down cyclically. The property cycle has four phases, as shown in Figure 10.1. The changes in supply and demand of properties play a role in influencing the property market, subsequently shaping the property cycle. The four phases of the real estate cycle are as follows.

> The changes in supply and demand of properties play a role in influencing the property market, subsequently shaping the property cycle.

- Expansion: After the market recovery, this phase contributes to the rise of property, rent prices, and construction activities. Also, the unemployment rates and vacancy levels fall. It is a good time for active investors who can oversee market fluctuations to remortgage their properties that have benefited from capital gains, release equity for reinvestment, and add more assets to their portfolios.
- Hyper-supply: Overbuilding projects due to higher demand during the expansion phase often leads to the hyper-supply of properties. During this phase, occupancy rates and rents fall because of lower demand. Property oversupply could lead to a housing bubble, which can cause financial crises and major problems in the housing market and economy. However, investors who were careful with their investments in terms of selection of property location, high-yield producing properties, and long-term lease agreements may choose to continue with their investment. They may decide not to sell despite the downturn and high risk.

> Property oversupply could lead to a housing bubble, which can cause financial crises and major problems in the housing market and economy.

- Recession: During the recession phase, demand, property price, rental income, employment, and occupancy rates fall. It is a tenants' market, so investors might be able to offer discounts to retain or attract potential tenants. It is a good time for active investors to look for opportunities and use their skills to find bargains and BMV properties for sale. However, using such options requires a lot of planning and preparation.
- Recovery: In this phase, the property market and employment rates improve. The economy starts to pick up during recovery, but property supply only happens due to oversupply during the previous two phases. However, limited construction activities might begin when

there is a demand for properties at specific locations. It is still possible for investors willing to take a risk to find good deals such as distressed properties, commercial to residential conversion projects, or adding value to damaged properties and selling them during the next phase. A distressed property is a type whose owner cannot keep up with regular mortgage payments. It is common for a distressed property to be offered for sale by the lender.

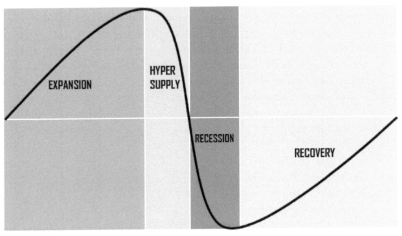

Figure 10.1 The four phases of the real estate cycle

Both the supply and demand rates are equal at the peak and trough of the property cycle. Although it is not easy to predict the length of each phase, active investors keep monitoring the real estate cycle regularly. This is to deal with the current phase and with market changes. Investors need to keep a close eye on the market's development and economic cycle to help them:

- determine which phase of the real estate cycle they are in;
- identify business opportunities;
- plan their investment strategies, and
- make informed investment decisions.

Sometimes, unexpected events occur, which could cause irregularity in the repetitive real estate cycle. The COVID-19 shock has brought the global economy to a near halt since early 2020. The lockdown measures by most countries, rise in unemployment rates, reduction in economic activities, and drop in GDP have had a knock-on effect on the real estate market and business growth.

2. SUPPLY AND DEMAND

Property prices and rents depend on the law of supply and demand in a free-market economy. The supply and demand mechanism in the property market is complicated. The demand for housing represents the number of residential properties buyers are willing to purchase at a certain price or

Factors significantly affecting supply and demand include the job market, interest rates, employment figures, demographic changes, etc.

Changes in property prices might affect not only property businesses' cash flow and investment, but also the country's economy as a whole, including its credit rating and GDP.

The property market behaves in accordance with the relationship between supply and demand, which is influenced by price variations and the number of properties available.

that tenants are looking to rent. The supply means the construction and flow of residential properties at a certain price. Various economic factors that affect the property market determine prices and rent charges. Factors significantly affecting supply and demand include the job market, interest rates, employment figures, demographic changes, etc.

Supply and demand for housing is a local market matter but is influenced by various conditions and local, regional, and national regulations and policies. Like many countries, the UK's economy and government rely heavily on the property market and hundreds of billions of overseas investments to generate income through tax and help the country's deficit. Changes in property prices might affect not only property businesses' cash flow and investment, but also the country's economy as a whole, including its credit rating and GDP. In his article in the *Independent* in 2017, Alexander Tziamalis stated that a 10% fall in the UK's property value would seriously affect the economy, equivalent to more than ten years of exported cars from the UK. The main economic factors that affect the rise in the price of properties in the UK are:

- expensive land;
- limited housing development;
- high development costs;
- limited social housing;
- high demand.

Decisions made by property investors, developers, local authorities, banks, and governments are also all responsible for price variations in the property market. The property market behaves in accordance with the relationship between supply and demand, which is influenced by price variations and the number of properties available. Figure 10.2 shows how price influences supply and demand and vice versa. For example, when demand exceeds supply, the price increases to a level known as an equilibrium state. The equilibrium state represents the price that matches the current demand to the available supply. It represents a compromise between what buyers are willing to pay for properties and what sellers are willing to offer regarding property specifications and asking price.

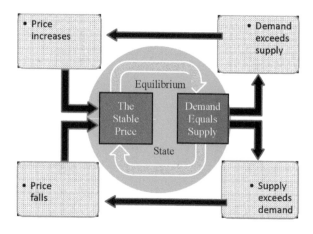

Figure 10.2 Demand, supply, and equilibrium

In property economics, the supply and demand relationship represents the properties in the market.

- Sellers wish to sell, or investors want to invest in and offer to let at various prices.
- Buyers wish to buy, or tenants want to rent.

This relationship is based on an economic theory used to model price determination in a market. Figure 10.3 shows the relationship between supply and demand. The x-axis represents the available stock, and the y-axis represents the property price or rent. Any change in the property price can be monitored along the demand and supply curves by holding constant all other non-price factors. However, any change in non-price factors would cause a shift in the demand and supply curves. The supply and demand curves intersect at the equilibrium, or market-clearing price P1, Q1. Assuming the available property stock N1 would provide a price P1, the remaining stock, i.e., above N1, represents the available stock.

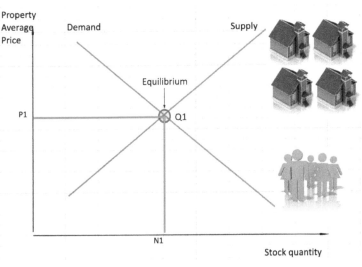

Figure 10.3 Supply and demand relationship

Owing to the limited number of buyers and the number of residential properties offered by the suppliers, the quantity of housing traded at any given price represents the realised demand and supply. When both the quantity buyers are willing to buy and the quantity suppliers are eager to provide to the market are equal, the price in this situation is called the equilibrium price (Stone and Fribbance, 2019). Understanding the basic economic principles can help investors decide the best time to invest in properties. The property supply and demand relationship operates in the following three ways:

- the higher the demand, the lower the supply;
- the higher the demand, the lower the number of available properties, and the higher the property price/rent. It is the sellers' or investors' market;

- the lower the demand, the lower the property price and the higher the number of properties available, i.e., the investors' market.

Notice that investors win in both cases, when there is high or low demand. Active investors can use the opportunity when property prices are high to remortgage and release equity, get funds to reinvest, and enlarge their portfolio. Also, they win when property prices are low by buying and investing in more properties at reasonable prices, getting good bargains, even BMV.

3. REAL ESTATE MARKET

The relationship between supply and demand and limited stock tends to affect real estate economics and prices. The issues of property supply, valuation, and pricing play a major role in the market dynamics.

There is a direct relationship between house prices and demand; however, some non-price factors affect the level of demand for housing and how able and willing buyers are to pay the offered prices.

The relationship between supply and demand and limited stock tends to affect real estate economics and prices. The issues of property supply, valuation, and pricing play a major role in the market dynamics. In addition, property-related tax has implications on the real estate market, property prices, and supply and demand. The UK government faces various economic challenges because of the shortage in housing stock and limited supply. These challenges include increased demand and inflated property prices, green belt destruction, lack of skilled builders, etc. Governments use taxation as a powerful tool to resolve such challenges.

Property price is a determinant of housing supply and demand. Any changes cause a movement along the demand curve, as shown in Figure 10.3. There is a direct relationship between house prices and demand; however, some non-price factors affect the level of demand for housing and how able and willing buyers are to pay the offered prices.

- Household size and income.
- Population.
- Property area and location.
- Regulations and legal requirements.
- Demographics.
- Interest rates.
- Preferences.
- Local amenities.
- Infrastructure.
- Public 'goods', e.g., good schools.

The non-price factors that influence the level of supply are:

- Cost of development.
- Local council regulations.
- Government laws.
- Housing policies.
- Labour cost.
- Material cost.

The market determines the property price, i.e., comparable neighbouring properties and the ability to supply enough properties. It often requires a lot of time and effort to deliver real estate's market needs and meet the demand.

Property development projects take time due to the development requirements and strict building regulations.

It takes a long time for developers to find suitable land for a project. It can take years to complete a new property development project. The planning process can affect project development as well.

In the UK, housing policies benefit individuals, such as owner-occupiers, first-time buyers, low-income households, elderly and disabled people, and tenants. For example, homeowners are exempt from SDLT when they sell their properties. Also, first-time buyers can benefit from the provision of additional support for the purchase of their first properties to get them on the property ladder. Housing policies are significant in providing social housing and housing for low-income households. Older and disabled people can benefit from housing policies in terms of getting the proper support and ensuring that the housing on offer for them is suitable. Moreover, housing policies are often used to control the private rental sector and to give necessary support to tenants who live in rented properties.

4. SUPPLY AND DEMAND IN THE PROPERTY MARKET

A fixed number of properties are always available for new tenants or the investment market. Rental prices are determined by the supply and demand rate and often depend on comparable properties. However, the property market is dynamic due to various factors such as the movement of tenants, demolition of existing properties, and development of new properties. As a determinant factor, price influences the demand and supply of the housing market. However, other factors, such as population, unemployment, average household income, crime rate, etc., are also important, and changes in these factors cause a shift in the supply and demand curves. According to economicsonline.co.uk, renting property is an alternative to ownership, and changes in rental prices influence the demand for private housing.

During periods of higher demand, individuals will pay higher rent due to limited supply or options. The market supply determines the existing available stock for tenants and investors. The increase in rent prices indicates a higher demand for housing. Similarly, if the number of properties available on the market is low, the demand would be high, as people would find it difficult to find affordable houses. This could be due to limited investment, expensive building materials or labour, lack of funding, or insufficient land to build new properties. However, if the number of available properties is high, people would not be willing to pay high prices or rent due to the options available.

When the population increases, demand for housing becomes high as more people are looking for properties to buy or rent and are willing to pay market prices. An increase in real household income is a demand shifter as well. When real income increases, individuals become more interested in buying better or bigger properties and are encouraged to move up the property ladder. This leads to a greater demand for housing, more competition among buyers, and a shortage of properties on the market.

Existing investors will try to expand their portfolios by developing new properties or remortgaging some existing ones. This allows them to raise

Property development projects take time due to the development requirements and strict building regulations.

Housing policies are significant in providing social housing and housing for low-income households.

Rental prices are determined by the supply and demand rate and often depend on comparable properties. However, the property market is dynamic due to various factors such as the movement of tenants, demolition of existing properties, and development of new properties.

The increase in rent prices indicates a higher demand for housing. Similarly, if the number of properties available on the market is low, the demand would be high, as people would find it difficult to find affordable houses.

funds to purchase more properties or to convert commercial properties to residential to meet demand. Also, new investors will try to enter the market, causing a further increase in the number of properties available.

Developing affordable and high-standard properties is vital for tenants' well-being, health, and life satisfaction (OECD, 2021). However, decisions about how to finance the purchase of our residential property, when to buy, and which area to live in are not easy, especially for first-time buyers, due to affordability issues (Stone and Fribbance, 2019). Knowing how property prices are determined and how their movements vary between regions is important to help people make informed decisions. This section discusses issues about the UK housing market, the demand and supply model, and the different factors such as income and affordability that have an impact on this model.

Knowing how property prices are determined and how their movements vary between regions is important to help people make informed decisions.

In the UK, residential property is viewed as an investment, a store of wealth, and is profitable for many people. Despite the ups and downs in the UK housing prices, the trend has been upward over the decades (1979–2017), and the rise over this period has been 169% (Lowe and Stone, 2018). UK banks, after careful consideration of the applicants, offer different mortgage products to eligible individuals to enable them to buy their properties with a secured loan . As part of the affordability assessment, banks review the income and expenditure of each mortgage applicant and check the source of funds for deposits to ensure that they use legitimate sources for their deposits and can afford their monthly payments (Stone and Fribbance, 2019; Mugleston, 2023).

House prices play a major role in household finances and future budgeting; therefore, it is useful to understand property market fluctuations to help us know how much we should pay and whether it is time to buy or sell (Stone and Fribbance, 2019). To understand how property prices change, we will use the 'demand-and-supply model' to simplify some aspects of the property market and predict future price changes. This model is developed to show how the quantity demanded by property buyers or supplied by developers varies with price. However, it doesn't consider some market segments, such as different types of buyers (e.g., first-time buyers and buy-to-let investors) or various countries. Still, it uses a single property marketplace for buyers and sellers (Stone and Fribbance, 2019; Myers, 2019).

To understand how property prices change, we will use the 'demand-and-supply model' to simplify some aspects of the property market and predict future price changes.

Figure 10.3 shows the market-planned demand and supply curves, represented by points on their relevant curves. The demand and supply curves reflect the number of buyers willing to buy and suppliers willing to supply at a given price. Other factors can affect demand and supply, even if prices are fixed. For example, if interest rates increase, more people will feel unable to afford expensive mortgages. This would mean that fewer people would be willing to buy and, therefore, cause a shift in the demand curve to the left from D1 to D2, as shown in Figure 10.4. This shift in the demand curve causes the supply to drop, the equilibrium point to move from Q1 to Q2, and the price to drop from P1 to P2. Another factor that could affect the demand for housing is household income.

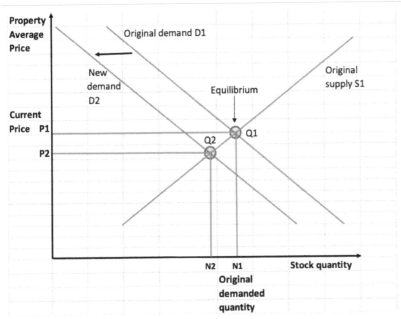

Figure 10.4 Decreased demand due to a change in a non-price factor.
Adapted from *Personal Finance* (De Henau and Lowe, p. 287)

The lower the income people earn, the lower the demand, resulting in a
shift in the demand curve to the left. Moreover, such a move would have a
knock-on effect on the price, which would be reduced, and on the quantity
demanded by the buyers from N1 to N2. As a result, the developers would
become reluctant to start new housing projects. The supply curve would
shift to the left and cause the equilibrium point to move from Q2 to Q3 and
the quantity of supplied properties to decrease from N2 to N3. However,
the reduced supply of new properties to the market would allow the price to
increase again and return to P1, as shown in Figure 10.5.

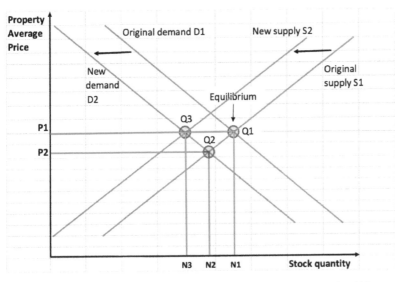

Figure 10.5 The effects of reduced supply of properties from N2 to N3

If the property price were too high, i.e., above the equilibrium price, the developers would plan to provide more properties, which could lead to an increased supply; because of that, sellers would be forced to drop their prices to a level acceptable to new buyers.

If the property price were too high, i.e., above the equilibrium price, the developers would plan to provide more properties, which could lead to an increased supply; because of that, sellers would be forced to drop their prices to a level acceptable to new buyers. Therefore, the market would settle gradually at a new equilibrium price and quantity point. Conversely, if the property price is below the equilibrium, i.e., too low, this attracts the buyers to buy more and compete for the available houses in the market. This would force buyers to offer competitive prices, leaving only those willing to outbid each other or even to gazump others to win the offered properties for sale. Due to increased demand, property prices would be pushed up; the market would attract more sellers, and gradually, property prices and offered houses for sale both settle at their new equilibrium levels (Stone and Fribbance, 2019).

The demand-and-supply model has been presented to show some aspects of the property market, understand the market fluctuations, and how property prices change.

Decisions about when and how to buy our residential property are not easy. In this section, issues about the housing market in the UK and the importance of how property prices are determined were introduced. The demand-and-supply model has been presented to show some aspects of the property market, understand the market fluctuations, and how property prices change. The model can help us to make well-informed decisions about whether or not it is time to buy or sell. It was developed to show how the quantity demanded by the buyers or provided by suppliers changes with price.

5. PROPERTY PRICING AND VALUATION

Property prices are determined by characteristics such as property struc-ture (e.g., property design and size), location (e.g., distance to the CBD), neighbourhood (e.g., safety), and environment (e.g., noise and air pollution). It is possible to determine a property price for its structure and location but not its neighbourhood and other nearby public 'goods' or public 'bads' which buyers can value differently. Property valuation is a different process

Various factors are used to value a property, such as its size, age, condition, location, etc. Surveyors often handle such a process and produce a valuation report with information about the valued property.

that involves the assessment of a property. Various factors are used to value a property, such as its size, age, condition, location, etc. Surveyors often handle such a process and produce a valuation report with information about the valued property.

The valuation of real estate is a complex process. It involves many factors related to the property, i.e., its features, such as the number of rooms, the size of the property, and external factors, such as public services, public goods or public bads. The prices for internal factors can be calculated but external factors are difficult to calculate. Public goods such as parks, safety, and clean air represent services that are often publicly financed, accessible to all members of a community and do not diminish (non-depletable) due to consumption by members of the community. A high crime rate represents a public bad opposed to a public good.

The property value is determined by the willingness of the buyer to pay for both property-related features and external factors. However, we must compromise or try to achieve an equilibrium between public goods and public bads. For example, living closer to a CBD, you pay a premium for city-style living and accept all the associated noise. The closer a property is to a CBD, the higher the prices, but the further the distance into the countryside, the greater are its beautiful views and calmness. Be aware that public goods and public bads do not have a price or are not offered in the market. Here is a list of some public goods and public bads.

Public goods:
- parks;
- countryside;
- safety e.g., crime control;
- quality infrastructure (e.g., streetlights, sewer system, motorway);
- public schools and hospitals;
- libraries;
- clean air;
- free-to-air media: free TV or radio broadcasting.

Public bads:
- crime;
- noise;
- polluted air;
- flooding;
- landfill sites;
- poor infrastructure.

Governments try to resolve different issues and minimise the effect of various problems in society in general and the property sector in particular. Taxation is a powerful tool the government uses to resolve economic issues and plan for the future. According to Danny Myers (2019), the main issues that are facing the government in the property sector include, but are not limited to:

> Taxation is a powerful tool the government uses to resolve economic issues and plan for the future.

- increased demand and limited supply;
- unfair competition;
- pollution;
- increased property prices;
- shortage of skilled labour;
- green belt destruction.

These problems represent external factors that create additional costs which the developers or property investors should have considered. Such additional costs should be added to the original expenses of property development projects. To achieve that, the government introduces different sorts of tax regimes, such as stamp duty, capital gains tax, etc., to the property business and transactions to help support the efforts to resolve those problems. Property-related tax does play a role in increasing property prices and development projects. Also, tax has implications for the real estate market, property supply, and demand.

> Property-related tax does play a role in increasing property prices and development projects. Also, tax has implications for the real estate market, property supply, and demand.

In England and Wales, a recent property tax system has been introduced by the government. From 6 April, 2020, Buy-to-let gross income (without a deduction for mortgage interest payments) became taxable. This has resulted in an increased tax bill for many landlords. Buy-to-let mortgage interest tax relief (MITR) for property mortgage costs will be limited to the basic 20% rate as a reduction in the rental tax bill. Running Buy-to-let expenses can still be deducted from gross rental income as before. Landlords with good rental cover (low mortgage costs relative to rental income) are less affected. However, higher rate and additional rate taxpayers (40% and 45%) are highly adversely impacted. Recently, many landlords have set up companies to manage their Buy-to-let property business and to minimise the costs associated with tax introduced by the government.

6. BANKS AND GOVERNMENT INTERVENTIONS

As a dynamic market, supply, demand, and other economic factors influence the real estate business. Factors such as interest rates, local authorities' planning rules, government regulations, etc., play a role in causing shifts in the supply and demand curves and, thus, shifts in the market. Without the money banks offer, investors would be unable to fund and develop their investment projects. Issues regarding funding, investors, and governments are covered first in this section. Investors need to be aware of inflation and its impact on mortgages, savings, property prices, buying power, and the value of money over time. This section briefly discusses inflation, its impact on real estate investment and people in general, and how banks and the government deal with it.

Money moves around the globe and the clock between individuals, organisations, financial institutions, and governments. With funds offered by banks, investors and businesses can fund their investments or develop their projects. Banks compete with each other to increase their market share by attracting more customers and real estate businesses that need capital to grow. Banks invest the money deposited by their customers by selling financial products, mortgages, providing loans, lending to property investors or businesses, or buying and selling assets. They are allowed by the central bank to lend about 90% of deposited money to other customers. This helps banks to make money and boost the economy. Banks make money from real estate mortgages to help them pay for their operational costs and generate profits through various other enhanced service offerings such as:

- transaction charges;
- charging mortgage fees;
- interest on their mortgage products;
- redemption fees;
- overdraft penalties, etc.

Governments use various options and financial tools to boost the economy and to minimise the effects of recession or depression, during which the money supply is restricted. During a recession, the economy shrinks, trading activities and wages fall, and unemployment rises. Due to the reduction in employment, people spend less and start to save, which will impact the economy in general and real estate in particular. A continued period of recession could lead to a more severe economic situation known as depression, which is much worse than a recession. To avoid that, governments tend to monitor the money supply in the economy, especially during times of recession, and adjust the cash reserves accordingly. This would allow them to decide whether to inject more cash into the economy and increase money circulation. Governments use three options to finance their budget:

Margin notes:

Without the money banks offer, investors would be unable to fund and develop their investment projects.

Banks compete with each other to increase their market share by attracting more customers and real estate businesses that need capital to grow.

Banks make money from real estate mortgages to help them pay for their operational costs and generate profits through various other enhanced service offerings.

A continued period of a recession could lead to a more severe economic situation known as depression, which is much worse than a recession.

- taxation such as CGT and SDLT;
- borrowing money;
- printing more money through central banks.

Real estate investors are expected to pay taxes to the government on their business profits. When the government's collected revenues from the tax are more than it is spending, it has a surplus. However, when the government's spending on its financial commitments exceeds income and additional funds are needed, it may have to borrow money or go for the risky option of printing money. The difference between the government's spending and income is known as the budget deficit. The deficit determines how much extra money the government needs to borrow or print to pay for public spending and fulfil its financial commitments. In addition to money printing, governments can create electronic money, but they need to be careful because increasing the money supply faster than economic growth will cause hyperinflation. Therefore, part of the central bank's job is to supply the required money, implement the government's monetary policies, and meet its economic targets.

> Governments can create electronic money, but they need to be careful because increasing the money supply faster than economic growth will cause hyperinflation.

Many economists believe government spending and investment are necessary to stimulate economic activities and maintain a balanced market. By injecting more money into the economy, unemployment could be reduced due to increased demand for products and services. However, governments also tighten their spending when inflation rises due to prolonged growth rates and an overheated economy, as shown in Figure 10.6. The government and central bank play a crucial role in the country's economy's money supply, circulation, and spending. Central banks are in charge of monetary policy, managing the national monetary system and responding to difficult economic situations, as shown in Figure 10.7. This includes setting the exchange rate and base rate, currency, country's reserve, and supply of money. All those measures have an impact on the property mortgage interest rate and property market.

> By injecting more money into the economy, unemployment could be reduced due to increased demand for products and services. However, governments also tighten their spending when inflation rises due to prolonged growth rates and an overheated economy.

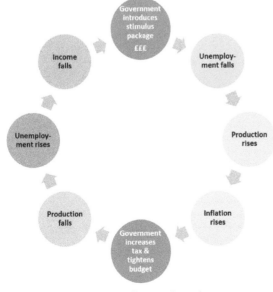

Figure 10.6 Economic cycle

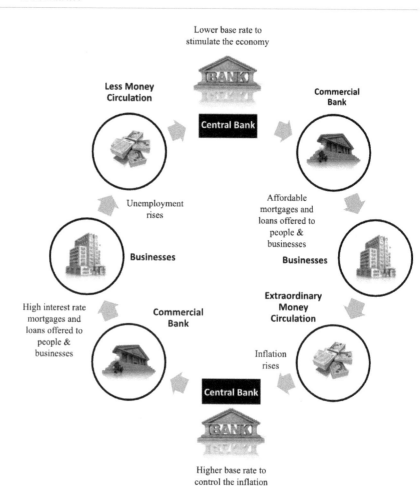

Figure 10.7 Central banks' response to the recession and rise of inflation

7. SUMMARY

The economic factors help investors make the correct market assessment and informed investment decisions.

Due to limited property stock and supply, the rental market dynamics and property valuation determine the available housing for tenants and their demand.

The real estate business is influenced by various economic factors such as interest rates, local authorities' planning rules, government regulations, etc., and their impact on supply and demand. These factors can cause shifts in the supply and demand curves and, thus, influence real estate market conditions and investment activities. The economic factors help investors make the correct market assessment and informed investment decisions. Property prices increase and decrease cyclically due to various economic factors. This chapter covered the property cycle, which includes four phases: expansion, hyper-supply, recession, and recovery. Due to limited property stock and supply, the rental market dynamics and property valuation determine the available housing for tenants and their demand. The relationship between supply and demand and their effects on real estate prices and economics was covered in this chapter.

The increased demand, limited supply, and sometimes inflated prices represent economic challenges to the UK government and central bank.

Therefore, various topics related to real estate pricing, valuation, taxation and its implications on the markets, and supply and demand have been presented. Governments are concerned with the shortage in housing stock and its impact on real estate supply and investment; this chapter covered the tools used by the UK government to deal with such challenges to resolve them. Due to the importance of inflation, investors need to be aware of its impact on property prices, mortgages, and the value of money over time. This should help them analyse and assess the real estate market and make the right investment decisions. Banks offer different financing options to investors to allow them to raise capital and develop their investment projects during various market conditions.

The next chapter covers various issues related to funding real estate investment projects, inflation, and its impact on real estate investment and economics. It will demonstrate how investors use creative financial techniques to conduct investment activities and leverage to expand their portfolios without using much of their capital.

Investors can use creative finance to benefit from certain market conditions, make the right investment decisions, and generate revenues and capital growth. The main idea of creative finance is for investors to arrange a deal to finance properties using funds from a third-party entity to build an income-producing portfolio and accumulate valuable assets. The next chapter introduces practical examples of how investors can leverage and expand their income-producing portfolios. Investors raise funds and identify deals such as BMV or distressed properties using capital offered by lenders through mortgage/remortgage products with appropriate LTV. However, using creative finance requires attention and skills in understanding the costs associated with mortgages and debt management. Another vital skill for investors is property accounting and how financial statements, including profit and loss reports and balance sheets, are prepared.

The next chapter introduces property accounting, which is essential for producing and reporting accurate financial statements from investment operations. It also discusses various issues about business operating and non-operating expenses, property tax considerations, and filing tax reports at the end of each tax year. Running a real estate investment business requires various management and risk analysis skills. The next chapter discusses risk management as an essential aspect of real estate investment. Investors need the necessary knowledge and understanding of risk tolerance to minimise losses and reduce the likelihood of adverse outcomes and unpleasant results. It covers the essential skills to manage risk to keep the possibility of failure to a minimum and develop risk tolerance to deal with unpleasant scenarios.

Due to the importance of inflation, investors need to be aware of its impact on property prices, mortgages, and the value of money over time.

Investors can use creative finance to benefit from certain market conditions, make the right investment decisions, and generate revenues and capital growth.

Investors raise funds and identify deals such as BMV or distressed properties using capital offered by lenders through mortgage/remortgage products with appropriate LTV.

REAL ESTATE INVESTMENT AND FINANCE

11

Don't let the fear of losing be greater than the excitement of winning.

Robert Kiyosaki

Real estate investors should always be prepared to pay a deposit when they purchase a property. However, investors must identify and get deals, preferably BMV opportunities. Banks are the main source of capital for providing different mortgage products and funding investment projects. In this chapter, the process of getting a mortgage and how to determine its LTV is introduced. This chapter discusses how investors can raise funds and expand their portfolios using creative financial methods such as remortgaging when property prices increase. Practical examples and real-life scenarios of remortgaging will be presented because of the importance of investors using creative finance to raise funds.

Real estate investment requires careful preparation, research, study, and risk analysis. Risk is the likelihood of losing part or all of your invested money in investing. Therefore, the importance of understanding and analysing risk in real estate investment will be covered in this chapter. Real estate investment and operations require careful management in terms of finances and risks. This chapter introduces the issue of risk management in the real estate business and its importance for investors to analyse risk, reduce failures, and maximise the likelihood of positive results. Different asset classes can be affected by varying levels of risk and, therefore, require accurate risk analysis and risk tolerance measures.

Investors need to acquire the necessary skills to mitigate risk to reduce potential losses, deal with worst-case scenarios, and ensure the likelihood of positive outcomes is as high as possible. This chapter highlights the issues of identifying and assessing risks associated with real estate investment, such as profit and loss, unexpected changes to the government's rules/regulations, or sudden changes in market conditions. Because there is no riskless investment, various topics related to risk awareness must be considered by investors during their investment journey. Risk tolerance is another issue investors should consider during their investment journey to deal with worst-case scenarios, withstand market fluctuations, and tackle unexpected revenue changes. At the end of the chapter, the issue of risk tolerance will be introduced.

Banks are the main source of capital for providing different mortgage products and funding investment projects.

Real estate investment requires careful preparation, research, study, and risk analysis. Risk is the likelihood of losing part or all of your invested money in investing.

Because there is no riskless investment, various topics related to risk awareness must be considered by investors during their investment journey.

Know what you own, and know why you own it.

Peter Lynch

1. INVESTMENT SELECTION AND FINANCING DECISIONS

Property investors often base the success of their investment on the amount of achieved rental yield. High rental yield indicates a tremendous demand for rental properties from those who cannot purchase their property and fuels the rental market and demand. Regarding property prices, renters expect to pay more when prices increase. However, homeowners would benefit from the capital gains when they sell their property. Still, investors must pay CGT for their income-generating properties if they decide to sell.

When property prices rise, active investors will try to expand their portfolios by remortgaging some existing properties that have benefited from the increased prices.

Property investors can benefit from increased prices, not only by selling but also through remortgaging and borrowing more. When property prices rise, active investors will try to expand their portfolios by remortgaging some existing properties that have benefited from the increased prices. This enables them to raise funds and use them to purchase or build more income-producing properties. Figure 11.1 is a flowchart that shows the main steps for selecting an investment property.

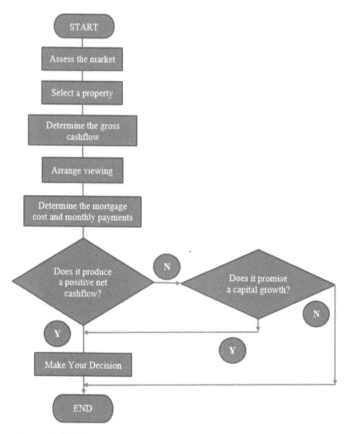

Figure 11.1 A flowchart for the selection of an investment property

Providing more properties will have a positive impact on the supply of residential properties and the rental market. However, owing to limited capital, investors often rely on lenders, such as non-high street banks, crowdfunding, and other investors, to expand their portfolios and fund their investment projects. Those with sufficient capital can still use mainstream lenders' funds to buy properties and leverage to improve their portfolios and magnify their returns.

> Those with sufficient capital can still use mainstream lenders' funds to buy properties and leverage to improve their portfolios and magnify their returns.

Most banks require investors to pay a deposit of 20–25% of the property's total purchase price, and they agree to pay the remaining balance of 75–80%. However, investors should try to get BMV deals, for example, from distressed properties or auctions. This has to happen before agreeing on a price with the vendor(s) or the estate agent, giving investors a chance to sell the purchased property for a profit. This can be achieved by adding value to the property through quality refurbishment works, adding an extension, or loft conversion. The achieved profits can be used to reinvest in the next property deals. So, investors need to be aware of the difference between the property's asking price, and the property value, which is what the surveyors think.

> Investors need to be aware of the difference between the property's asking price, and the property value, which is what the surveyors think.

Artificial intelligence, or AI, is becoming a useful technology and tool for business intelligence, market assessment, and property legal matters. AI uses various online accessible data repository platforms to extract valuable information. It offers cost-effective solutions to a number of real estate business challenges, opening opportunities for serious investing, earnings, and time and cost savings. Property investors and developers became aware of the power of AI and started using it to analyse the real estate market and for evaluation and assessment purposes. I asked ChatGPT (Chat Generative Pre-trained Transformer), a large AI-based natural language processing model, two questions about the current property market in England. The questions were regarding the best areas to invest in in England in properties in general and buy-to-let in particular. I couldn't disagree with ChatGPT; the responses were as shown below.

> AI uses various online accessible data repository platforms to extract valuable information. It offers cost-effective solutions to a number of real estate business challenges, opening opportunities for serious investing, earnings, time and cost savings.

You

Where are the best areas in England to invest in buy-to-let properties?

ChatGPT

Choosing the best areas for buy-to-let properties depends on various factors, including rental yields, demand for rental properties, economic growth, and local market conditions. As of my last update in January 2022, here are some areas in England that were often considered promising for buy-to-let investments:

1. **Manchester:** The city has a strong rental demand, particularly from a large student population and young professionals. Areas like the city center, Salford Quays, and Didsbury have been popular among investors.

2. **Liverpool:** With regeneration projects and a growing economy, Liverpool has become a hotspot for buy-to-let investors. Areas like the city center, Baltic Triangle, and Kensington have seen increased interest.

3. **Birmingham:** The city's economic growth, redevelopment projects, and a high demand for rental properties make it an attractive option for buy-to-let investors. Areas such as the city center, Digbeth, and Edgbaston are often considered.

4. **Leeds:** A vibrant city with a large student population, Leeds has been a popular choice for buy-to-let investments. Areas like the city center, Headingley, and Hyde Park are frequently targeted by investors.

5. **Sheffield:** The city's affordable property prices and growing student population make it appealing for buy-to-let investors. Areas such as the city center, Ecclesall Road, and Crookes are commonly considered.

6. **Nottingham:** With a significant student population and affordable property prices, Nottingham has been attractive for buy-to-let investments. Areas like the city center, Lenton, and Beeston are popular choices.

It's important to conduct thorough research and stay updated on the latest market trends before making any investment decisions. Consider factors such as local amenities, transportation links, employment opportunities, and the overall economic climate. Additionally, changes in government policies and regulations can impact the buy-to-let market, so it's advisable to seek advice from real estate professionals and financial experts.

You

Where are the best areas in England to invest in properties?

ChatGPT

I don't have real-time data, and property markets can be highly dynamic, so it's important to conduct thorough research and possibly consult with local experts before making investment decisions. As of my last update in January 2022, some areas in England were considered promising for property investment due to factors like economic growth, demand for rental properties, and overall market trends. However, these conditions might have changed.

Historically, cities with strong economic growth, good infrastructure, and high demand for housing tend to be attractive for property investment. Some cities that have often been mentioned include:

1. **London:** Despite high prices, London remains a global financial hub, and certain areas may offer good investment potential.
2. **Manchester:** Known for its strong economy, cultural scene, and a growing population, Manchester has been a popular choice for property investors.
3. **Birmingham:** As the second-largest city in the UK, Birmingham has seen significant development and investment, making it an attractive option for property investors.
4. **Liverpool:** With regeneration projects and a thriving cultural scene, Liverpool has attracted attention from property investors.
5. **Leeds:** This city has a diverse economy, a large student population, and ongoing development projects.
6. **Bristol:** As a vibrant city with a strong economy, Bristol has been considered a good option for property investment.

It's crucial to consider various factors such as local job markets, transportation links, educational institutions, and future development plans. Additionally, changes in government policies, interest rates, and the overall economic climate can impact the property market.

Keep in mind that property investment involves risks, and it's advisable to seek advice from financial and real estate professionals to make informed decisions based on the most recent market conditions. ↓

2. MORTGAGE LOANS AND CASH FLOW

Investors must under-
stand the mortgage
process, the difference
between LTV and
equity, and buy-to-let
and buy-to-sell
mortgages.

For an investor to get a mortgage accepted, banks require them to pay a deposit depending on the offered LTV, i.e., the percentage of the property price offered as a loan to the investor by the bank. Therefore, investors must understand the mortgage process, the difference between LTV and equity, and buy-to-let and buy-to-sell mortgages. Figure 11.2 shows how a mortgage started with a balance of 75%; as the investor pays the mortgage, the LTV decreases, and their equity increases. Notice that the investor will own the property 100% by the end of the mortgage period.

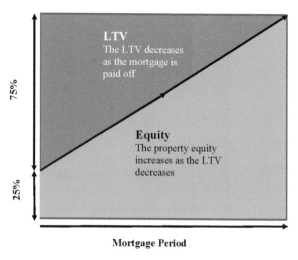

Figure 11.2 LTV and equity

The property value
might fall due to a
market downturn to a
lower value than the
mortgage amount owed
to the bank, and then
the property is said to
be in negative equity.

Risk management,
market analysis,
economics, and finan-
cial intelligence are all
essential aspects of the
property business.

Banks are willing to
finance various real
estate assets such
as buy-to-let, devel-
opment, commercial
properties, etc.

The property market plays a role in determining the value of any property. The property value might fall due to a market downturn to a lower value than the mortgage amount owed to the bank, and then the property is said to be in negative equity. In other words, the property has a negative equity value when the market value drops below the mortgage loan amount. For example, if a buy-to-let investment property is bought for £600,000 and has 80% LTV, then the mortgage loan value is £480,000 interest only, and the equity value is £120,000. Assuming that the property value dropped to £350,000, below the mortgage loan amount of £480,000, this would result in the property being in negative equity. Like any market, the real estate business has its ups and downs. Therefore, risk management, market analysis, economics, and financial intelligence are all essential aspects of the property business. Also, knowing how to assess the market, identify the right deal, and when to buy, hold, refinance, sell, or exit is vital to a successful investment.

Investors borrow money from banks to fund their investment projects in the property business. Investors need to pay interest, a percentage of the money they borrowed for their investment. The type of mortgage and interest rates offered will depend on the market conditions and the bank's risk appetite. Banks are willing to finance various real estate assets such as buy-to-let, development, commercial properties, etc. They are the primary source of capital and mortgage products for property investors. Recently, banks started to offer most of their services online and use mobile banking to support their customers. High net worth (HNW) customers with large portfolios and financial assets are well looked after by banks. HNW customers are offered boutique financial services such as wealth planning, family services, and investment advisory services unavailable to average customers. Being an HNW customer has its advantages; the banks also allocate them financial advisers.

To make the right investment decision about a particular property purchase, investors must ask themselves two questions to evaluate the deal: does it generate cash flow? And does it have a high yield and ROI? To check whether or not an investment stacks up, they must calculate the net yield, monthly cash flow, and ROI. To achieve that, investors would know the market rent and the mortgage cost (monthly mortgage payment). The cash flow is the profit made from property rent after deducting all expenses, as follows:

Cash flow = Monthly rent – Monthly expenses (Running cost)
Monthly expenses = Mortgage payment + Ground rent +
Building insurance + Service charge + Contingency (5%)

The contingency is mainly for other expenses such as management fees, extra maintenance work expenses, rental voids (lack of rental income), if any, and annual gas safety checks.

In January 2023, our property business company, Anzar Property Investors Limited, bought a four-bedroom house in Manchester through an auction with Pugh Auctions for £200,000, as shown in Figure 11.3. The property is a three-story building with one family bathroom, a top-floor ensuite, and a ground-floor toilet (WC), as shown in Figure 11.4. We had to spend £16,600 for the complete refurbishment of this property. Table 11.1 presents all financial figures related to this property in terms of the purchase and remortgage costs, the achieved rental yield, cash flow, and ROI.

This property was featured in a well-known TV property programme, the BBC's *Homes Under the Hammer*, in May 2023. The production team invited me to participate in the show to discuss the auction purchase of this property, refurbishment works, and development activities. It was recorded and available on my YouTube channel as a memento, and accessible using this link https://www.youtube.com/watch?v=p8MD_GdhzZg. This particular episode is highly likely to be repeated on the same BBC *Homes Under the Hammer* programme several times over the coming years. It was an enjoyable experience and exciting activity.

To make the right investment decision about a particular property purchase, investors must ask themselves two questions to evaluate the deal: does it generate cash flow? And does it have a high yield and ROI?

Figure 11.3 The four-bedroom property. Image courtesy of Pugh Auctions: https://www.pugh-auctions.com/

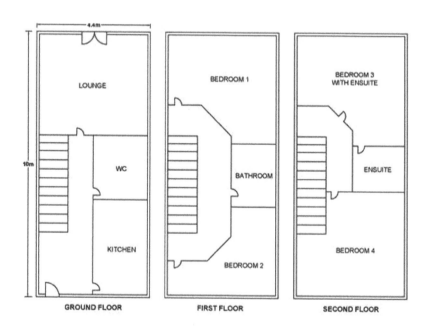

Figure 11.4 Property plan. Image courtesy of Pugh Auctions: https://www.pugh-auctions.com/

Table 11.1 Rental yield, monthly cash flow, and ROI calculations

Item	Amount (£)
Property price	200,000
Mortgage 75%	150,000
Purchase costs:	
Deposit 25%	50,000
Buy-to-let Stamp duty (SDLT) 3%, 5%	6000
Refurbs + legal fees (20,000 + 1600)	21,600
Interest rate	6.99%
Monthly paid interest	967
Interest charges for 6 months = 967 x 6	5802
Yield = (1550 x 12) / (200,000 + 6000 + 16,600)	9.23%
Remortgage:	
New value of the property	270,000
Re-mortgage funds	202,500
Mortgage fees	4085
Repayment charges for the first year (4% of the mortgage loan)	6000
Investment income:	
Raised funds = 202,500 – (150,000 + 6000)	46,500
Rent	1750
Cashflow & ROI:	
New lender interest rate 5.09%	876.2647083
Insurance (monthly)	18
Ground rent – leasehold (monthly)	22.5
Contingency 5% per annum = (1750 x 12 x 5%) / 12	88
Monthly cashflow = 1750 – (876.26+18+22.5+88)	746
ROI = (746x12)/(50,000+6000+21,600+5802–46,500)	24%
Number of years to get back initial investment = 1 / 21%	4.1

3. FUNDING INVESTMENT PROJECTS

Various options and mortgage products are available to investors to fund their investment projects. However, raising the necessary funds for an investment project requires the investor to meet certain conditions and possess marketing skills. A mortgage is a long-term loan taken out by an investor to purchase real estate such as a residential property, land, or commercial unit. The mortgage covers a percentage of the property value known as LTV and is secured against the property purchased until it is fully repaid by the end of the term. An investor is expected to put down a deposit as a percentage of the property value and as part of the mortgage agreement.

The common characteristic of all mortgages is that they will eventually have to be repaid by the investor with interest and mortgage charges. The bank can only repossess the property if the investor cannot keep up their regular repayments or fails to abide by the agreed terms and conditions. In such a case, banks can take back the property and sell it to regain their capital. Any remaining money will be paid back to the landlord.

The mortgage covers a percentage of the property value known as LTV and is secured against the property purchased until it is fully repaid by the end of the term.

The bank can only repossess the property if the investor cannot keep up their regular repayments or fails to abide by the agreed terms and conditions.

The main sources of funding for real estate investment projects are as follows:

* savings;
* joint venture;
* high street banks;
* non-high street banks;
* non-bank financial institutions.

When using an interest-only mortgage, the buyer repays only the interest on the borrowed loan monthly. The buyer must repay the borrowed loan amount at the end of the mortgage period.

In terms of mortgage provision, there are different types of mortgages with different rules and regulations that govern the financial services sector. The two common mortgage types are repayment mortgages and interest-only mortgages. In the repayment mortgage, the property buyer has to pay back the interest and the loan every month. The buyer owns the property 100% once the interest and loan amount is repaid. When using an interest-only mortgage, the buyer repays only the interest on the borrowed loan monthly. The buyer must repay the borrowed loan amount at the end of the mortgage period. The three common types of mortgages are listed below.

* Fixed-rate mortgage: The interest an individual is charged stays the same for the whole mortgage term period regardless of the central bank's base rate.
* Standard variable rate (SVR) mortgage: The interest an individual is charged can change regardless of the central bank's base rate.
* Tracker mortgage: The interest an individual is charged tracks the central bank's base rate.

Figure 11.5 summarises the difference between all three mortgage rates.

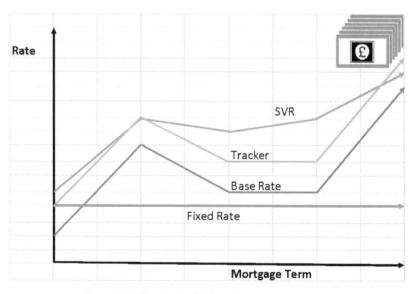

Figure 11.5 Fixed-rate, SVR, and tracker mortgages

Asking a mortgage adviser to get a 'no redemption fees/penalties' mortgage product is helpful if the investor plans to remortgage their property and raise funds for their next project. Lenders often expect investors to reinvest the raised funds by buying more income-producing properties. This should help the investors to grow their property portfolio and investment. The next time the investor remortgages both their old and recently bought properties that were added to their portfolio, they should use the raised funds to reinvest and buy more income-producing properties, and so on. Reinvestment helps investors grow their businesses, produce better and bigger returns, and has what is known as the snowball effect. As we all know, a snowball gets bigger and bigger when rolled down a hill until it becomes a giant ball.

> Lenders often expect investors to reinvest the raised funds by buying more income-producing properties.

4. PROPERTY ACCOUNTING

Accounting is about producing, summarising, and reporting financial records and transactions resulting from business operations over a specified period. Organising business accounts is key to managing real estate financial transactions and records and preparing financial statements. This section introduces the concepts and principles of property accounting and the importance of accurate accounting in property investment. It covers financial statements, including profit and loss reports and balance sheets produced using accounting software known as Xero. Xero has been presented because we use it at Anzar Property Group, but other accounting software is available to support businesses. With proper planning and understanding of their financial situation, investors should be able to develop accurate projections for their future revenues, expenses, and tax commitments. Investors must file their tax reports at the end of each tax year, so they need to be aware of the main types of property tax.

> Organising business accounts is key to managing real estate financial transactions and records and preparing financial statements.

> With proper planning and understanding of their financial situation, investors should be able to develop accurate projections for their future revenues, expenses, and tax commitments.

An essential aspect of any business, in general, and real estate, in particular, is to ensure that financial records and income reports are accurate and comply with tax laws. The produced reports are essential to managing investment operations and decision-making and to lenders, investors, employees, and the government. The accounting records are essential because they show the business's current financial status, how the company is progressing, and how profitable it is. Financial accounting is concerned with the following.

> The accounting records are essential because they show the business's current financial status, how the company is progressing, and how profitable it is.

- Designing all the internal controls necessary for management and auditing.
- Developing a system for analysing the data recorded from bookkeeping and minimising errors.
- Recording transactions, developing financial reports, and measuring out revenues and expenses for a business to determine profits and losses during a particular period.
- Analysing data from bookkeeping to report the business financial results, financial statements, tax returns, and performance measures.

Real estate investors need to ensure that they have an accurate view of the financial situation of their business and that it is reported to them regularly. Accounting reports are very useful in helping business owners to develop their financial strategies and to make important financial decisions whenever necessary. Another aspect of the accounting business is bookkeeping, which supports accounting activities and operations. Bookkeeping is an essential aspect of real estate investment operations that complements the accounting business. It is the process of tracking, gathering, organising, and recording business financial transactions and activities. Bookkeeping is important for preparing financial reports (e.g., profits and expenses) and tax returns.

Financial statements are essential documents that HMRC (His Majesty's Revenue & Customs) requires to show different financial information about the business and maintain its transparency. Lenders often request such documents to check how the company is performing before granting funds to investment projects. The two main financial statements are:

I. profit and loss statement, and
II. balance sheet.

Let us get into the details of each one of these financial statements.

I. Profit and loss statement

A profit and loss statement is required to report a company's financial status and performance over a specific period. As part of the company's annual report, it summarises how it will incur its revenues and expenses or the net loss and net profit. Also, it provides information about the company's earnings before it pays taxes. For example, the profit and loss statement in a buy-to-let property business is divided into four parts, as listed below.

1. Operating expenses: Provides information about the costs that come from regular business activity, such as initial refurbishment, building insurance, and repairs.
2. Non-operating expenses: Provides information about the costs that do not come directly from regular business activity, such as accountancy fees, marketing, and training.
3. Gross profit = revenue − operating expenses.
4. Net profit = revenue − (operating + non-operating expenses). The investor will have a net loss if the outcome is negative. Net profit is the most common indicator of how profitable the business is.

Note that the net profit produced on the profit and loss statement is before tax. It is often helpful to show the profit and loss figures as a percentage of the rental income because it is easy to:

- analyse the statement, including all revenue and expense figures;
- compare how the business is performing in comparison to previous years;
- manage losses and identify which of the costs make up the most significant portion of the income.

II. Balance sheet

A balance sheet is a financial statement that includes the following three crucial pieces of information about a business:

1. A company's assets, e.g., all business Buy-to-let properties, cash or cash equivalents.
2. A company's liabilities, e.g., total mortgage values.
3. Shareholder(s) or owner's equity.

The balance sheet provides a clear snapshot of the financial state of the company in terms of its capital owned and debt, using the following formula:

Owner's equity = Assets – Liabilities

The balance sheet helps to evaluate the business's financial structure and perform financial analysis at a particular time. It is an important document used to value a specific business and helps an understanding of how the outside world views it. Banks often ask for such a document to check if the business is in an excellent financial position, establish the company's debts or financial obligations, and determine whether to fund the investment project. A profitable business with significant debts is fine if it can show a healthy financial status and generate good profits.

Banks and investors like to receive a detailed balance sheet to help them make the right decisions. It is helpful to use the balance sheet as part of an investor pack to attract potential investors so that they are happy to fund investment projects or join current or future joint venture projects.

For a real estate business, the balance sheets represent a company or an investor's property portfolio. Some property portfolio details are available on the Companies House and Land Registry websites. Whenever investors ask their mortgage adviser for options to refinance or buy a property, they expect to be asked for an updated copy of their portfolio, regardless of its size. This allows them to send a copy of the portfolio to potential lenders. After the 2008 global financial crisis, lenders have become stricter with their lending criteria and procedures. They ask investors to provide their up-to-date portfolios whenever they ask for funds or remortgage loans.

Beginner investors need to know about refinancing, the power of compounding yields, gearing/leveraging, and good debt. Ex-council dere-lict properties for sale could be an excellent way to learn about property investment, especially if they are at the right location, e.g., close to a city's CBD or amenities. Often, they help a person to learn the purchase process, legal matters, and renovation skills before renting them out. Such proper-ties could make good investment opportunities if they are in the correct location. They can attract specific communities and may produce good yields. Property investment could be an exciting and enjoyable game, but it requires attention and discipline.

The liabilities in a real estate portfolio are the mortgage loans the banks or lenders provide to support the property investment projects. It is the debt that the company owes to the banks or lenders. The assets are the residen-tial or commercial properties that help the business generate income. The generated revenue could be used to support business operations or reinvest-ment. The primary property business operations are as follows:

- managing the assets, i.e., properties;
- preparing the tenancy agreements;
- arranging building insurance, boiler insurance, gas, and electric safety;

The balance sheet helps to evaluate the business's financial structure and perform financial analysis at a particular time.

A profitable business with significant debts is fine if it can show a healthy financial status and generate good profits.

Whenever investors ask their mortgage adviser for options to refinance or buy a property, they expect to be asked for an updated copy of their portfolio, regardless of its size.

The liabilities in a real estate portfolio are the mortgage loans the banks or lenders provide to support the property investment projects.

The assets are the residential or commer-cial properties that help the business generate income.

- organising and managing repair works;
- managing resources.

5. PROPERTY TAX

Taxation has been used for centuries, even before the modern state, to raise funds, develop social and economic projects, and control and manage the state and its economy. Governments now use it to collect data about citizens' and businesses' expenditures, forecast the economy, and plan for budgets. Regardless of the type of business investors have, they must file their taxes before the end of the tax year. Therefore, it is crucial to have accurate financial statements and accounting records ready for filing these taxes. Real estate investors are required to keep records of their financial transactions and to produce accurate accounts whenever requested by legal entities such as HMRC in the UK.

With the help of their accountants and accurate financial statements, investors should be able to complete their relevant tax forms and use applicable deductions. Accurate accounts help accountants to offset every expense and to take all costs into account. Tax deadlines are strict, so late tax returns are liable to fixed penalties and interest charges. Knowing the current financial situation will help investors develop accurate projections with realistic expenses and tax commitments estimates. With proper financial planning and robust recording systems, real estate investors should be able to predict their future rental income and revenues.

Real estate investors should be able to accurately manage their capital and forecast their capital position to plan early for their financial and tax obligations. In this way, they can avoid unexpected events, overspending, and delayed tax payments. As an employer, any real estate investor should act as a tax collector for the government by maintaining accurate financial records and an effective employee payroll system. Simplicity and using quality tax accounting tools and bookkeeping packages play a significant role in developing an effective accounting system and tax accounting for the company. Tax accounting is an accounting process that uses complex operations and focuses on the following:

- preparing and filing taxes;
- helping investors to track all their financial activities, such as incoming funds, expenses, revenues, and business financial obligations;
- reducing tax liabilities;
- following the necessary rules to complete tax returns.

Governments use systems to collect different types of tax. In the UK, HMRC is the tax, payment, and customs authority. According to HMRC, they have the authority to 'collect the money that pays for the UK's public services and help families and individuals with targeted financial support' and 'help the honest majority to get their tax right and make it hard for the dishonest minority to cheat the system'.

> Regardless of the type of business investors have, they must file their taxes before the end of the tax year.

> Accurate accounts help accountants to offset every expense and to take all costs into account.

*In this world, nothing can be said to be
certain, except death and taxes.*

Benjamin Franklin

5.1. INCOME TAX

Property investors in the Buy-to-let business must complete a tax return under the 'Residential Lettings' rules. As part of their and the company's income, rental income tax cannot be offset against income earned from other jobs. They might be able to claim tax relief on their business expenses. HMRC sets out these expenses; for some claims, investors must keep records, e.g., receipts of what they have spent. HMRC states, 'Income Tax is a tax you pay on your income. You do not have to pay tax on all types of income'.

HMRC's income tax collection depends on a tax allowance and rate. An allowance is the income investors can earn without paying income tax, i.e., non-taxable income. However, they must pay tax at the applicable tax rate on all taxable income above the non-taxable earnings, i.e., their allowance. The tax rate determines the percentage that investors have to pay to HMRC. As their income increases, the percentage they must pay as tax increases. Another form of tax by the government is the National Insurance Contribution (NIC), which is deducted from anyone in employment.

Property investors in the Buy-to-let business must complete a tax return under the 'Residential Lettings' rules.

An allowance is the income investors can earn without paying income tax, i.e., non-taxable income.

5.2. Stamp Duty

Another type of tax the government collects to manage its public finance and budget is Stamp Duty Land Tax (SDLT). In England, SDLT is the main tax on property transactions that must be paid when an investor buys a property or land over a specific price. There are different SDLT rules if an investor is buying their first home. Legally, it is their responsibility to make sure that their stamp duty/transaction tax is paid before the deadline set by the government. The tax rate they must pay varies depending on the property price.

Another type of tax the government collects to manage its public finance and budget is Stamp Duty Land Tax.

5.3. Capital Gains Tax

Capital Gains Tax (CGT) is paid by an investor or asset owner to the government when they sell the asset (e.g., buy-to-let property) for more than the original price for which they bought it and the capital spent on it. The CGT is paid on the capital gained, i.e., a tax on the profit when an asset owner sells an asset that has increased in value, not the full amount of capital they receive. Not all assets are taxable. Asset owners also do not have to pay CGT if all their annual gains are below their tax-free allowance. So, they only pay CGT on capital gains above their tax-free allowance, i.e., the Annual Exempt Amount. For more details and up-to-date rates, check the UK government website https://www.gov.uk/capital-gains-tax.

Capital Gains Tax (CGT) is paid by an investor or asset owner to the government when they sell the asset (e.g., buy-to-let property) for more than the original price for which they bought it and the capital spent on it.

5.4. Corporation Tax

Corporation Tax is imposed on limited companies' profits and capital gains. It is a legal obligation the investment business owes the government. As a limited company, the business must register for Corporation Tax when it

Corporation Tax is imposed on limited companies' profits and capital gains. It is a legal obligation the investment business owes the government.

starts doing business and must keep its accounting records current. Taxable profits gained from a company business and from which the company must pay Corporation Tax include the income the company managed to make from the following activities:

- trading business;
- successful investment;
- selling assets for more than they cost, i.e., chargeable gains.

Check the https://www.gov.uk/corporation-tax website for up-to-date rates and more details.

6. RISK MANAGEMENT IN REAL ESTATE BUSINESS

Risk management is a process that allows investors to identify, evaluate, and mitigate the impact of potential losses. Investors have to keep the effects of such risks when they occur to a minimum. They must consider any changes in the market in terms of how they could affect future income from a potential investment. The main risk management issues in the real estate business are highlighted next. Risk management aims to identify and evaluate the financial risks associated with the business and its earnings and resources. Property investment, in general, and buy-to-let in particular, is a long-term business; therefore, such a business requires a long-term vision and careful planning.

As risk-takers, successful property investors are willing to deal with risk and accept large amounts of capital to fund their investment projects and business activities. They take the risk of setting up property companies and investing a lot of time in acquiring the know-how and knowledge to deal with banks, mortgage advisers, solicitors, local authorities, estate agents, insurance, developers, planners, utility service providers, etc. In property investment, an increased value of debt due to deflation must be considered part of the risk. Higher debt levels are part of leveraged finance, but debt becomes problematic if the property cannot maintain a good yield or tenants cannot pay their rent. That is why it is essential to ensure tenants pass a rigorous affordability check before signing a tenancy agreement. During the COVID-19 pandemic, which started in early 2020, furloughed workers received support from the UK government, so that most tenants could pay their rent.

We witnessed how UK businesses, such as hospitality, airlines, and sports industries, struggled. But the situation was different in other businesses, such as e-commerce – they were booming during the lockdown. There is always a risk, which is the case with any business or investment. Real estate investment involves the risk of losing out financially if the portfolio does not achieve its target and produce the expected income. For example, some properties become empty for a long period, or tenants cannot pay their rent due to unemployment or unexpected circumstances.

Investors must be aware of the changes that might happen to the market regarding supply and demand. Unexpected changes to the market can occur due to various factors, and changes to tenants' circumstances can happen

Risk management aims to identify and evaluate the financial risks associated with the business and its earnings and resources.

In property investment, an increased value of debt due to deflation must be considered part of the risk.

There is always a risk, which is the case with any business or investment.

Investors must be aware of the changes that might happen to the market regarding supply and demand.

for different reasons. The demand for rentals can go up and down, and stock availability can also change. Likewise, the supply of properties depends on changes in the rental market and demand for residential or commercial properties. The significant risks in property investment and development include, but are not limited to:

- unexpected changes to supply and demand;
- increases in tax such as stamp duty, CGT, or income tax could have a knock-on effect on supply and demand;
- extra costs associated with buying or selling investment properties;
- difficulty in selling a property due to high competition or time constraints;
- unexpected changes to government rules or tax regulations.

The major risks of buy-to-let investment include, but are not limited to the following:

- on-time rent payment is not guaranteed;
- void periods could be unavoidable;
- increased costs associated with ground rent and service charges for leased properties and apartments;
- falling demand;
- an increased cost of lending.

Active investors are willing to learn marketing, sales, technology, real estate economics, property law, project management, finance, accounting, tax rules, operations management, business strategy, and, most importantly, how to deal with clients and customers. Experienced real estate business investors with many property mortgages would be as concerned about Bank of England interest rate fluctuations as any starting business owner. Therefore, diversifying the business portfolio across different strategies would give the investor options to reduce risk.

When an interest rate increases, it will significantly impact the cost of tracker types of mortgages and new property purchases. At the same time, revenues and rental yield will decrease. For example, a property investment company that owns and rents many buy-to-let properties might need to use its risk profile to investigate and analyse the business exposure to interest rate fluctuations. The rise in interest rate will increase their monthly mortgage payments and decrease their monthly cash flow income. The investor needs to consider taking specific measures to reduce that exposure, for example, by regularly reviewing their rents and monthly expenses and considering fixed-rate mortgages or different investment strategies.

Insurance is a form of risk management by which businesses undertake to transfer the risk of potential financial losses or accidental damages to an insurance service provider in return for guaranteed compensation. Insurance service providers are willing to take on the risk in return for a premium paid by the insured business. The insurance policy would include all the terms and conditions agreed upon between both parties, the insurance company, and the policyholder or insuree. Without insurance, real estate businesses would be vulnerable to unexpected losses of their investment portfolios, properties, and earnings.

Experienced real estate business investors with many property mortgages would be as concerned about Bank of England interest rate fluctuations as any starting business owner.

The investor needs to consider taking specific measures to reduce that exposure, for example, by regularly reviewing their rents and monthly expenses and considering fixed-rate mortgages or different investment strategies.

Insurance service providers are willing to take on the risk in return for a premium paid by the insured business.

Uninsured investors
could become unable
to grow and might face
bankruptcy in the case
of adverse events.

Uninsured investors could become unable to grow and might face bankruptcy in the case of adverse events. For example, properties could be insured against adverse events such as flooding or fire. Banks want a building insurance policy before transferring a mortgage loan to a property investor. Investors should make the necessary arrangements to pay a fee to the insurance company in exchange for compensation if an unexpected loss happens. Also, investors must know the importance of tenancy rules and regulations, including contract agreements. Such issues determine the legal rights and responsibilities of both parties, investors and tenants. The tenancy agreement should specify how much rental income will be received from the tenant.

Investors or landlords
should be able to use
technology and avail-
able tools to support
their business and
management activities.

Investors or landlords should be able to use technology and available tools to support their business and management activities. For example, they can use online banking apps to manage their financial transactions or a tool such as MileIQ to track their mileage, travel expenses, etc. They can use online deposit protection services to manage their deposit protection accounts for their tenants. Also, they can use an online service such as the DocuSign eSignature tool to get the tenant to sign the tenancy agreement. The tenant should be able to set up their account and use this online service to sign future tenancy agreements. This will speed up the process of signing and exchanging the contracts.

All available tools and functions are important and require proper attention because they can affect the business's and investment's progress. Investors must have the skills of buying and selling, operating and managing real estate businesses, and using technology to deliver a quality service. All such skills and activities are useful to build a successful investment and keep the risk of failure to a minimum. In the property business, to minimise risk, investors might need to:

- acquire the necessary knowledge of management, finance, and technology;
- actively assess the market and adapt to changes;
- consider diversifying their business portfolio in different property investments such as REITs, HMOs, SA, etc.;
- be accredited by the industry's key governing bodies, such as NRLA, IoD (Institute of Directors, for company directors);
- attend property investment events such as seminars, workshops, and network meetings;
- think about investing in different regions or even countries if appropriate;
- learn to budget for contingencies;
- develop an exit strategy to minimise losses.

The only strategy that is guaranteed to fail is not taking any risks.

Mark Zuckerberg

7. RISK TOLERANCE

Risk tolerance is another issue that investors need to be aware of. It is about an investor's ability to withstand market fluctuation and deal with changes in investment returns. Real estate investors must deal with all scenarios and review worst-case scenarios and situations to predict future losses during bad times. This requires a regular assessment of their short-term and long-term circumstances and financial situation. Investment risks include loss of initial investment, reduced rental demand, increased interest rates, increased inflation, and rental voids.

The idea behind risk tolerance is to make investors ready for the unexpected, determine which investment best suits them, and assess how much they are willing to lose. Regardless of the investment type or asset class, investors must improve their risk knowledge, understand risk tolerance, and assess it as it applies to them. Different asset classes can be affected by varying levels of risk. Buy-to-let investment has a medium risk, but investing in REITs is medium to high. Property prices tend to change due to various factors and market situations. During the 2008 credit crunch, the unemployment rate increased, leading to high levels of repossessions, and property prices dropped in value. It took the market about six years to recover to the pre-crisis levels. The rewards are high in the REITs stock market, but the risk of stock shares dropping is also high, as discussed previously. The key risks for real estate investment are as follows:

- Price tends to change.
- Property tax may change.
- Rental voids can affect your ROI.
- Interest rate changes.
- Properties require maintenance and repairs regularly. Unexpected repairs may result in high losses.
- As mentioned previously, monthly mortgage payments may increase in the case of a tracker mortgage, which implies more financial commitment.

A high-risk property investor is not restricted to safe investment. Such an investor should plan to mitigate certain losses, such as rental voids, to maximise their profits and improve their portfolio. Managing tenants and collecting rent is challenging. Avoiding rental voids is like trying to avoid the unavoidable; therefore, to mitigate the risk of voids, investors might need to do the following:

- Get actively involved in the selection process of tenants by arranging interviews before signing contracts.
- Check the tenant's affordability.
- Request a guarantor.
- Carry out a credit check.
- Avoid overcharging.
- Communicate regularly with their tenants to show support and care to their families.
- Invest in their property by keeping it up to scratch with regular checks and maintenance.

Risk tolerance is another issue that investors need to be aware of. It is about an investor's ability to withstand market fluctuation and deal with changes in investment returns.

The idea behind risk tolerance is to make investors ready for the unexpected, determine which investment best suits them, and assess how much they are willing to lose.

Different asset classes can be affected by varying levels of risk.

A high-risk property investor is not restricted to safe investment. Such an investor should plan to mitigate certain losses, such as rental voids, to maximise their profits and improve their portfolio.

- Keep their tenants informed about any upcoming changes or maintenance works.
- Develop a void period strategy to minimise losses. An investor can avoid losses due to an empty income-producing property by arranging rental voids insurance or a guaranteed rent agreement.
- Look after their employees, business operations, and management.

8. SUMMARY

Creative finance introduces an intelligent solution for investors to structure their investment deals and build their portfolios. It is a useful way to help investors arrange a good deal and finance a real estate purchase using capital from a third-party institution or OPM legally. This chapter covered various issues related to this topic, including financial techniques and management as a key tool for planning and controlling investment projects. Applying creative finance, such as leveraging available financial products to real-life investment deals, can help investors use the minimum of their capital. Practical examples supported with real-life scenarios and cash flow and ROI calculations have been presented in this chapter. Investors should be able to exploit creative finance and benefit from the real estate market regardless of economic conditions and price fluctuations.

Creative finance provides an opportunity to resolve the issue of limited access to capital and makes leveraging possible. To achieve this, investors should ensure that their income statements and balance sheets are ready for lenders and have access to funds from high street or non-high street banks. In this chapter, I introduced real estate financing to support investors and fund their deals; however, this requires some preparation from the investor's side, such as identifying BMV properties and ensuring that deposits are ready in their bank accounts. Banks provide funds in the form of mortgage products with different options for interest rates depending on the length of the term. The process of applying for a mortgage/remortgage, how to receive a mortgage/remortgage offer, and determining its interest rate and LTV have been discussed.

All investment businesses require accounting operations and financial accounting knowledge to process their financial data, report their financial records, and file their accounts at the end of each tax year. Various topics have been presented about how investors can finance their investment projects, raise funds using creative finance, and remortgage using real-life leveraging scenarios. Real estate investment operations produce various financial transactions requiring recording and financial accounting. Real estate investors must understand how property accounting operates and how financial statements, including profit and loss documents and balance sheets, are prepared. This chapter introduced property accounting and highlighted the importance of recording all financial transactions resulting from property investment operations. Running a real estate investment business requires careful management of its operations, finances, accounts, and risk analysis.

This chapter introduced risk management as an essential aspect of real estate investment. Investors require the necessary knowledge and understanding of risk analysis for different asset classes to minimise losses and

Applying creative finance, such as leveraging available financial products to real-life investment deals, can help investors use the minimum of their capital.

Banks provide funds in the form of mortgage products with different options for interest rates depending on the length of the term.

Real estate investors must understand how property accounting operates and how financial statements, including profit and loss documents and balance sheets, are prepared.

increase the likelihood of positive results. Different levels of risk can impact different investment strategies and asset classes, which require accurate risk analysis. The necessary skills to manage risk to keep the likelihood of failure to a minimum and develop risk tolerance to deal with unpleasant scenarios have been discussed.

The final chapter introduces our family property business, Anzar Property Group, its main activities, challenges, and the skills gained by the management team. The company focuses on buy-to-let and a property development strategy, growing its assets portfolio in the UK, and managing the business risks. Different topics about our business, including the set-up of Anzar Property Investors Limited, its main operations, investment activities, social responsibility, and contributions, are covered. The story of Anzar Property Group is presented, supported by real-life scenarios about the company's business activities, business model, structure, and operations.

> Different levels of risk can impact different investment strategies and asset classes, which require accurate risk analysis.

ANZAR PROPERTY GROUP

We are a family property business based in Manchester, UK, set up in 2017, focusing on buy-to-let. We built our multi-assets portfolio, generated revenues, and expanded our property portfolio using the BRR (buy, refurb, refinance) model. Financial independence was my goal; I always wanted to be self-employed and become my own boss. This chapter discusses various topics about our family business, including its story, the set-up of the company Anzar Property Investors Limited, its primary operations, money management abilities, and investment activities. It covers our business activities, such as our annual property seminar, publications, media participation, etc. Sharing our story with you aims to inspire you in case you plan to set up your business and build your assets portfolio.

Anzar Property Group is an expanding family-run business that manages multiple real estate companies, and each owns a property portfolio. The family business members had to operate outside their comfort zone and deal with many challenges and difficult situations, but we managed to make it work. We learnt how to deal with many property stakeholders and built trustworthy relationships with various entities such as estate agents, auction houses, mortgage brokers, solicitors, suppliers, etc. Anzar's investment philosophy is to acquire properties in areas of high demand which produce high yield and capital gains to minimise risk and maximise returns for long-term sustainable growth. In this chapter, my family business story covers information supported by real-life scenarios about the family business and its structure, business strategies ,and operations.

Anzar Property Group invested heavily in different technologies and tools to implement automated processes and solutions such as Google Cloud and drives to store all the business data and file management, Signable to sign tenancy agreements, etc. We use an online management system, Arthur, to help us manage all the business operations and deal with the tenants' enquiries. Investing in knowledge is essential to any business; therefore, we had to learn about investing, finance and wealth management, and leadership to manage our business effectively. This enabled us to understand managing and tolerating risk and making informed investment decisions. This chapter presents the company's significant activities, such as annual events, membership of professional bodies, and participation in media. We understand the property investment business and our social responsibility as a housing service provider; therefore, we try to play our role in society and local communities by sponsoring local and international sports teams and events.

Sharing our story with you aims to inspire you in case you plan to set up your business and build your assets portfolio.

Anzar's investment philosophy is to acquire properties in areas of high demand which produce high yield and capital gains to minimise risk and maximise returns for long-term sustainable growth.

Investing in knowledge is essential to any business; therefore, we had to learn about investing, finance and wealth management, and leadership to manage our business effectively.

1. OUR STORY

We managed to build our multi-assets portfolio in Manchester and generate decent annual revenues for our company, which we set up in 2017. I used to be a university lecturer and worked at different universities in the UK, but in 2019 I had to leave my full-time job. Despite owning our first property, it was another six years before we bought our residential property in Watford. We started expanding our property portfolio later using the BRR model. I arrived in the UK in December 1997, accompanied by my wife, Fathia, and two sons, Adrar and Axcel, to study a postgraduate Masters's programme in data communication, followed by a PhD in Cybersecurity. In 1998, my third son, Efaow, was born in Manchester during my postgraduate study. Before coming to the UK, I worked as a teaching assistant at various educational institutions in Tripoli, Libya. I set up a computing services business in Tripoli, providing various computing and network training courses, technical support, and sales. I always had the ambition to be self-employed and become my own boss.

During my PhD study at Sheffield University, I was doing another teaching course called PCHE, which I managed to complete while studying. I also delivered tutorial sessions and, occasionally, had the opportunity to give lectures to help my supervisor. I had to do my PhD, study a teaching course, and work part time simultaneously to help me achieve my career goals and aspirations. Studying and working to get extra income and support my family was challenging. In 2004, a few months before completing my PhD, I was offered my first full-time lecturer post in Internet Computing at Hull University. I left Hull University in 2006 to work at the University of Sheffield and other universities. I was passionate about my area of expertise in Internet Computing and Cybersecurity and lecturing, but being a university lecturer was insufficient for my family's living expenses. I had to work part time for other universities and during weekends to mark students' work and prepare tests and exam papers to earn extra income to support my family, but it was unsustainable and very hectic.

Following the birth of my daughter, Natir, in 2007, I was offered a senior lecturer post at Hertfordshire University. In 2008, we all moved from Sheffield to Watford, where we lived for ten years before our departure to Manchester in 2018. During our stay in Watford, we self-managed our property remotely in Manchester, which was not an easy thing to do. As an academic specialising in technology and cybersecurity, my property finance and management knowledge could have been improved. Still, the property could help us improve our lives, and it definitely worked. Being a university lecturer for many years helped me develop project management skills and research experience to gather information about property investment and management, and legal obligations and regulations.

1.1. Property business location

Between 2014 and 2018, before we left Watford, all family members tried their best to offer help and support the business and are still committed to doing so. Knowing each other's strengths and limitations helped us allocate tasks to each individual and try to keep mistakes as minimal as possible. Our first few property investment projects in Manchester were straightforward regarding refurbishment works because we couldn't afford time and effort,

Knowing each other's strengths and limitations helped us allocate tasks to each individual and try to keep mistakes as minimal as possible.

allocate enough resources, and project manage larger extensions or development works. We used to travel frequently to Manchester via the motorways M1 and M6 almost every week during 2017 to either resolve specific property-related issues or to view properties advertised on rightmove.co.uk for sale. Therefore, we thought it was better to be closer to our business in Manchester and so decided to move to Manchester in 2018.

To keep our business simple and manageable, we focused on a specific area of Manchester, the northern part of the city. This helped us remotely manage our properties from Watford, build relationships with local estate agents, builders, and suppliers, and learn more about the local market and services. Also, I wanted to know the prices of the properties and the limits of our offers for the properties we were interested in. Getting things right and moving smoothly in the first few buy-to-let purchases is not easy. We had to put in a lot of blood, sweat, and tears, learn the hard way, and navigate many obstacles and challenges. We got used to unpleasant surprises and mistakes but had limited options and no way back, so we had to make it work.

1.2. Our business network is our net worth

We learnt how to negotiate prices with estate agents and sellers and figured out how to refurbish and redecorate derelict properties. We managed to create nice homes that are modern and desirable to local community families and new arrivals to Manchester. When we first started our property journey, we had to rely on high street banks to fund our investment projects, but when we exceeded ten properties, we had to rely on non-high street banks and lenders to fund the purchase of our buy-to-let properties. We managed to build an excellent relationship with a few mortgage brokers to offer us options for lenders and buy-to-let mortgage products with competitive rates suitable for our needs and circumstances. We also used investors' money often for one year to support some of our successful property investment projects and fund specific refurbishment works.

We developed a trustworthy relationship with our solicitors, which was essential for us and made them comfortable working on our behalf for many purchase and refinance projects. We provide them with all the documents they request and ensure that our ID documents, proof of funds, and proof of address are always up to date. Over the years, we learnt what they wanted, the format of their documents, and their way of operating and dealing with our files; on the other hand, they understood our business and investment strategies, which we have used for many years. We often use Manchester-based solicitors to carry out all conveyancing business even though it is unnecessary to use local solicitors.

In the property business in general and the private rented sector in particular, local knowledge, networking, and building relationships are essential, especially if you want to be informed about properties coming to the market from their owners and about potential tenants. Many of our current tenants contacted us after they received recommendations from tenants who had lived in our properties for years. Sometimes we receive calls from professional people and families moving from abroad to Manchester because of jobs offered to them. Developing such relationships and connections helps to build bridges with the local communities and businesses and build trust.

> We managed to build an excellent relationship with a few mortgage brokers to offer us options for lenders and buy-to-let mortgage products with competitive rates suitable for our needs and circumstances.

> We developed a trustworthy relationship with our solicitors, which was essential for us and made them comfortable working on our behalf for many purchase and refinance projects.

We managed to get excellent deals from local neighbours who wanted to sell their properties and from others who knew our tenants through word of mouth. This helped us deal directly with the property owners and the sellers, who were satisfied and happy to deal with someone introduced to them by friends or family members they know and trust. The vendors managed to receive the money they wanted for their properties and avoided paying hefty fees to estate agents or auctioneers. Buying investment properties closer to each other helps with the management and investment point of view. For instance, property checks such as energy performance certificate (EPC) or gas certificate checks, repair work, and maintenance can be carried out easily with less time and minimum costs.

> Buying investment properties closer to each other helps with the management and investment point of view.

We learnt how to develop joint venture projects with other investors that can lead to a win–win situation. We built a good relationship with many local estate agents operating in our investment area in Manchester. We bought many buy-to-let properties from in-house auctions and smart online auctions. Developing a good relationship with all other stakeholders is crucial for any business. During our property investment projects, we deal with local builders, electricians, gas engineers, estate agents, etc. We built a great relationship with mortgage brokers who helped us receive excellent mortgage offers from different lenders. Our favourite mortgage broker knows very well our simple business strategy in terms of adding value to any buy-to-let property we buy to maximise the potential and rent the property out. After six months, we remortgage to raise funds to reinvest.

> We learnt how to develop joint venture projects with other investors that can lead to a win–win situation.

2. ANZAR PROPERTY INVESTORS LIMITED

Real estate investment has changed my view of business in general and property in particular and allowed me to set up our family property company, Anzar Property Investors Limited, in May 2017 with my family's support. Financial independence was my goal, and I had to work hard and smartly. Anzar Property Group is an expanding family-run business that owns and manages a property portfolio. It is a property investment company that maintains a strong record and delivers consistent results in buy-to-let business through buying, renovating, and renting properties in Manchester. Anzar Property Group works with many stakeholders in the UK. Figure 12.1 shows the main stakeholders of our company to allow it to achieve its business goals. Table 12.1 shows a comprehensive list of stakeholders as well as both their power over our business and activities (low/medium/high) and their level of interest in it (low/medium/high) in terms of finance and operations.

We have applied our core principles on purchasing the best deals from on- and off-market properties while adding value through refurbishments to minimise risk and maximise returns. The company's vision, mission, and values are shown below.

> We have applied our core principles on purchasing the best deals from on- and off-market properties while adding value through refurbishments to minimise risk and maximise returns.

Vision

Build, develop, and manage excellent accommodation for residents in Greater Manchester, and consistently build on our property portfolio.

Mission

- Strictly adhere to our high profit margins and high yields criteria by selecting the best deals.
- Scale quickly while maintaining low levels of risk.
- Add value to our customers.

Values

- Trust and transparency. We remain open and honest as a family business.
- Win together. We want everyone working with us to grow and benefit.
- Care for the community. Company profits are used to hold seminars with the aim of educating the community and to fund relevant charities for cultural education and social work activities.

Figure 12.1 Anzar's main stakeholders

Table 12.1 Anzar Property Investors stakeholders

No	Stakeholder	Power (low/medium/high)	Interest (low/medium/high)
1	Property Sellers/Owners	Medium	High
2	Employees	Medium	High
3	Tenants	Medium	High
4	Lenders/Banks	High	High
5	Mortgage Advisors	Medium	High
6	Estate Agents	Medium	High
7	Solicitors	High	High
8	Surveyors	Medium	High
9	Building Insurance Providers	High	High
10	Land Registry	High	High
11	Local Authorities / City Council	High	High
12	Freeholders	High	High
13	Service Management Companies	High	High
14	Utility Providers (Gas, Electricity, Water)	Medium	High
15	EPC Provider	Medium	High
16	Gas Engineers (Maintenance and Gas Safety)	Medium	High
17	Electric Engineers (Maintenance and Electric Safety)	Medium	High
18	Contractors (building, painting, flooring, plumbing, windows and doors)	Medium	High
19	Deposit Protection Providers	High	High
20	Regulators	High	High
21	Suppliers	Medium	High
22	Local Community	High	High
23	Accountants	High	High
24	HMRC	High	High
25	IT Service Providers (Internet, cloud storage, email, software, hardware)	High	High

The main business within Anzar Property Group focuses on four main activities: operations and marketing, finance and accounting, investment and development, and IT management.

In 2018, we sold our residential property in Watford, which had increased in value since 2009, and the whole family moved to Manchester to be closer to the business. We left Watford to ensure we manage our properties professionally and care for our tenants and family business. When we moved to Manchester, we had about 12 properties. We used the cash from the residential property in Watford, which we sold, to invest in many other buy-to-let properties on the northern side of Manchester and to expand the portfolio. We wanted to create an extensive portfolio of great accommodation for the family rental market in Greater Manchester. The main business within Anzar Property Group focuses on four main activities: operations and marketing, finance and accounting, investment and development, and IT management, as shown in Figure 12.2. Since starting our property investment journey, we have focused on one strategy, buy-to-let, to build our business. Table 12.2 demonstrates the SWOT analysis for Anzar Property Investors Limited, which describes the strengths and limitations of the company.

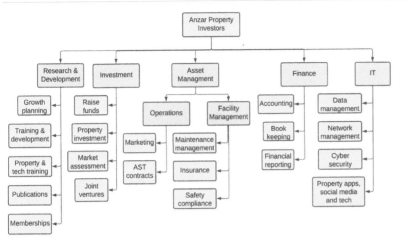

Figure 12.2 The four primary business activities
of Anzar Property Investors Limited

Table 12.2 The SWOT analysis for Anzar Property Investors Limited

STRENGTHS	WEAKNESSES
• Strong brand recognition within communities in North Manchester • High demand area of investment • Quality family homes provision • Quality services for our tenants • Strong network teams (suppliers, solicitors, professional builders, estate agents, lenders) • Quality operations management • Excellent knowledge of local areas • A rigorous selection process for our tenants • Minimal employee turnover (family owned business)	• A limited supply of properties (unable to meet the demand for residential properties) • Not easily affordable for a limited income household (Premium Price Policy)
OPPORTUNITIES	**THREATS**
• Easy access to the local property market (local networks, automated online tools) • The property portfolio is within new development plans by the Manchester city council • High capital appreciation areas close to Manchester CBD (Central Business District) • Predicted increased demand for homes in Manchester in the next few years	• Increased interest rates • Limited access to funds • Reduced demand

As a real estate investment business, Anzar's philosophy is to acquire properties in areas of high demand which produce high revenues and yield to achieve financial independence and meet our financial goals, as shown in

Our way of property investment, business strategy, and belief in our financial goals requires us to make effective planning decisions.

Figures 12.3 and 12.4. Anzar Property Investors company built up a stock of profitable properties and developed a successful business in Manchester. Our way of property investment, business strategy, and belief in our financial goals requires us to make effective planning decisions. We need to utilise the necessary resources to manage our operations and focus on our investment options based on what we are interested in and capable of.

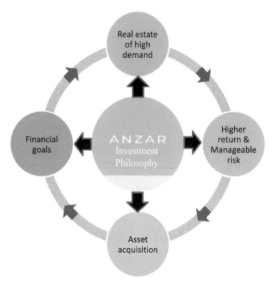

Figure 12.3 Anzar Property Investment philosophy

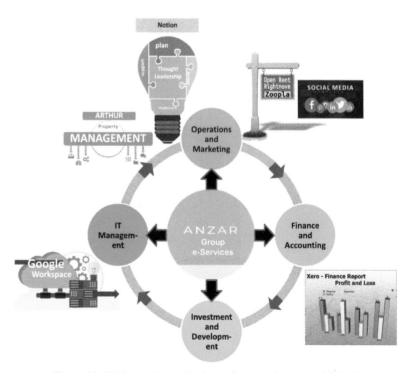

Figure 12.4 Main tools used by Anzar Property Investors Limited

3. INVESTING IN THE TECHNOLOGY

Property business e-Service is concerned with providing the company with different techniques and tools to deliver its services using the web and IT systems. Our online systems use automated technological processes and components to allow us to improve our services. At Anzar Property Group, we are determined to improve the quality of our services and operations. To achieve that, we are exploring different options to implement e-Services throughout all aspects of our business. We are interested in using technology and online services to resolve some of the complex problems and challenges which are having an impact on our business, as listed below.

- Keep our business operating effectively and capable of productively delivering its services to our customers.
- Effective monitoring of operations and more measurability of results and completed tasks. (If you cannot measure it, you cannot improve it.)
- Ensure agility and accountability to minimise errors.
- Speed up activities and workflow and improve service support.
- Minimise wastage in effort and time and avoid the use of *ad hoc* measures.
- Develop a dynamic and efficient business that is capable of resolving its problems and challenges and is able to change.
- Better satisfaction of business members and employees.
- Reduce rental voids and blocks to the income flow.
- Minimise the risks of human errors and make informed decisions.

A successful business is a profitable systemised enterprise that operates using powerful automated processes and business tools. We learnt about digital marketing to help us understand how to use social media to market our properties and attract good tenants. After completing the refurbishment works for any property, it is then advertised on the rental market using various online platforms to find suitable tenants. Property accounting is very important, so we had to invest time and money to educate ourselves and ensure that we do things right with the support of our accountants. We applied various technology tools to support the business, such as Xero for accountancy and filing tax, Arthur to manage all properties and receive and record all tenants' enquiries, Google Cloud and drives to store all the business data and file management, Signable for signing tenancy agreements, etc. Figure 12.4 shows the main tools used by our company to support all four business activities: operations and marketing, finance and accounting, investment and development, and IT management.

4. INVESTING IN KNOWLEDGE

I read many valuable books about investing, business, finance, accounting, and management to improve my knowledge, help me figure things out, and manage our family business. We used many useful resources, enabling us to understand how to manage and tolerate risk and make informed investment decisions. All family members are involved in the property business, have attended many property networking events, and have joined many

> Our online systems use automated technological processes and components to allow us to improve our services.

> We are interested in using technology and online services to resolve some of the complex problems and challenges which are having an impact on our business.

> We learnt about digital marketing to help us understand how to use social media to market our properties and attract good tenants.

> Property accounting is very important, so we had to invest time and money to educate ourselves and ensure that we do things right with the support of our accountants.

> We used many useful resources, enabling us to understand how to manage and tolerate risk and make informed investment decisions.

investment and social media groups. We spend thousands of pounds yearly for property and business education and training in all aspects of real estate, from finance and accounting to managing wealth and leadership. This ensures that all family members involved in the business are well educated and have the proper knowledge and skills to help them support and manage the business.

Fortunately, much information about the real estate business and its aspects is available online. Still, sometimes it is vital to get the necessary knowledge about specific areas from its sources. Getting the right information from experts and professionals is essential, especially when it comes to creative finance and accounting, tax matters, and wealth management. For instance, we learnt that we could raise a little cash upfront to get into property investment and buy-to-let properties in particular. We learnt how to analyse the property market, gather relevant information, and select the right properties and good deals and value to them. Such skills are essential for anyone intending to get into real estate investment and business.

We figured out how to raise funds by remortgaging our properties that meet the lenders' requirements and conditions in terms of the refurbishment works and then repeating the process again and again over the years. We have to meet the lenders' requirements in terms of the stress tests, which they use to ensure that the rental income is sufficient to pay the refinance costs. Stress testing is used to weigh the mortgage loan amount against the rental income and interest cost. This remortgaging process helped us raise funds to reinvest and grow the family business and build our asset portfolio. All family business members gained the necessary experience by dealing with mortgage brokers, solicitors, and lenders and negotiating deals with estate agents and sellers.

Recently, we managed to buy an uninhabitable three-bedroom house and had to claim SDLT back from HMRC, which was a good saving. Before completion, the solicitor included the SDLT in his completion statement, and we paid it fully. After the purchase completion, we learnt that paying SDLT for the uninhabitable property was a mistake on the solicitor's side. Landlords are exempted from paying such a tax when they buy uninhabitable properties. So, we contacted HMRC and provided all documents and evidence to support our claim for requesting back the SDLT that we paid back. After a week or so, we received £5,000 back, which had been paid mistakenly as SDLT to HMRC.

After we set up our property company in 2017, we joined NRLA to help us manage our properties and tenants and comply with the regulations and legal obligations. In 2021, I became a member of the IoD to get support from this organisation on how to lead and manage our business and understand my responsibilities as a company director. Members are kept informed regularly with up-to-date information and changes in rules and regulations. We subscribed to a few property magazines and online resources such as *YPN* (*Your Property Network*), *Property Investors*, and *NRLA Property Magazines*.

NRLA helped us provide many materials and documents and access to many resources such as tenancy agreements, section 21 letters, regular newsletters, etc. NRLA also offers different business products and services and quality discounted training courses for landlords to help them understand the business better, keep them updated and manage their portfolios professionally. All the business members of the family attended property professional training programmes with either NRLA, expert investors, or

Getting the right information from experts and professionals is essential, especially when it comes to creative finance and accounting, tax matters, and wealth management.

We figured out how to raise funds by remortgaging our properties that meet the lenders' requirements and conditions in terms of the refurbishment works and then repeating the process again and again over the years.

All family business members gained the necessary experience by dealing with mortgage brokers, solicitors, and lenders and negotiating deals with estate agents and sellers.

specialised training institutions. They invested a lot of money in learning and knowledge. We reached a level where we are ready to take on larger-scale conversion and refurbishment projects such as commercial to residential development and set up our own estate agent.

5. COMMUNITY SUPPORT

Businesses should play their role and have a positive effect on their local communities and societies; giving is the best way to gain more and achieve better. Offering cash to those in need and sharing it with others will help you receive more, speed up money flow, and grow more. We should not care about the external forces outside our control; instead, we must be practical and focus on using the available resources and leveraging the knowledge and opportunities to make a positive change. We must plan for the worst, and there is no need to wait for perfection because that will never happen. Being aware of others' needs is important, so we do our best to help, but at the same time, we must be careful not to overspend.

We understood the property investment business and finances well and developed firm relationships with various business stakeholders, banking, accounting, lawyers, and property valuation professionals. This assisted us with our responsibility as a housing service provider and managing our tenants. All our properties are remortgaged, and many have been more than once. In 2019, we organised our first real estate investment seminar in Manchester, and many community members and professionals attended this event. In the second event, organised in 2022, as shown in Figure 12.5, a few investors and mortgage brokers delivered interesting presentations to the audience.

In November 2023, I was invited by the real estate group at the School of Science, Engineering and Environment, Salford University, to participate in their Real Estate Research and Consultancy Cluster Workshop. My presentation was about our business investment strategy and growth model, which helped us to scale up. A quiz about calculating ROI for a property investment case study was given to the audience. Two winning students who are studying at Salford University and attending a real estate investment and finance course were presented with Anzar Medals and copies of my book about real estate investment, as shown in Figure 12.7. Since 2021, I have participated in the ECIE (European Conference on Innovation and Entrepreneurship) and presented my entrepreneurial perspective of real estate investment and the company's business operations as a case study.

We reached a level where we are ready to take on larger-scale conversion and refurbishment projects such as commercial to residential development and set up our own estate agent.

In 2019, we organised our first real estate investment seminar in Manchester, and many community members and professionals attended this event.

Figure 12.5 Anzar Property Investment's second seminar in Manchester (2022)

Figure 12.6 Anzar Property Investment's third
seminar in Manchester (October 2023)

Figure 12.7 Two winning students were presented with Anzar
Medals and copies of my book about real estate investment

We also sponsored different sports activities in Manchester, Liverpool, and Germany. We helped fund the Inner City World Cup Tournament in Liverpool and Manchester. We supported our Anzar Football Team, sponsored the Libyan Community Football League in Manchester in 2023 and the Libyan football team in the Socca World Cup 2023 in Essen, Germany, as shown in Figures 12.8 and 12.9, respectively.

We also sponsored different sports activities in Manchester, Liverpool, and Germany.

We make a living by what we get, but we make a life by what we give.

Winston Churchill

Figure 12.8 The Libyan Community Football League in Manchester, UK (May 2023)

Figure 12.9 The Libyan Football Team in the Socca World Cup League in Essen, Germany (June 2023)

In 2021, I wrote my first book, titled *Real Estate Investment: In the Pursuit of Building Income-Producing Assets to Grow Your Wealth*, in which I developed my wealth generation model.

In 2021, I wrote my first book, titled *Real Estate Investment: In the Pursuit of Building Income-Producing Assets to Grow Your Wealth*, in which I developed my wealth generation model, as shown in Figure 12.10. This book will describe this model in greater detail, including all its four gears. The book is available on many online platforms, such as Amazon, Waterstones, and many others. I am a regular guest on the BBC Arabic TV channel, discussing real estate investment in the UK and technology-related development. In early 2023, the BBC *Homes Under the Hammer* team visited some of our buy-to-let properties, which we bought from auctions. All my BBC interviews and *Homes Under the Hammer* visits to our buy-to-let properties are available on my YouTube channel.

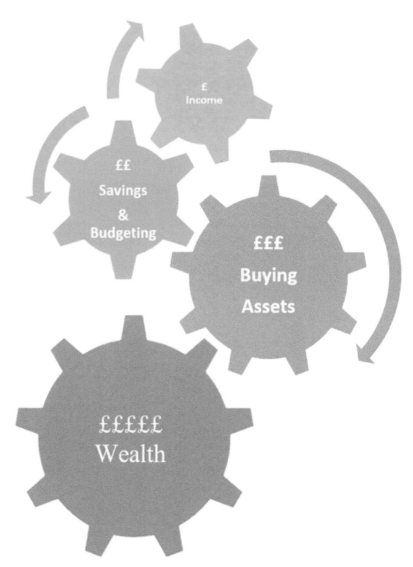

Figure 12.10 The wealth generation engine

In 2023, we were on the air with the BBC property programme, *Homes Under the Hammer*. We participated in the show a few times to talk about residential properties we bought from auctions and development projects. Some of my family members who manage the development projects also participated. The episodes are available on my YouTube channel. It was an interesting media exercise.

6. FAMILY BUSINESS

As a family business, we allocated tasks to each member based on their strengths and abilities. This helped us self-manage our property portfolio, and we didn't need to rely on letting agents to carry out such jobs for us. All the family members are entrepreneurs, know the property business very well, and know each other's skills and limitations; therefore, all support each other in all aspects of the business. Even though all members work in all business activities, each focuses on a specific area, such as project management, maintenance management, accounting, finance, and investment, etc. Some of the business members are full time, and some work part time, but the plan is to have all family members work full time in the property business in future.

An entrepreneur is 'someone who starts their own business, especially when this involves seeing a new opportunity'.
Cambridge English Dictionary

Despite working full time in property, everyone is enjoying being financially independent. The better the social relations among the family business members, the easier are the business activities and management tasks. Having a supportive team around you is essential for building a successful business. Despite the recent business challenges, potential legislative proposals, and complicated rules and regulations, we manage to run the business smoothly and professionally. We implemented the right tools and have built all the necessary systems to support all the business activities and processes. This is to ensure that all the business managers are well supported and keep tenants' complaints as minimal as possible and well managed.

Before making any important decisions about whether or not to go ahead with a new investment, business strategy or project, we discuss the issue together and arrange a meeting if necessary to understand the details. It is essential that we

- listen to each other;
- get opinions from the management team;
- look at all aspects of the issue or project;
- do our proper due diligence on relevant matters;
- raise any concerns;
- share ideas; and then
- make informed decisions.

Having a supportive team around you is essential for building a successful business.

We implemented the right tools and have built all the necessary systems to support all the business activities and processes.

This ensures the investment or development project succeeds and avoids unpleasant outcomes, bad results, and rushing decisions.

7. SUMMARY

We are a family property business based in Manchester, UK, focusing on buy-to-let and property development. We managed to build our multi-asset portfolio and generate decent annual revenues for our company, Anzar Property Investors Limited, which we set up in 2017. We expanded our property portfolio using the BRR model. During our stay in Watford, we self-managed our property remotely in Manchester, which was challenging. However, financial independence was my goal, and I had to work hard and smartly. I always had the ambition to be self-employed and become my own boss. This chapter covered various topics about our family business, including the setting up of Anzar Property Investors Limited, its main operations, investment activities, and contributions. Business activities, such as our annual property seminar, publications, media participation, etc., have been presented. The purpose of sharing our story with you was to inspire you if you want to start your business journey and build your assets portfolio.

We had to put in much time and effort, learn the hard way, and navigate many challenges. Operating outside our comfort zone and dealing with many unpleasant situations was challenging, but there was no way back, so we had to make it work. We learnt how to negotiate prices with estate agents and sellers and built a trustworthy relationship with a few mortgage brokers and property solicitors. Local knowledge, networking, and relationships are essential; developing such connections helps build bridges with businesses and trust. Some brokers offered us excellent options for lenders and buy-to-let mortgage products with competitive rates to fund our investment and development projects. We learnt how to buy from auctions and managed to develop joint venture projects with other investors that could lead to a win–win situation. We bought many buy-to-let properties from in-house auctions and smart online auctions. Developing a good relationship with all other stakeholders is crucial for any business.

Anzar Property Group is an expanding family-run business that manages multiple real estate companies, and each owns a property portfolio. It is a property investment business that maintains a strong record and delivers consistent results in the buy-to-let business through buying, renovating, and renting properties in Manchester. In this chapter, my family business story covered information supported by real-life scenarios and diagrams about the family company, its business model, structure, and operations. We have applied our core principles to identifying and purchasing the best deals from on- and off-market properties. We add value to those properties through quality refurbishments to minimise risk and maximise returns for long-term sustainable growth. Anzar's investment philosophy is to acquire properties in areas of high demand which produce high yield and capital gains that enable us to achieve financial independence and meet our financial goals.

At Anzar Property Group, we are determined to improve the quality of our services and operations and use technology and AI to resolve complex business problems. The company invested heavily in different technologies and tools to support the business and deliver its services using the web and

---

We learnt how to negotiate prices with estate agents and sellers and built a trustworthy relationship with a few mortgage brokers and property solicitors.

We learnt how to buy from auctions and managed to develop joint venture projects with other investors that could lead to a win–win situation.

We have applied our core principles to identifying and purchasing the best deals from on- and off-market properties.

The company invested heavily in different technologies and tools to support the business and deliver its services using the web and IT systems.

IT systems. Our online systems use automated technological processes and components to allow us to improve our services. We developed a digital marketing strategy and applied various online platforms and social media networks to market our properties and attract good tenants. We use an online management system to help us manage all properties and receive and record all tenants' enquiries, Google Cloud and drives to store all the business data and file management, Signable for signing tenancy agreements, etc.

Investing in knowledge is essential to any business; therefore, we had to allocate the necessary financial resources for real estate investment and finance education and training. All the family business members must read lots of valuable books about investing, business, finance, accounting, and management to improve their knowledge and manage our business. This ensures all members are well educated and have the proper knowledge and skills to help them support and manage the business. This enabled us to understand managing and tolerating risk and making informed investment decisions. We attended many property networking events and joined property networks and social media groups. We joined a few professional organisations, such as NRLA and IoD, to help us manage our business, comply with the regulations and legal obligations, and get the necessary support.

We understood the property investment business and our social responsibility as a housing service provider and managing our tenants. We organise our annual real estate investment seminar, which many community members and professionals attend. A few property investors and mortgage brokers have delivered interesting presentations to the audience. We participated in the annual ECIE, where I presented our business operations as a case study. In 2020, I wrote my first book, titled *Real Estate Investment: In the Pursuit of Building Income-Producing Assets to Grow Your Wealth*, in which I introduced my wealth generation model. I am a regular guest on a BBC TV channel, discussing real estate investment in the UK and technology-related development. The BBC's *Homes Under the Hammer* team visited some of our buy-to-let properties, which we bought from online smart auctions. All my BBC interviews and *Homes Under the Hammer* visits to our buy-to-let properties are available on my YouTube channel.

As a family business, we allocated tasks to each member based on their strengths and abilities, which helped us self-manage our property portfolio. All of us are entrepreneurs; everyone enjoys being financially independent, understands the property business, and knows each other's strengths and limitations. All members support each other in all aspects of the company; therefore, having a supportive team around you is essential for building a successful business and running the business smoothly and professionally. Making crucial decisions about whether or not to go ahead with a new investment requires a clear vision and an effective business strategy. This ensures building a successful business and continued growth and avoids rushed decisions and unpleasant situations.

> Investing in knowledge is essential to any business; therefore, we had to allocate the necessary financial resources for real estate investment and finance education and training.

> We understood the property investment business and our social responsibility as a housing service provider and managing our tenants.

Bibliography

Antonopoulos, A. M. (2021) *Mastering Bitcoin: Programming the Open Blockchain*. Sebastopol, CA: O'Reilly.

Base, D. (2022) Should you get an interest-only or repayment mortgage? Edited by Jessica Bown on 15 March, 2022. Available at: https://www.money.co.uk/mortgages/should-you-get-an-interest-only-or-repayment-mortgage (accessed: 6th June, 2022).

BBC Business News (17th June, 2022) Big pay rises could push prices up, says minister. https://www.bbc.co.uk/news/business-61846102 (accessed: 27th November, 2022).

Blundell, J., Machin, S., and Ventura, M. (March 2021) Covid-19 and the self-employed – ten months into the crisis. Covid-19 Analysis Series, No. 019.

British Medical Association (29th September, 2023) Junior doctors' guide to strike action. Available at: https://www.bma.org.uk/pay-and-contracts/pay/junior-doctors-pay-scales/junior-doctors-guide-to-strike-action (accessed: 30th December, 2022).

Brueggeman, W. and Fisher, J. (2019) *Real Estate Finance and Investment* (16th Edition). New York: McGraw Hill.

Camus, A. (1969). *Notebooks 1935–1942*. New York: Knopf.

Cribb, J. Delestre, I., and Johnson, P. (2021) Who is excluded from the government's Self Employment Income Support Scheme, and what could the government do about it? Available at: https://ifs.org.uk/publications/15276 (accessed: 25th February, 2022).

De Henau, J. (2018a) 'Week 7: Income', DB125 You and your money. Available at: https://learn2.open.ac.uk/mod/oucontent/view.php?id=1882692&printable=1 (accessed: 5th April, 2022).

De Henau, J. (2018b) 'Week 9: Expenditure', DB125 You and your money. Available at: https://learn2.open.ac.uk/mod/oucontent/view.php?id=1882696&printable=1 (accessed: 16th April, 2022).

De Henau, J. and Callaghan, G. (2019) 'Income', in J. De Henau and J. Lowe (eds), *Personal Finance* (pp. 55–106). Milton Keynes: Open University Press.

De Henau J. and Lowe, J. (Eds) *Personal Finance*. Milton Keynes: Open University Press.

Department of Business (2020) COVID-19 financial support for businesses. Available at: https://www.gov.uk/government/collections/financial-support-for-businesses-during-coronavirus-covid-19 (accessed: 25th February, 2022).

Experian (n.d.) How does your credit score compare? Available at: https://www.experian.co.uk/consumer/credit-score-map-uk/ (accessed: 1st November, 2022).

Google Finance (updated daily). Bitcoin to pound sterling. Available at: https://www.google.com/finance/quote/BTC-GBP (accessed: 12th February, 2022).

HMRC (2020) Check which employees you can put on furlough to use the Coronavirus Job Retention Scheme. Available at: https://www.gov.uk/guidance/check-which-employees-you-can-put-on-furlough-to-use-the-coronavirus-job-retention-scheme (accessed: 25th February, 2022).

Investopedia (n.d.) Financial planning. Available at: https://www.investopedia.com/financial-planning-4427750 (accessed: 3rd December, 2022).

Livingston, A. (12th August, 2022) 7 effects of inflation and how to protect yourself from the consequences. Available at: https://www.money-crashers.com/protect-effects-inflation-loss-purchasing-power/ (accessed: 30th December, 2022).

Lowe, J. and Higginson, M. (2019) 'Expenditure', in J. De Henau and J. Lowe (eds), *Personal Finance* (pp. 107–151). Milton Keynes: Open University.

Lowe, J. and Stone, H. (2018) You and your money. Available at: https://learn2.open.ac.uk/mod/oucontent/view.php?id=1882710 (accessed: 7th June, 2022).

Moore, R. (2018) *Money: Know More, Make More, Give More*. London: John Murray One.

Morgan, C. (2020) *Financial Independence: The Ultimate Guide to Exploding Your Income, Dropping Out of the Rat Race, and Achieving Financial Freedom*. Independently published.

Mugleston, P. (31st July, 2023, updated) Mortgage affordability checks. Available at: https://www.onlinemortgageadvisor.co.uk/mortgage-affordability/mortgage-affordability-checks/ (accessed: 14th July, 2021).

Myers, D. (2019) *Economics and Property* (Fourth Edition). Routledge.

Narayanan, A., Bonneau, J., Felten, E. *et al.* (2016) *Bitcoin and Cryptocurrency Technologies: A Comprehensive Introduction*. Princeton, NJ: Princeton University Press.

Office for National Statistics (March 2020) Saving for retirement in Great Britain: April 2018 to March 2020. Available at: https://www.ons.gov.uk/peoplepopulationandcommunity/personalandhouseholdfinances/incomeandwealth/bulletins/pensionwealthingreatbritain/april2018tomarch2020 (accessed: 23rd October, 2022).

Office for National Statistics (7th January, 2022) Household debt: wealth in Great Britain. Available at: https://www.ons.gov.uk/peoplepopulationandcommunity/personalandhouseholdfinances/incomeandwealth/datasets/householddebtwealthingreatbritain (accessed: 31st October, 2022).

Organisation for Economic Co-operation and Development (OECD) (2021) OECD focus on housing: 14–18 June 2021. Available at: https://www.oecd.org/newsroom/oecd-focus-on-housing-14-18-june-2021.htm (accessed: 13th July, 2021).

Partington (2020) UK consumers repay record £7.4bn of debt in Covid-19 lockdown. Available at: https://www.theguardian.com/money/2020/jun/02/uk-consumers-repay-record-74bn-of-debt-amid-covid-19-lockdown (accessed: 11th April, 2022).

Plummer, R. and Palumbo, D. (2021) Covid: What impact has the furlough scheme had? Available at: https://www.bbc.co.uk/news/business-54601117 (accessed: 25th February, 2022).

Rand, A. (1992[1957]). *Atlas Shrugged*. New York: Penguin.

Shipman, A. (2018) 'Week 11: Borrowing and debt', DB125 You and your money. Available at: https://learn2.open.ac.uk/mod/oucontent/view.php?id=1882700&printable=1 (accessed: 20th April, 2022).

Shipman, A. (2019) 'Borrowing and debt', in J. De Henau and J. Lowe (eds), Personal Finance (pp. 153–195). Milton Keynes: The Open University.

Shipman, A. and Stone, H. (2019) 'Personal finance – setting the context', in J. De Henau and J. Lowe (eds), *Personal Finance* (pp. 7–54). Milton Keynes: Open University Press.

Stone, H. (2019) 'Savings and investments', in J. De Henau and J. Lowe (eds), *Personal Finance* (pp. 197–247). Milton Keynes: Open University Press.

Stone, H. and Fribbance, I. (2019) 'Housing', in J. De Henau and J. Lowe (eds), *Personal Finance* (pp. 249–294). Milton Keynes: Open University Press.

Twain, M. (n.d.) BrainyQuote. Available at: https://www.brainyquote.com/quotes/mark_twain_100303.

UK Government Dept of Business (2020) https://www.gov.uk/government/collections/financial-support-for-businesses-during-coronavirus-covid-19 (accessed: 25th February, 2022)

UK Government HM Revenue & Customs (2020) https://www.gov.uk/guidance/check-which-employees-you-can-put-on-furlough-to-use-the-coronavirus-job-retention-scheme (accessed: 25th February, 2022).

Wikipedia (n.d.) Conspicuous consumption. Available at: https://en.wikipedia.org/wiki/Conspicuous_consumption (accessed: 11th December, 2022).